Also By Michael Maccoby

SOCIAL CHARACTER IN A MEXICAN VILLAGE
(with Erich Fromm)

THE GAMESMAN

THE LEADER

SWEDEN AT THE EDGE
(editor)

WHY WORK?

MOTIVATING THE NEW WORKFORCE

MICHAEL MACCOBY

SECOND EDITION

Miles River Press

1009 Duke Street, Alexandria, Virginia 22314

First Edition, Simon & Schuster Inc., 1988

Second Edition, 1995
Published by
Miles River Press
1009 Duke Street
Alexandria, Virginia 22314

Ordering Information
Orders by individuals and organizations. Miles River Press publications are available through bookstores or can be ordered direct from the publisher at the MRP address or by calling (800) 767-1501.

Quantity sales. Miles River Press publications are available at special quantity discounts when purchased in bulk by corporations, associations, and others. For details, write to "Special Sales Department" at the MRP address or call (703) 683-1500.

Orders by U.S. trade bookstores and wholesalers. Please contact Atrium Publishers Group, 3356 Coffey Lane, Santa Rosa, CA 95403; tel (707) 542-5400; fax (707) 542-5444.

Orders for college course adoption use. Please contact Miles River Press, 1009 Duke Street, Alexandria, VA 22314; tel (703) 683-1500; fax (703) 683-0827.

Miles River Press Team
Peg Paul, Publisher
Elizabeth Katz, Editor
Libby Schroeder, Marketing Coordinator
Raue & Associates, Art Direction & Cover Design
Coda Graphics, Production

Library of Congress Cataloging-in-Publication Data:

Maccoby, Michael, 1933
Why Work?: motivating the new workforce/Michael Maccoby. — 2nd ed. of Why Work.
p. cm.
   Previous ed. has subtitle: Motivating and leading the new generation.
Includes bibliographical references and index.
ISBN 0-917917-05-7
1. Leadership. 2. Employee Motivation. 3. Organizational effectiveness.   I. Title.
HD57.7.M33   1995
658.4' 092—dc20   95-2939
                                                          CIP

10 9 8 7 6 5 4 3 2

Dedication

To Sandylee, Annie, Izette, Nora, and Max

ACKNOWLEDGMENTS

In working out my theories of motivation in the workplace, I have made use of findings from a number of separate studies that employ social-character theory and methods. While I directed some of them, others were done independently, in which cases I was a consultant to the research. I am grateful to the following research associates, students, and colleagues who have participated in the studies, which form the basis for the first edition of this book.

Richard Margolies, a clinical psychologist, has been my principal research associate. He helped me design the survey and interview questions, and he interviewed many government and business employees. He wrote papers on the expert and helper types, and offered useful suggestions about revising drafts of these chapters.

Cynthia Elliott Margolies, a clinical psychologist and my other research associate, conducted interviews and wrote papers on the self-developer and defender types. She was particularly helpful in the study of the self-developer.

Barbara Lenkerd Cortina, an anthropologist, and Margaret Molinari, a sociologist, contributed interviews of government employees. Dr. Lenkerd and I jointly authored a report on the ACTION Agency, Ideals and Interests: Final Report on the Participatory Work Improvement Program at ACTION/Peace Corps, 1977-1980 (Discussion Paper Series, John F. Kennedy School of Government, Harvard University, May 1984). Dr. Molinari authored a study of government auditors, which helped develop understanding of the bureaucratic character, reported in Michael Maccoby et al., Bringing out the Best: Final Report of the Project to Improve Work and Management in the Department of Commerce, 1977-1979 (Discussion Paper Series, John F. Kennedy School of Government, Harvard University, 1980).

Mauricio Cortina, a psychiatrist, studied doctors and nurses in a county health center. Jody Palmour, a philosopher, allowed me to use his excellent interviews with police officers.

Using the questionnaire in Appendix C, Marilyn Stahl, Tony Wagner, Scott Camlin, Veena Kapur, and Ruth Fort contributed employee interviews. John Paul MacDuffie interviewed managers and workers at Westinghouse Furniture Systems.

Linda Streit and Tony De Nicola provided statistical analysis of some of the survey data. Gay Mount worked with me on the State Department study of leadership. Douglas Wilson, a clinical psychologist and management consultant, shared his interviews with entrepreneurs in California as did Åke Beckérus and Berit Roos in Sweden.

Jan Erik Rendahl, a psychologist, studied change and social character in the Swedish criminal system. With Anders Edstrom, an economist, he also shared studies of social character at Scandinavian Airlines. In Australia, Trevor Williams applied the social-character questionnaire to managers in Australian Telecom. The pattern of responses proved similar to those of U.S. telephone company managers.

David Riesman shared his interviews with college and university presidents and was, as always, a helpful critic. Berth Jönsson, Bo Ekman, Russ Ackoff, Richard Normann, and Gunnar Hedlund have contributed to my thinking about business leadership in the age of information and service.

Elsa Porter has also been very helpful in working out my ideas about leadership. In 1990, she and I prepared a report to the Swedish Employers Federation, which reviewed the research on leadership. She has also confirmed the social character findings in a number of seminars she has given.

I especially appreciate the support of Hal Burlingame who first brought me into AT&T in 1977 and who as senior vice president of Human Resources at AT&T has led the innovative approaches that have resulted in Workplace of the Future.

Harvey Brooks has contributed to my understanding of technology and work, and Mike Wolf has encouraged me to clarify my ideas in *Research Technology Management*.

Goran Lindahl of ABB engaged me to study the cultural and social characteristic differences in that company, and has been a stimulating collaborator.

Others who have supported the combination of consulting and participative study of social character include: Goran Collert and Reinhold Geijer of Swedbank; Gerhard Larsson of Samhall; Bjorn Mattsson of Cultor; Jack Fearnsides and Barry Horowitz of MITRE; Jack White and Bill Wiley of Battelle; Bill Ketchum, Tapas Sen, and John Petrillo of AT&T; Peter Janson, Paul Kefalis, and Borje Fredriksson of ABB Canada; Morty Bahr and Jim Irvine at CWA, Al Shanker of AFT, and Jack Joyce of BAC.

For the first edition, I had useful suggestions from Steve Roday, Robert H. Gaynor, Anne Maccoby, Alice Mayhew, and Diana Hanson.

In preparing the second edition, *Why Work?* I have been very fortunate to have the excellent editorial help of Elizabeth Katz and secretarial support of Maria Stroffolino.

I am also grateful to Peg Paul and to Libby Schroeder of Miles River Press for their publishing and marketing advice.

TABLE OF CONTENTS

PREFACE

It is much easier to change technology and organizational roles than it is to change people. In my work with organizations trying to change, I have seen a need for all those involved — managers, employees, union officials — to understand why people work and especially what motivates them to help make an organization succeed. Managers need to understand how and why people, starting with themselves, differ in their motivation. They also need to be able to turn this diversity into a source of strength rather than conflict. Knowing about what motivates people at work can make leaders more effective, companies more competitive, and government more efficient. At the same time, this knowledge can inoculate employees from manipulation by management, since they will better understand themselves and their bosses.

When I wrote *Why Work* in 1988 (It was first published without the question mark in the title), it was clear to me that the theories of motivation taught in business schools and management seminars did not fit the changing workplace and the values of the workforce. These theories were and are misleading and have, in fact, impeded change. Employees were dissatisfied with their leaders, and the leaders did not understand why. This is still the case today. According to every survey I have seen, a majority of employees do not trust their leaders.

Since publishing the first edition of this book, I have surveyed hundreds of senior managers on the gaps between what is most important in their leadership roles and how well they are practicing these functions or tasks. In every case, one of the largest gaps they indicate is that of motivating people. I have chosen to revise this book because my understanding of the motivating values of today's workforce has become clearer as I have used the theory of social character described here to help leaders adapt to the dramatic economic, social, and technological changes transforming our world. People are energized by their values. The theory of social character explores the dominant values that determine motivation, and it allows us to differentiate five value types:

the expert, helper, defender, innovator, and self-developer. These value types cut across categories of gender, generation, and culture or ethnic group.

In fact, different cultures have found the book useful in understanding the changes in family structure and the nature of work that are forming the new social character in their milieu. The first edition of this book has been translated into ten languages, including Japanese, Chinese, and Russian. In Germany, the title was made more explicit: *Warum Wir Arbeiten* or Why We Work. In Sweden, where the book was a best seller, a question mark was added: *Arbeiten Var För Det?*, Work, Why Do It? The Spanish edition is called *Por qué y para qué trabajar?* or Why and For What Reason to Work? The French title also has a question mark: *Travailler Porquoi?* or Why Work? I have added a question mark to this second edition, since in citing the first edition, most people put one in anyway and only the Germans seemed to understand what I had in mind by leaving it out. However, the book is meant to answer the question it raises: Why do we work?

In July, 1994, the leading Japanese business magazine *NIKKEI*, cited *Why Work* in helping to understand the reasons why Japanese firms had to downsize white collar work and how this change was having a positive as well as negative human impact on people who had entered the workplace expecting lifetime employment.

In this second edition, I have added new material describing what I have learned during the seven years since the publication of *Why Work*. Much has happened to the companies referred to and to some of the people described in Chapter 3. First of all, AT&T has transformed itself from a national monopoly to a competitive global company. Since 1992, I have been the principal consultant to the Workplace of the Future, an innovative agreement to improve customer service, profitability, and employment security between AT&T and its unions, the Communications Workers of America (CWA) and the International Brotherhood of Electrical Workers (IBEW) (see Appendix E for the contract language). This agreement is still fragile and depends on how well management and union understand each other and how willing they are to transform their relationship. However, the Workplace of the Future was reaffirmed tin the 1995 contract between AT&T, CWA, and IBEW.

Since 1988, I have also been a consultant to ABB (Asea Brown Boveri), a global company specializing in electrical engineering, and I have interviewed ABB managers in 20 countries, in Europe, Asia, and North America to help them understand social character differences among their different cultures.

In Sweden since 1988, I have worked as consultant to the management of Swedbank, the largest bank in Scandinavia, which was created in 1992 by the merger of 11 savings banks and 700 branches. This bank has flattened its hierarchy and developed an empowered front line similar to the motivating organization described in Chapter 9. During this time, I have also been a consultant to Samhall, a Swedish company of 30,000 employees, which hires handicapped employees and succeeds in developing many of them for jobs in other companies. Samhall has also used *Why Work* in management seminars. In addition, the concepts of social character were used in a collection of studies about Swedish leadership and organization which I supervised.[1]

In Finland since 1990, I have met regularly with the top management group of Cultor, a company producing sweeteners, animal nutrition and bakery products, which has transformed itself from the Finnish Sugar Monopoly to an innovative international company. In the U.S. from 1990-94, I worked with managers of the MITRE Corporation and from 1991-92 with those of Battelle's Pacific Northwest Laboratory. Both are high-tech cultures of expert engineers challenged to adapt their culture to their customers' needs. Their customers are asking for partnerships that help them succeed, rather than for, as in the past, products "thrown over the wall." Both MITRE and Battelle have used the concepts of this book to understand resistances to change and as a part of their management training. From 1990-92, I also served as consultant to the American Federation of Teachers (AFT) in developing their future strategy. The new generation of teachers has made it clear that this union should help them develop themselves and should facilitate participation in the management of schools.

---

[1]Michael Maccoby, ed. *Sweden at the Edge* (Philadelphia: University of Pennsylvania, 1991).

The innovators I described in the first edition of this book, Larry Lemasters from AT&T, Russ Nagle from Westinghouse Furniture Systems, and Jan Carlzon from SAS, have all left those companies. In Chapter 3, I discuss lessons to be learned from them about the fate of many innovators in times of tumultuous change.

I have also used the first edition to teach executives from a number of companies, and in the process have been challenged to clarify the concepts of this book. During the period of 1988 to the present time, I have written three articles a year for a feature called "The Human Side," published in the bimonthly journal, *Research Technology Management.* In this second edition, I include material from some of these articles as well as from an article, "The Innovative Mind at Work" written for *Spectrum,* the journal of the Institute for Electrical and Electronic Engineers.[2]

The research my colleagues and I have carried out, much of it in the context of transforming organizations, has convinced me that change is a never-ending process. Even the best of organizations can fall apart without good leadership. Many of the most heralded models of organizational excellence have become complacent and unable to adapt to the ever-changing business environment. Markets change, new competitors emerge, new products and methods are created; but organizations still depend on motivated people. To build and lead the great organizations that create wealth, leaders will continue to need motivated followers. In the modern organization, creative energy and commitment will not be gained by hype and will not be bought by money alone. They will be developed and strengthened by leaders who understand, respect, and engage the productive values of people at work, leaders who do not manipulate but who motivate with integrity.

Michael Maccoby
Washington, D.C.
May, 1995

---

[2]*IEEE Spectrum,* 28, 12 (December 1991): 23.

INTRODUCTION

During the past seven years, the historical changes described in the first edition of *Why Work?* have become more apparent. These changes require a rethinking of what motivates people at work.

The first historical change is that *the nature of work continues to shift from manufacturing to service.* Over 70 percent of the workforce is now in the service sector. Technicians as well as clerks, wholesalers, and professionals have customers. Even manufacturing work has become a form of technoservice with the application of total quality management techniques that transform work processes into customer-supplier relationships.[1] Hierarchies have been flattened, and managerial roles have changed. Instead of directing subordinates (who are fully capable of directing themselves), the best new managers formulate strategy, facilitate teamwork, and teach employees how to redesign work. They also benchmark best practices in other companies, and use the four Rs — responsibilities, relationships, rewards, and reasons to create a motivating organization (see Chapter 9).

Unlike the industrial-bureaucratic expert who prized functional autonomy, the new manager practices the give and take of the interactive process because business success demands it. However, many attempts to transform organizations have run into resistances from experts who feel threatened, or they have been led by innovators who demand that followers become true believers. In one global company, an executive asked to evaluate all the total quality management and customer focus programs reported that he had found 40 different "religions." Each proponent claimed to have the truth, each had part of it, and none were eager to learn from each other.

---

[1]I have used the term *technoservice* to describe a mode of work using technology (including tools and information) to satisfy internal as well as external customers as part of customer-supplier processes. Technoservice contrasts with the industrial-bureaucratic work organization where the worker has no direct relationship with customers or suppliers.

The second dramatic historical change that I believe affects motivation is that *people can no longer count on lifetime careers in a single company.* Competition, information technology, and process re-engineering have caused large companies and government agencies to lay off employees at all levels. Change is a constant and there is no job security. Employability depends on one's competencies and values. While those companies that ask employees to help the company succeed should offer them opportunities to develop their skills, each person needs to accept responsibility for continual self-development. We discuss the meaning of that concept in Chapter 8.

A third transformation occurring in today's workplace is that *the social character of the workforce continues to change from the traditional experts adapted to functional roles in the industrial bureaucracy to the new generation of self-developers who are better adapted to service in the age of information technology.* The traditional experts were typically raised in families headed by sole male wage earners. This was the dominant family of the '50s and '60s. Most of today's top managers grew up with the model of the good manager as a father-figure and the good mother at home raising children. Success in that model required individual achievement and bonding with authority.

The new generation of today's self-developers has typically been raised in a family with dual-wage earners who share work and child-rearing roles. At an early age, these self-developers learn they cannot always count on their parents to be around when needed. Today's children have to learn interpersonal skills early to get along with one another in day care centers and nursery schools, and to support each other in the absence of their parents. These childhood experiences form people for whom both self-reliance and teamwork feel natural. Sharing ideas and networking are easy for them. Knowing that they can't count on lifetime employment in an ever-changing market, they naturally put a premium on self-development in order to maintain their employability. This shift in family structure continues (see Chapter 1).[2] During the

---

[2]This conclusion is supported by a national study, carried out in 1992, *The Changing Workforce* by Ellen Galinsky, James T. Bond, and Dana E. Friedman of the Families and Work Institute. Notably, 75% of couples interviewed by random selection for that study were both employed.

21st century, most employees in the U.S. and Western Europe, at least, will be self-developers, shaped by the combined forces of changing technology, education, and family life.

The social character types described in this book — expert, helper, defender, innovator and self-developer — describe values that are shared by people everywhere. These types are somewhat different from the way Americans usually categorize themselves. Americans enjoy describing themselves by place and historical generation. In an extremely mobile society, one way of forming fast friendships is to connect with people who come from the same place in time as well as space. Thus people will say: "We are from Texas" or "We are both from the '60s; we are Baby Boomers." People are also characterized by others as representing a time, as in "He is an '80s person," implying that he is greedy and hedonistic. Some Americans also type themselves by ethnic groups as in African-American, Italian-American, or Swedish-American.

Today, there is a diversity of values in how people approach their work, but this kind of diversity cuts across gender, generation, culture, and ethnic groups, although these variables do interact with the social character types. For example, there is an increasing percentage of self-developers among the young today.

However, while some academics maintain that women manage differently from men because they care more about relationships, the research presented in this book indicates that this difference is more characteristic of the older generation. In the traditional workplace, women were more likely than men to be helpers, and men more likely to be experts. In the new generation of self-developers, there is little difference between values of men and women at work.

Strong cultural differences imply different values embedded in the family, religious, ethnic, and national traditions that form social character. Thus, Asian Confucian values emphasize family obligation as contrasted to the Western value of individualism.[3] This influence affects all types, and particularly the style of leadership that most motivates (Chapter 10). Furthermore, groups that have been oppressed or

---

[3]See Michael Maccoby, "Creating Quality Cultures in the East and West" *Research Technology Management*, 37, 1 (January-February 1994).

marginalized, such as African-Americans, are more likely to develop defender values (see Chapter 6).

This book provides concepts that explain how values determine not only individual differences in motivation at work but also styles of work and leadership. Understanding these different styles enables one to describe and understand the logic that determines a person's choices, emotions, and behavior at work.

Although *Why Work?* describes the factors essential to motivation, it is not a book on how to motivate. Doing that depends first on understanding the complex interaction between people and organizations, which determines the way people work. The book is intended to provide that understanding and to be used both to increase understanding of differences among individuals and to evaluate the tools or systems that organizations use to motivate employees. The book is also useful in helping readers to understand the people who serve us when we are customers and those in government who regulate, guard, or police us. The better we understand one another, the better our relationships will be.

Managers from some of the most technically advanced companies in the world have found my theories of social character useful in understanding differences in approaches to work and management styles. These companies require high levels of knowledge matched with increased teamwork, both within their organizations and with customers. Such corporations are bridging the gap between the old bureaucratic-industrial world and the new world of technoservice. They find that the more people understand each other, the better they communicate and work together.

I have arranged the plan of this book in the following way:

Chapter 1 describes the nature of motivation and the differences between the ideas in this book and theories currently being taught in business schools and management seminars.

Chapter 2 discusses the values that motivate us and how they are formed.

Chapters 3 through 7 delineate the five social character types: innovator, expert, helper, defender, and self-developer. How do they approach work? What makes work meaningful to them? What does each find satisfying and dissatisfying? What do they want from a boss, and how do they behave in the role of manager? What are their strengths and weaknesses? How can they best develop themselves for the new workplace?

Chapter 8 focuses on the meaning of self-development and the role of individual responsibility in achieving it.

Chapter 9 brings together the lessons of how to motivate different types of people for empowerment in the new workplace in terms of the 4Rs: responsibilities, relationships, rewards, and reasons.

Chapter 10 describes the style of leadership required to create the motivating organization. This chapter includes a matrix of the positive and negative qualities of each leadership style, which executives have found useful for evaluating themselves and each other.

When using the concepts presented in this book, readers need to keep in mind that no value type is good or bad. Each type has positive and negative potentialities. It is also important to remember two principles:

Those people who are the most extreme examples of a type are the ones who have the most difficulty adapting to change.

Those people who tend to balance the values of expert knowledge, helping others, respect for individuals, innovation, and self-development are most adaptive and effective.

Organizations will succeed in motivating people with different values when their organizational responsibilities, relationships, and rewards are all aligned with peoples' values at work, and when employees believe there are meaningful reasons for performing their work. This book describes motivation at work as a relationship between individual values, leadership styles, and organizational practices. To understand these relationships and the differing values underlying them is to understand what will motivate the new workforce.

CHAPTER 1

THEORIES OF MOTIVATION

The concept of motivation describes the impetus to act with energy and purpose. We are all motivated to: eat, sleep, have fun, make love, and work. The challenge for management is to discover what motivates people at work to do what is necessary for the organization to succeed. In the past, in the industrial-bureaucratic era of rigid hierarchy and electromechanical tools, management's task was to motivate employees to obey orders and perform set tasks. Today, in the age of service industries (and especially information-age technoservice), management's task is to motivate employees to take responsibility for: solving problems, responding to customer needs, cooperating with team members, and continuously improving products and services. In the industrial-bureaucratic era, motivation for most workers was mostly compliance, showing up on time, and doing what they were told to do. Only a small percentage of managers and professionals was expected to exercise personal judgment. In the technoservice era, this kind of compliance is not enough; another type of motivation becomes essential. The organization requires people who are motivated, enabled, and empowered to achieve results by exercising judgment.

There are two kinds of motivation. One is extrinsic motivation, which has to do with control, getting people to do something they may not want to do. Extrinsic motivation is caused by positive or negative incentives. Carrots and sticks. These are most effective when people are in need or afraid. Well-fed people do not jump for carrots, and self-confident people do not allow bosses to beat them.

The theories of psychologist B.F. Skinner describe how the use of rewards, or "positive reinforcement," increases the probability of occurrence of a behavior. Skinner's theory is particularly useful for motivating animals and people to repeat simple tasks. Skinner motivated rats and pigeons by first starving them and then doling out pellets of food when the "correct behavior" occurred. In human terms, this approach would imply making people afraid that if they did not perform well, they would not eat. In the workforce of the information age, it is necessary to drive out fear. Employees are not expected to repeat the same simple task, but to use their judgment and communicate with customers and each other. They need to be engaged and challenged by their work, not afraid of what will happen if they make a mistake.

Intrinsic motivation, the second kind of motivation, results when internal drives and values are engaged at work. In the 1950s, another psychologist, Harry Harlow, demonstrated that monkeys learned to solve problems that appeared to be interesting challenges for them.[1] When the monkeys were subsequently rewarded with bananas for solving a problem, such as opening the lock on a door, their performance deteriorated. Harlow was showing that fully fed and secure animals are intrinsically motivated to solve problems. There was no need for other incentives. Rewards, in fact, may have confused them. Rather than pursuing the enjoyable task of problem solving, where they were in control, the monkeys started working for bananas, over which they had no control. For monkeys, there is intrinsic motivation to solve problems. And so it is for human beings.

People want to express themselves and exercise their skills at work, but self-expression is the expression of values and capabilities, and people differ in the mix of values that most determine their intrinsic motivation at work. For a person who has a deep value of helping others, the opportunity to help is what most motivates intrinsically. For an innovator, it is the opportunity to create. For an expert, it is the

---

[1] H. F. Harlow, "Mice, Monkeys, Men, and Motives," *Psychological Review*, 60 (1953), pp. 23-32.

chance to demonstrate knowledge. For the defender, it is the opportunity to right wrongs. And for the self-developer, it is the chance to take on new challenges and to enjoy the give and take of the team.

When I ask today's employees to rank what they most value in their work, they choose a combination of extrinsic and intrinsic factors. Extrinsic factors include better pay and benefits, employment security, opportunity for advancement, and working conditions. Intrinsic factors include challenging work, enjoyable work, meaningful work, and above all, opportunity to experience a sense of accomplishment. However, what is challenging, enjoyable, and rewarding depends on employees' individual values (and skills), which differ among people at work.

Sometimes, as we shall see, the distinction between intrinsic and extrinsic becomes blurred. Pure intrinsic motivation implies that people would be motivated to work, even if they were not paid, as is the case when people play a game for fun. Pure extrinsic motivation implies that people would not be motivated to do something unless they were paid. In fact, most people need to be paid for their work, even though they may put as much or more of themselves into games and volunteer activities. As we shall see in Chapter 7, an increasing number of new generation self-developers take a job for the pay and benefits, but they are intrinsically motivated by other work such as artistic or volunteer activities.

The What Motivates? graphic on page 10 indicates the relationships between intrinsic and extrinsic motivation. The motivation to do what is needed for the organization to succeed results from:

1. The fit between positive intrinsic motivation and work, including tasks, responsibilities and relationships;

2. Positive extrinsic incentives including pay, benefits, and working conditions.

Thus people are motivated when they are engaged by their responsibilities, and, at the same time, are satisfied by the organization because incentives (compensation, benefits) are considered fair and appropriate. Fear of losing pay or position is also an extrinsic motivator, but fear depresses performance over the long run. Those people

What Motivates?

+	Compliant	Motivated
Extrinsic Motivation		
−	Alienated	Frustrated

— Intrinsic Motivation +

who are positively motivated intrinsically but negatively motivated extrinsically, i.e. dissatisfied by their rewards, become frustrated or resentful. Even if they do enjoy their work, they will complain about how they were treated and look for better jobs. Those people who are positively satisfied extrinsically but unengaged or negatively motivated intrinsically will be compliant and do only what they are told to do. The job will not motivate them to give more of themselves. And the alienated, turned-off, and often angry employees, are neither engaged nor satisfied by their work. They are negative on both dimensions and can contribute to a climate of bad feeling.

Motivating employees requires designing jobs that engage their values and provide satisfying rewards. This requirement is a challenge not only to managers, but also to employees whose values (intrinsic motivation) are adapted to the bureaucratic-industrial world and not to that of technoservice.

The chapters of this book present examples of how different types of people are motivated. To give an example, the experience of police officers (as discussed in Chapter 5) illustrates the difference between intrinsic and extrinsic motivation. In terms of intrinsic motivation, there are three types of police officers, each driven by different constellations of values. Most are *experts* who are motivated to work within the rules, solve problems, and apprehend perpetrators who break the rules and commit crimes. A small percentage of the officers are *defenders* who are motivated by their desire to protect society from bad people and punish criminals. These officers are often frustrated by rules and technicalities, which can be used by criminals to escape what they consider their just deserts.

A former New York City police officer said he finally quit his job after he had arrested the same person for drug selling three times, and each time the judge had let him go free because there was not enough evidence. Being a defender, the former police officer yelled his frustration at the judge, accusing him of irresponsibility and ineptitude. When the officer was cited for contempt of court, he decided to resign.

The third type, the *helpers*, want to help people avoid trouble. Police officers who are helpers are frustrated by demands that they spend their time in ways that may lead to arrests, but do little to prevent future troubles. The extrinsic motivations used by police departments typically reward and promote police officers for the number of arrests they make. This approach is motivating for the expert type, but not for the helper types, who are seldom promoted. They are not appreciated for resolving conflicts on the street or engaging teenagers in sports or other activities that direct the young people away from crime.

While these three types of people and kinds of intrinsic motivation are most common among the police officers we interviewed, in business organizations we often find a different distribution of intrinsic motivation and social character types, including *innovators* and *self-developers*. This distribution exists because businesses have had to change and have attracted and retained people who are not satisfied with the status quo.

Partial Man Theories

The major theories of motivation at work that are still taught at business schools and in managerial courses are *partial man* theories, which do not distinguish between extrinsic and intrinsic motivation. Nor do they help us understand differences in the values that motivate people at work. These theories see man as *economic man, sociological man, political man*, and *psychological man* motivated by money, power, status, or a hierarchy of needs. Each of these theories is partially true; none is fully true. These theories were relevant for the bureaucratic-industrial age, not for technoservice. Like functional departments in an intellectual bureaucracy, these theories focus on one motivating factor at the expense of the whole person. They are designed for partial people in narrow, routinized jobs at the bottom, and for those engaged in specialized functions at higher levels of the industrial-bureaucratic workplace.

These theories do not explain how to motivate people to use their judgment, solve problems for customers, or work interdependently. They do not explain differences in values that determine the quality and intensity of motivation for the new workplace. They assume that everyone is motivated in the same way, that managers do not need to understand people, but can employ formulas that work with everyone. Furthermore, such partial theories leave out key psychological concepts that are essential for motivation in the information age: trust, caring, meaning, self-knowledge, and respect.

Economic Man

The theory of economic man is based on the view that people can be motivated by the promise of money. Managers are attracted to this theory of motivation because money is the motivator that they themselves control best. Managers would like to believe they can design a system in which each employee, by working to maximize individual gain, makes the whole company prosper. It is an idea that brings to mind the image of a well-made watch. Yet the theory of economic man does not even fully explain top management motivation.

Although they are motivated to maximize the bottom line, even chief executives in most American companies are not pure economic men. Although they want to make as much as they can, top managers are not motivated to be more effective solely by the promise of making more money. The executive making $250,000 does not work harder to make $500,000 or $5,000,000 or $50,000,000. The bottom line has meanings other than money for chief executives. Like most of us, their sense of self-worth depends in large measure on the esteem of people they consider their peers. Chief executives spend much of their time with other CEOs, bankers, and financial analysts who judge them on their quarterly statements and share price. Doing poorly is humiliating. Doing well gives them a glow of success.

The theory of economic man is popular, because the drive to make money has some meaning for everyone. It has been the most reliable theory of motivation for the industrial age. Although the meaning of making money may be different according to our values, everyone wants it. Money provides a sense of security. It is proof of one's mastery and a means for buying pleasure. Having money means freedom from suffering indignities. With enough of it, one can tell any boss to take a walk. Freedom-loving Americans dream of making enough money to be financially independent, and this is a major reason why the entrepreneurial spirit remains strong in the U.S.A. Some of the most courageous businesspeople are willing to carry a huge load of debt and risk their own money in hopes of a big payoff. But within the new workplace, everyone cannot become financially independent, and money alone will not motivate the good relationships required for effectiveness. For most employees, with the exception of people working on sales commission or with the chance to become independent, money is more a satisfier than a motivator.

Sociological Man

Sociological man is the structural complement to economic man. This theory maintains that people are motivated by their organizational role and their desire for the status gained as they advance up the hierarchy. This is a traditional view of bureaucracy. It is the picture of the organization man of the '50s and '60s who works to please the boss and get promoted up another rung of the bureaucracy. It is still a powerful motivator for the experts in large companies, who are motivated to become part of the officer's club with all its perquisites.

Because most people enjoy status, the sociological man theory worked well enough, as long as American corporations could afford layers of management. It has fit the values of snobbish bureaucrats educated to measure success in terms of promotion in school. But today, the status hierarchy dampens the productive motivation of people with high school or college degrees who are at lower levels, particularly if managers at higher levels come to believe their positions prove they do not need to learn from people on the front line.

Political Man

Another partial man theory, that of political man, holds that people in organizations act to increase their power and influence. Its roots lie in Machiavelli's classic studies of Roman and Renaissance leaders. In his best-known work, *The Prince*, Machiavelli maintains that the prince is motivated to gain power, and only by collectively creating countervailing power can the people avoid oppression. Marxist theories of political man also say that managers design work to maintain their control over the workers. They claim that workers would be more motivated if they gained control of the means of production and the fruits of their labors. But a sense of ownership does not necessarily motivate employees, especially in large companies. Despite Marx's theory, many workers who "own" their companies and elect the managing director have felt alienated and turned off by boring work. Despite ownership, they have had little or no say about how work will be done. Nor do most workers understand why management makes decisions that change technology and jobs.

For example, workers who owned the Vermont Asbestos Company sold their shares to make a profit. They saw no compelling advantage to ownership because management did not become more participative and they did not have enough power to make a difference.[2] To feel whole at work, people must have a meaningful say over conditions that affect them. They must participate in designing their work, and they must be empowered to use judgment. Workers can gain the right to have a say by contractual agreement as in AT&T's Workplace of the Future or Bell

---

[2] William F. Whyte, et al., *Worker Participation and Ownership* (Ithaca, N.Y.: ILR Press, 1983).

South's quality program that was bargained with their unions. In these companies employees take part in planning councils and process change teams and are empowered to make decisions to better satisfy customers. Whether or not they own the company, to participate meaningfully they must be educated about the business.

The experience of work in industrial bureaucracies has caused a sense of powerlessness and provoked employees to protect themselves by using power against power, either collectively in unions, or individually by rising up the hierarchy to gain a strategic role. The theory of political man, that people are motivated to gain power at work, describes a defense mechanism against exploitation and manipulation.[3]

Psychological Man

Psychological man is another of the partial man theories, which states that people are motivated by the satisfaction of needs. Edward Lawler III has summarized the psychological research on motivation.[4] He concludes that both intrinsic needs for competence and achievement and extrinsic needs for money are motivating. He shows that the theory of economic man is incomplete. Pay combined with participation in designing jobs and open communication are more effective than pay alone. Despite this, his attempt to expand economic man is incomplete for two reasons.

First, Lawler does not describe the different types of intrinsic motivation. Second, while he discusses how responsibilities and rewards motivate, he does not focus on the importance of relationships that

---

[3] See Michael Crozier, *The Bureaucratic Phenomenon* (Chicago: University of Chicago Press, 1964) for a description of the bureaucrat as a political man. See also Melvin L. Kohn and Carmi Schooler, *Work and Personality: An Inquiry into the Impact of Social Stratification* (Norwood, N.J.: Ablex Publishing Corporation, 1983). They show that the bureaucrat's ideal is a job with authority and autonomy. As we shall see, this is still the case for the expert and it remains true as long as people at work need to protect themselves from arbitrary authority.

[4] Edward E. Lawler III, *Motivation in Work Organizations* (San Francisco: Jossey Bass, 1994).

create trust or on the reasons that give meaning to work. His concept of intrinsic motivation best fits those people whose dominant value is mastery and not those motivated by helping, innovating, defending, or by self-development. As a result, his psychological man theory is inadequate for understanding how to motivate different types of people for the information-age workplace.

Another psychological theory types people according to their temperaments. The Myers-Briggs test types in this way using categories described by the Swiss psychoanalyst C.G. Jung, e.g. introvert-extrovert.[5] Topologies based on genetics or temperament are different from those presented here, which are based on values and developed from the systematic study of how people approach work. Unlike the Myers-Briggs test, which describes patterns of feeling and behaving but does not explain how they developed, the social character types of *Why Work?* can be understood as adaptations of human drives to particular cultural institutions such as family, school, and workplace.

Abraham Maslow's theory of motivation still remains the most popular and influential psychological theory taught to managers. Maslow appears to integrate the other theories with a hierarchy of needs. He presents a typology that describes lower-level needs as more extrinsic and higher-level needs as more intrinsic.[6] He calls the lowest-level needs physiological: feeding, drinking, sex. These are the needs for relief of tension, pain, and discomfort. Next come what he calls the safety needs (security, dependency, protection, etc.), which are felt once the physiological needs are gratified. These are the needs of economic man. If both the physiological and safety needs are satisfied, Maslow then postulates that the next level of needs for love and affection will emerge. Once this next level of needs is satisfied, a person will experience needs for status, achievement, and autonomy, the sociological and political needs, and finally self-actualization, the need to express one's

---

[5] Isabel Briggs Myers, *Gifts Differing* (Palo Alto, Calif.: Consulting Psychologists Press, 1980).

[6] Abraham Maslow, *Motivation and Personality* (New York: Harper & Row, 1954), p. 3.

creative potential. All managers from big business and government learn this theory, either in business school or in advanced executive seminars, and the hierarchy-of-needs chart can be found in offices around the globe.

According to Maslow, people are motivated by money, status, and power only at lower and middle levels of the organization. But through success, partial man can become whole and transcend the bureaucratic condition. This theory is used by both conservative and liberal managers. Conservative managers cite Maslow's hierarchy of needs to justify and rationalize their reluctance as managers to change their organizations. They argue that workers are still at lower levels and do not want more demanding and responsible roles. In reply, liberal managers contend that with affluence, the needs of workers have moved up the hierarchy, and unless organizations provide more opportunity for self-actualization, these people will not be motivated.

Maslow's theory appears to integrate all the others and satisfy everyone. What is wrong with it? Two things. First, it does not fit the facts of what motivates people. It is not based on studies of the different values people bring to work. Second, while it works well enough for the industrial bureaucracies, it seriously misleads management for the age of information and service (technoservice).

Starting with the first objection, we see that the evidence does not support the concept of a needs hierarchy. Superficially, the concept appears to make sense, but the theory ignores all the cultural and psychoanalytic evidence of the role of values, of human character informing intrinsic motivation. No evidence shows that satisfaction of lower needs triggers higher needs, or that any of these needs can indeed ever be satisfied. One thinks of hungry artists or generous villagers who transcend lower needs without satisfying them. One never satisfies needs for safety, food, or love, once and for all. We may learn better ways to satisfy these needs; we may raise the aesthetic quality of these needs, but the needs never disappear. Nor can we humans ever achieve all our potentials. How we develop depends on opportunity, discipline, and commitment.

Once character is formed, satisfaction of needs does not necessarily change the motivation to work. And when it does, the result may be negative rather than positive. Empire builders are never satiated in their needs for money and power. Conquests whet their appetite for more. Narcissists of any type can never receive enough acclaim. Nor do people become more productive if they are given what they have not earned. This I observed when an idealistic innovator, a believer in Maslow, gave half his multimillion-dollar company to the workers. He expected that the sense of security would move them to higher levels of self-actualization. In fact, as owners, they complained about too much work and criticized the innovator for not giving them more money and time off. Satisfying "needs" increased dependency and did not stimulate greater responsibility or creativity.

Maslow's partial person theory is contradicted not only by everyday experience, but also by neurophysiology and cognitive psychology, which show that all humans from birth strive to organize experience, infuse it with meaning, and master the environment. Our very perception of the world requires from infancy that we actively organize ambiguous stimuli. Human development results from opportunity combined with discipline, knowledge, and practice. In fact, we often grow by frustrating, not satisfying, our needs. Needs have been made to sound biological, genetically determined, even though we continually manufacture new ones. Instead of automatically serving all our needs, we would be wiser to analyze each of them in terms of whether or not it does contribute to self-development.

For the second objection, the theory misleads. If managers embrace Maslow's theory, they will be misled into believing that what worked for the industrial bureaucracies will fit the new service world. The theory does not fit. For instance, in the industrial bureaucracy, managers can treat the lower-level worker as economic man, motivated by security needs. If this treatment does not guarantee good workmanship, it does at least gain compliance. Middle managers need their self-esteem bolstered; they can be controlled with the symbols of success and the chance to exercise power. The financially independent at the top are so driven to succeed that they need no further incentives; they are fully capable of negotiating their own rewards to satisfy themselves. Although this theory does not fit every case, it has been good enough to keep the industrial bureaucracy running, especially in Maslow's time.

Like Maslow, Tom Peters and R. H. Waterman, the authors of the best seller *In Search of Excellence*,[7] described middle managers as motivated by status and self-esteem. But they went further and emphasized that all of us need meaning in our lives and will sacrifice a great deal to institutions that provide it for us. The "excellent companies" that Peters and Waterman cited practiced strong values emphasizing excellence, winning, and the respect for individual dignity. The employee in such an organization either accepts these values or gets out.

Most of these successful companies reflected the values of strong owner-entrepreneurs. The organization was held together when the employees identified with the culture-shaping paternal leader. However, the present generation of self-developers will be motivated not by praise from fathers but by opportunities for self-expression and career development, combined with a fair share of profits. I believe that Peters and Waterman do, in fact, describe the spirit of successful American companies as studied by them in the late 1970s. But some of these companies, like IBM and General Motors, did not do so well in the 1980s. They and the others will continue to be successful in the 1990s only if their culture matures beyond the paternalistic model. This development means increased understanding of the new generation as well as information-age requirements for empowered people.

To summarize, the new workplace not only requires higher levels of motivation, but it also asks people to work cooperatively, share information, solve problems, and care about customers, fellow employees, and the success of the business, even if that means sacrificing short-term personal gain. Motivation for service in the information age requires attention to psychological concepts totally lacking in partial man theory: trust, caring, meaning, self-knowledge, and respect.

---

[7] T. J. Peters and R.H. Waterman Jr., *In Search of Excellence* (New York: Harper & Row, 1982).

Intrinsic Motivation: Social Character Types at Work

To understand the fit between work and intrinsic motivation, we must describe the values that drive behavior and how they are affected by the nature of work and management. To describe these values, I have used the theory and methods of social character research, as I did in my previous books, *The Gamesman, The Leader,* and *Sweden at the Edge.*[8] Through family, school, and workplace, a culture molds human drives — that is, dynamic behavior patterns — into values that are adaptive to work and social relations. The values shared by a group are the "social character" of that group. Many managers use their own categories to explain motivation, such as, "She's a real marketeer; she loves to put on shows," or, "He's an engineering type; he has to measure everything." The most effective managers continually modify their categories according to experience.[9] The purpose of my social character types is to refine these categories, sensitize perception, enrich experience, and deepen understanding of individuals at work.

A social character typology is a conceptual tool. It should not be used to pigeonhole or caricature people, but to understand better what motivates them and why this is so. Social character types are "ideal" types based on dominant values. They are like photographs that show one figure in high focus while the rest of the picture is blurred. Unlike other typologies based on needs or temperament style (such as Carl Jung's introvert-extrovert dichotomy), social character describes shared values and how they are formed. The theory helps us to understand ourselves within a particular culture. It shows us how different patterns of upbringing cause variations in the dominant values that motivate us

---

[8] See also *Social Character in a Mexican Village,* with Erich Fromm (Englewood Cliffs, N.J.: Prentice-Hall, 1970); *The Gamesman* (New York: Simon and Schuster, 1976); *The Leader* (New York: Simon and Schuster, 1981), *Sweden at the Edge* (Philadelphia: University of Pennsylvania Press, 1991). The theory of social character was developed by the psychoanalyst Erich Fromm (1900-1980).

[9] Donald A. Schön shows how professionals use and modify practical theories to solve problems in his classic study, *The Reflective Practitioner: How Professionals Think in Action* (New York: Basic Books, 1983). The most effective people are those who can modify their theories to take account of new experience.

at work. Although most people are a mixture of types, *The Gamesman* research team of psychologists and psychiatrists agreed that in over 80 percent of the cases they studied, including practically all of the most successful managers, one of the four types clearly predominated. The other 20 percent fell into many small groups of mixed types, and for the purpose of generalizing, we left them to one side.

In *The Gamesman, The Leader*, and *Sweden at the Edge*, I studied managers in business and government. For this study, I used the managerial character types described in those books as conceptual tools, expanding and modifying them where they did not fit, to develop a typology for managers and employees at all levels of business and government. The social character types described in the first edition of this book, *Why Work*, integrate the high-tech managerial types with people at all levels of business and government, from executives and professionals to the front line of operators, agents, and clerks.

Since 1988, my associates and I have continued to test these types, because we find that they help people at work to understand themselves and others. Social character research is a systematic method of differentiating people in terms of value differences that cut across demographic categories. These differences determine motivation and style of leadership. However, if these differences are not named, they will not be noticed and taken seriously in the design of organizations and the education of leadership. Since each human being is unique, categorizing people into types can be limiting. Yet we cannot avoid it. We think about and describe people in terms of age, gender, intelligence, generation, race, religion, and national origin, even as we recognize that no one can be fully understood by these stereotypes. But these categories only marginally explain motivation (e.g., working parents want day-care facilities; younger workers want higher wages instead of pension benefits).

In *The Gamesman*, I described managerial social character based on 250 interviews with managers in 10 successful high-tech companies at the cutting edge of change in the early 1970s. (Four of the companies — Hewlett-Packard, International Business Machines, Schlumberger, and

Texas Instruments — were also included as exemplary models within *In Search of Excellence*.) These managers participated in the study and helped shape the conclusions because they were interested in better understanding themselves, what made them effective at work, and how their work shaped their values. After analyzing their responses, I distinguished four variations on corporate social character. I called these types *craftsman, jungle fighter, company man*, and *gamesman*, terms the high-tech managers were able to use meaningfully to describe differences in motivation and meaning among themselves. These four types are still valid, and managers use them to describe themselves and each other.

Craftsmen and *craftswomen* value making, building, and designing high-quality products and systems. They tend to be responsible, self-contained, prudently conservative, and paternalistic. This type fits easily into a system of masters and apprentices. As leaders, they tend towards perfectionism. They seek one best way to do things, and find it difficult to delegate.

Jungle fighters live in a psychological world where they see everyone as either predator or prey. At their worst, they fit the cut-throat stereotype of the American business executive so favored by Hollywood. At their best, like the lion, they defend their workplace families. Some of the builders of American industry were jungle fighters, and today there are still lion-like entrepreneurs such as Ross Perot of Electronic Data Systems in Dallas, who risked his life to protect his employees imprisoned in Iran. Protectors at the top can create freedom for front-line employees, but jungle fighters at middle levels resist sharing power and block the open exchange of information necessary to effective technoservice.

Company men and *women* value harmony, cooperation, and identification with the organization. They are other-directed careerists who climb the corporate ladder by making themselves useful to bosses. This type flourished in the age of rapid growth of fat American corporations. They are the communicators and integrators between functions. Their drive for consensus can smooth over conflict, but it can also drag the organization toward mediocrity. As corporations struggle to become lean and competitive, the negative side of the company man or woman is fueled by fear of the future. Managers of this type have been the major victims of corporate downsizing because their roles are disappearing as hierarchies flatten.[10]

Gamesmen see developing projects, human relations, and their own careers, all in terms of options and possibilities, as if they were a game. Their characters are collections of near-paradoxes understood in terms of adaptation to the needs of the business. They are detached and playful, but compulsively driven to succeed; team players, but would-be superstars; team leaders, but often rebels against bureaucratic hierarchy; tough and dominating, but fair and unprejudiced.

Each of these four types has both positive and negative potentials. The positive side is more productive and flexible; the negative side is more defensive and compulsively driven. Formative experiences and current opportunities determine which side will be expressed. When there is a good fit between the requirements of work and values, people become more successful, respond to opportunity, and gain the incentive for more positive development. When conditions no longer allow a type to adapt, negative traits become stronger. People feel frustrated, unappreciated, resentful, and defensive. Consider, for example, the hard-working, self-reliant proprietor of a general store, put out of business by Wal-Mart. Lacking the managerial skills and values to work in a large company, his social character no longer fits; it is not adapted to the business environment. He becomes increasingly isolated, angry, and paranoid about the politicians and bankers whom he blames for his failure.

Think also of the committed factory worker or helpful telephone operator who has enjoyed a middle-class income and is displaced by technology. The new jobs require technical and social skills he or she lacks. Frustrated and resentful, these workers blame the "inhuman" bosses and "inept" labor leaders who have been unable to protect them.

In my book about pioneers in the changing workplace, *The Leader*, I predicted the emergence of a new social character type for whom the dominant meaning of work would be self-development. Since writing that book, my associates and I have interviewed many self-developers at work, and through surveys we have charted the continual growth in their numbers and in their significance for the new workplace.

---

[10] See Charles Heckscher, *White Collar Blues* (New York: Basic Books, 1995).

The New Types

In the process of interviewing employees at all levels of business and government for the first edition, *Why Work* and for this new book, I found that the four high-tech managerial types of *The Gamesmen* described above did not quite fit. Like the craftsmen, many accountants, doctors, executives, salesmen, and clerks valued mastery and excellence, but not necessarily designing and building products and systems. The values of government lawyers and whistleblowers are in some ways similar to those of corporate jungle fighters. Both feel they must fight to defend their dignity, vanquish people who might harm them, and protect those who are loyal to them. But in contrast to the jungle fighter's striving to be the head monkey, the most positive values of the defender transcend the jungle and promote the public good. So I developed a new social character typology in which my original types become subtypes.

I decided to make the gamesman a subtype of a new type I called the *innovator*, because the term *gamesman* for many people suggests only the compulsive drive to win and willingness to gamble, in contrast to the positive values of playful creation and daring strategy to develop markets and organizations embodied in the term innovator. Furthermore, I wanted a gender-neutral name that comfortably fit women as well as men.

I named the new types according to positive values that motivate them at work and determine their leadership style. These types — *expert, helper, defender, innovator,* and *self-developer* — are broader than those of *The Gamesman,* and one can see more easily the possibility of a combination of types. Experts include craftsmen; a subgroup of helpers with defender values are institutional helpers or company men and women; lion-like jungle fighters are a type of defender; innovators are creative gamesmen.

The following lists show the relationship between the social character types of *The Gamesman* and *Why Work.* Those appearing in all capital letters are the new types; those in initial-only caps are from *The Gamesman* study.

SOCIAL CHARACTER TYPES

Type	Dominant Values
EXPERT	Mastery, control, autonomy
Craftsman	Excellence in making things
HELPER	Relatedness, caring for people
Company man, institutional helper	Helping authorities, resolving conflict
DEFENDER	Protection, dignity
Jungle fighter	Power, self-esteem, survival
INNOVATOR	Creating, experimenting
Gamesman	Glory, competition
SELF-DEVELOPER	Balancing competence, play, knowledge, and personal growth

Most people balance more than one of these value types, and the best managers are a mixture of all of them. Usually, however, one type describes the dominant meaning of work for people. In subsequent chapters, the strengths and weaknesses of each type, their character development, and how each views service, work relationships, and management are described. I have focused particularly on service since this is the dominant mode of production in the new workplace.

For *experts*, service means providing technical excellence and professional knowledge. Their highest values relate to mastery and achievement. Experts enjoy analyzing how things work. Their search for autonomy in an organization pushes them up the hierarchy through functional specialization and toward professionalism. Typical experts are surgeons, lawyers, engineers, investment bankers, foreign service officers, auditors, air traffic controllers. But would-be experts are found among salespeople, computer operators, public relations personnel, and policemen.

For *helpers*, service means caring for people, responding to their needs. Helpers value relationships above all and seek to make the workplace a family. They represent a secondary American value, oriented to caring rather than to individualistic achievement or self-development. Typical helpers are teachers and nurses, but they can be found in most fields. A subgroup of helpers, *institutional helpers*, combines the values of helpers and defenders. For them, service means helping leaders. Although they are not a distinct character type, I included institutional helpers as a separate category in the survey questionnaire on values at work I developed for *Why Work* (see Appendix C) because this group seemed sufficiently different from the helper. However, people who find meaning in helping the leader *do not* necessarily care about people. The most productive institutional helpers care about defending the organization and its values. The less productive merely want to share the leader's strength; their desire to help is the company man or woman's need to identify with the powerful organization. I have not written a separate chapter on the institutional helper. Since most are mixtures of helpers and defenders, I include positive examples of institutional helpers in Chapters 4 and 5.

For *defenders*, service means policing and protection. Defenders are most concerned with values of survival and are also strong in the defense of human dignity. For them, this implies gaining power in order to enforce good values. They include both the corporate empire builders and their critics like Ralph Nader and government whistleblowers.

For *innovators*, service means creating new products or implementing a new competitive strategy. They value the play of creativity or the game of business for its own sake and the glory of winning, or in some cases, changing the world. They are naturally enterprising, like Bill Gates of Microsoft.

For the new generation, the *self-developers*, service means facilitating a problem-solving process with customers and clients. It is also an opportunity to learn, grow, and gain a sense of competency and independence. Self-developers value an egalitarian workplace where authority belongs to the one who is in the best position to deal with an issue or problem.

With these four types in mind, we can show why a partial man theory like that of economic man is not sufficient to describe what motivates different people. While it is true that for everyone, money as a reward is not satisfying if it is not considered fair market value, beyond this, money as a reward has different meanings that determine motivation. (See Value Drives and the Meaning of Money graphic.) For the expert, money is a form of status and recognition. For the helper, money

Value Drives and the Meaning of Money

indicates appreciation, and is a means for helping others. For the innovator, especially the gamesman, money is either a score that determines whether or not one is a winner or it is a resource to be used for new ventures. For the defender, money means dignity and justice, and is a means for power.

The union leader is not satisfied with gaining for members wages based on market value. Wages should provide enough money to live with dignity. In contrast for self-developers, monetary rewards should be a form of information, i.e. feedback on performance. Money is also a means for having fun and new experiences. Ideally, it will provide the independence to leave a frustrating or alienating job and look around for work that motivates. The Value Drives and Meaning of Money Circle summarizes these differences. It shows that while money is a motivator for all types, the reasons why this is so are different. This has implications concerning which rewards motivate best (see Chapter 9).

To study the distribution of the new character types in a workplace, a short questionnaire was constructed based on brief descriptions of each type. The questionnaire asks employees how and if they identify with the values motivating each type, and whether or not they are able to express these values in their own jobs. The first part of the questionnaire is reproduced below. After you fill it out you will be able to compare yourself to the people described in the next chapters. (Findings from administering the questionnaire to people in business and government are reported in Appendix C.)

The Values At Work Survey

How well does each statement describe your approach to work?

1. Very much   2. Somewhat   3. A little   4. Not at all

A. You approach your work as an expert. Whatever your job, you want to provide high-quality work and to exercise your skill and competence.

1   2   3   4

B. You approach your work as a helper. You want to help people.

1   2   3   4

C. You approach your work as a defender. You want to defend against those who do not respect the law, who do harm, or who undermine the values essential to a good organization.

1   2   3   4

D. You approach your work as a helper to those in positions of leadership. You want to strengthen your organization by serving well those who have the authority to make decisions.

1   2   3   4

E. You approach your work as an innovator who knows how to play the bureaucratic game. You want to win by making the organization more successful.

| 1 | 2 | 3 | 4 |

F. You approach your work as the means to a self-fulfilling life. You want your work to further your own development.

| 1 | 2 | 3 | 4 |

Which of the above approaches to work are most important to you? Please write the letters of those choices.

1st Choice _____

2nd Choice _____

To what extent does your current job permit you to take this positive approach?

	Very much	Somewhat	A little	Not at all
First choice	1	2	3	4
Second choice	1	2	3	4

To what extent does the following statement apply to you? You came to your job with a positive approach but have found that the system and its leaders keep you from working in this way.

| 1 | 2 | 3 | 4 |

Changing Social Character

The surveys support the view that we are in a time when the social character is changing. The expert character which fit the bureaucratic industrial world is sharing the stage with the self-developers. The experts still dominate leadership roles, which may account for the fact that so many people who feel they can express their intrinsic values in their job are dissatisfied with leadership at work. We shall return to these issues in the chapters that follow. But first, a note on the causes of the change in social character.

In the 1960s, social character began to change in the U.S.A., Canada and Western Europe. Why did social character change? Why does this change continue? First, general prosperity in the '60s undermined the frugal, self-sacrificing, and dutiful values of the social character formed in the first half of the century. The majority of the population in the U.S.A. and Western democracies became citizens of consumer-oriented societies, where they continually sought new forms of pleasure. Television flooded minds with images, ambitions, and wants. Affluent parents accepted and paid for their children's new needs for clothes, travel, and education. Employees with more years of schooling expected to continue their learning at work.

Second, political movements of both the New Right and New Left attacked bureaucracy as dehumanizing and set the stage for organizational change and the attitudes that have flourished in the '80s and '90s. In the U.S.A. in 1962, writing for a Left audience, Tom Hayden called for a new community, acceptance of one whole man by another whole man, not those forms of partial contact fostered by bureaucratic life. On the Right, Michael Bernstein's 1961 "Goldwater Manifesto" spoke for the "total man" against the crippled liberal bureaucrat who was seen as dependent on institutions and unable to stand up for liberty.[11] Both models of freedom aroused the national psyche.

In Europe, the rebellions in 1968 against bureaucratic authority followed the U.S. lead. Then in the '80s, young people began to see business rather than government as the place where they could best express themselves. In the '90s, however, they have lost the belief that government can solve many problems. Rather than hoping to change the world, today's young people have increasingly come to believe that progress means changing one's self. In the '90s, although Bill Clinton has more belief in the possibilities of government helping people than does Newt Gingrich, both share the view that government cannot help people on welfare unless these people take more responsibility for themselves.

---

[11] Garry Wills, *Nixon Agonistes* (New York: New American Library, 1979), p. 330.

The third reason for these social character changes is that the 1960s brought a new sense of individual rights and criticism of authority, which has continued in subsequent years. Workplace protections lessened fear of speaking out. The civil rights and antiwar movements reinforced the challenge to traditional authority. Activists identified authority with old men who hoarded power, sent the young men to war, and lied to the public about Watergate. Haunted by the threat of nuclear war and made indignant by reports of ecological damage, young people questioned the authority of science and technology that threatened the planet. These movements for rights and environmental protection still remain today as challenges to traditional authority.

The fourth change factor is that information technology, much of it developed in the space program, created new opportunities for entrepreneurs. Young engineers and scientists outstripped their elders and became impatient with outmoded ideas. These irreverent innovators modeled a new style of participative management in high-tech companies such as Hewlett-Packard and Texas Instruments. In the early '90s, the re-engineering movement flattened organizational hierarchies and empowered front-line employees, especially in service work. People took orders from customers rather than from bosses.

The fifth, and perhaps most important influence is the mass entry of women into the workplace. This pattern signaled the end of the family with a sole male wage-earner, and with it the traditional sex roles and the paternal model of managerial authority.

The dramatic rebellions of the '60s are over, but despite some backlash, trends begun then have continued and in the '80s and '90s have begun to transform the workplace. Although America is pulling back from sexual excess and self-indulgence, and rediscovering the need for discipline and good leadership, the forces changing values at work have not receded. The graphic, Increasing Responsibility of Women Workers for Family Financial Needs, shows these trends from 1975 to 1993. The percentage of dual-career families and those with a sole female working has been steadily increasing. The percentage of households with a sole male breadwinner has decreased from 69 percent in 1954 to 21 percent

The Increasing Responsibility of Women Workers for Family Financial Needs

Percent of All Families with Children in Each Family Type

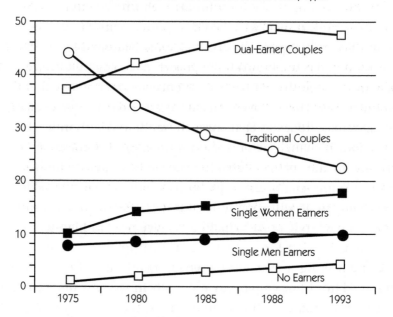

in 1993, while that of families in which both husband and wife work has jumped from 28 percent to about 50 percent, and those with a single female wage earner have increased from 4 percent to 16 percent.

Influence of Dual-Career Families

The self-developers tend to come from families where both parents worked. At an early age, they have had to adapt to strangers and develop interpersonal skills. Increasingly, American children are being raised to become self-developers by parents who are away at work much of the day. Between 1960 and 1990, the percentage of working mothers with children under one year of age jumped from 20 percent to over 50 percent, and working mothers with children ages 6-17 went from 40 to over 70 percent. The new social character no longer models itself on the paternal image at work, or on the maternal image at home.

The two-wage-earner family requires shared authority and trade-offs between work and family. Self-development means that both men and women must create their own models of maturity. It means a different motivation at work.

We are in a period of value transformations, pushed along by changes in work and family structures. Traditional and new value orientations exist side by side in organizations. Self-developers tend to be younger, but it is important to emphasize that a significant percentage of the young still identify with the traditional generation. Also, there is a communication gap between value types, even within the same age group. The traditional experts and helpers see the self-developers as egotistical and superficial, and do not recognize their greater flexibility and potential for cooperation. In turn, self-developers underestimate the value of knowledge and expertise. To motivate members of the new generation, we need leadership that understands them. To work more effectively, we need to understand ourselves and each other.

CHAPTER 2

WHAT MOTIVATES?

Why **do** we work?

When I traveled around the U.S. promoting the first edition of this book, some TV and radio interviewers said, "It is obvious why we work, to make money." Or, "We have to work, to survive." I responded by asking, "What would you do if you had all the money you needed?" The answer always was, after a brief pause, "I'd come to work." Some added, "I like this job."

Today, many people are not as satisfied as these TV or radio interviewers were with their jobs. Many people would be happier with jobs that make better use of their abilities, and stimulate them to learn. Even so, people do not work for money or survival alone. The peasant farmer, factory worker, service technician, and professional may employ different skills and knowledge, but all find personal and social meanings in work. Even when necessity forces us to take a job, financial need is not the only reason why we work.

Beyond Economic Motivation

Work ties us to a real world that tells us whether or not our ideas and visions make sense; it demands that we discipline our talents and master our impulses. To realize our potentialities, we must focus them in a way that relates us to the human community. We need to feel needed. And to feel needed, we must be evaluated by others in whatever coinage, tangible or not, culture employs. Our sense of dignity and self-worth depends on being recognized by others through our work. Without work, we deteriorate. We need to work.

Marie Jahoda, who studied the effects of unemployment, contrasted the manifest consequence of employment, losing one's income, with latent consequences based on five psychological functions of employment:

1. Imposition of time structure on the working day;

2. Regular shared experience and contacts outside of the nuclear family;

3. Linking individuals to goals and purposes that transcend them;

4. Personal status and identity; and

5. Daily exercise of activity and skill.[1]

While some people can structure their lives and to some extent satisfy these functions through self-directed activity, most people need to be employed, either by a company, or in the case of independent professionals, by their clients. Recent studies show that this is still true for most people.[2] However, in a world where employment becomes more scarce, people are being challenged to find goals, purposes, and structure through cooperative and volunteer activities.

Through work we express ourselves and practice commitment. When activity that springs from a spirit of play, like music or painting or sports, moves to the category of work, this implies a seriousness of purpose beyond pleasure in activity for its own sake. However, we differentiate work that expresses a vocation, work we love to do, from work we agree to do as a means of gaining a livelihood, having status as being employed, or paying our dues so that we can do "our own work." This is the way some university professors talk about teaching, as a chore that allows them to do research and writing. Assembly-line workers in a southern factory called this work "public work," which provided

---

[1] "Work Employment and Unemployment," *American Psychologist* 35, 2, 1981.

[2] Barbara Lenkerd, *Psychosocial Consequences of Unemployment* (Stockholm: City University Press, 1995).

enough money to support real work as parents, farmers, and craftsmen and craftswomen. Some new generation employees at AT&T said they needed their jobs to support their work as musicians.

Hope also drives us to work. We expect different kinds of rewards depending on our values. We hope our work will bring us money, pleasure, appreciation, fame, power, knowledge, independence, a better world, and possibly the satisfaction of creative fulfillment. The underside of hope is fear of not reaching our goals or measuring up to expectations. The urge to work is an emotional necessity directed by our values and opportunities.

Thus, the strongest universal motivators to work are self-expression, hope, and fear. Neurobiological research illustrates how necessary hope is to the survival drive. David Ingvar's research with the positron emission tomography (PET) scan shows computer-generated pictures of the brain during different states of mind. Ingvar finds that the brain turns off when people cannot anticipate a positive future.[3] We cannot solve problems without hope. People who face a dead end need to spark a facsimile of hope. Some retreat from life and seek hope where they can, in compulsive gambling or in a lottery ticket. Hope can come from denying unpleasant reality and escaping to a wishful future. But even optimism that is irrational becomes habit-forming, because it allows people to function. It motivates them to work for an elusive pay-off.

Of course, hopefulness depends not only on seeing opportunity, but also on a feeling of optimism. We all know people with sunny, optimistic dispositions, and we like to be around them. This emotional attitude of hope seems to be a natural quality or an inborn gift in some people. The attitude of hope attracts us to possibilities for growth, opportunities for productive relationships. For most of us, a hopeful attitude was nurtured by loving parents who satisfied our infant needs and promised us a bright future if we worked for it. Hope is bolstered by disciplined learning and achievement that make us feel we can take

---

3 David Ingvar, "Memory of the Future: An Essay on the Temporary Organization of Conscious Awareness," *Human Neurobiology*, 4, 1985.

advantage of opportunities. It is strengthened when as adults we take responsibility for creating a better future in every way we can. For those people whose hope wavers, and that is true some of the time for most of us, leadership can rekindle hope, at least for a while. Franklin Delano Roosevelt has been a model for Republican as well as Democratic leaders because he sparked hope in people during the depression of the 1930s. Ronald Reagan admired Roosevelt for this reason, and despite his sometimes fuzzy visions, while he was President, Reagan's optimism encouraged many Americans who wanted to believe him. Thus, the perennial appeal of motivational speakers preaching, "We can do it." But positive thinking can also become a narcotic, blurring unpleasant realities that require painful decisions and action.

Although even good leaders cannot create intrinsic motivation in others, they can direct and amplify it. Optimistic and supportive leaders bring out a positive attitude in those they lead, while worried, pessimistic leaders make everyone feel worse.[4] A skillful coach can pump up a team's intensity and drive to win. But the leadership that helps motivate best depends primarily on understanding the values of those led, as we shall discuss in Chapter 10.

To understand what motivates ourselves and others, we must identify the dynamic values that determine our needs. Such an understanding leads the way to both organizational productivity and to the development of our individual potential at work. Values are slippery concepts. They can be defined as "a principle, standard, or quality considered worthwhile or desirable."[5] This is the way we think of a statement of corporate values. They are principles or ideas considered desirable by top management. They may or may not correspond to group behavior. We also think of human values in a broader sense as

---

[4] Goran Ekvall and Jouko Arvonen, in Leadership Styles and Organizational Climate for Creativity, (Working paper, The Swedish Council for Management and Worklife Issues, Stockholm, 1984), show that 75 percent of the workplace climate, defined as feelings of optimism, openness to and support of subordinates' ideas, etc., is determined by leadership style.

[5] *American Heritage Dictionary of the English Language,* New College Edition, ed. William Morris (Boston: Houghton Mifflin Co., 1981).

the energized patterns of perceiving, thinking, wanting, and acting that determine individual and group behavior. I call these patterns value drives.

All of us are born with dynamic tendencies, drives that direct our actions. For example, we respond to pain with flight or fight; we are driven to repeat pleasures, master the environment, and communicate.[6] While all human beings share these dynamic tendencies, they express and direct these different values according to the culture, acting through family, school, and workplace. Those value drives or energized values shared by members of a social class or culture comprise their "social character."

Social character is a biologically necessary function of culture. Human decision making is less genetically programmed than that of other creatures. Our shared values (social character) allow us to act instinctively, as it were, in ways that are common to members of a culture and that facilitate effective social relations. Otherwise, we would be overwhelmed with conflicting impulses and paralyzed by the constant demand to evaluate and decide what to do and how to interpret the behavior of others. Enough must be programmed into us to participate in the culture. But we also need flexibility to adapt to change. In our education, we human beings need a balance between structure and freedom.

As we grow up, we can develop these values by defining ourselves, deciding what we should do or not do in different situations, and disciplining ourselves with good habits so that we can achieve desirable goals. However, few people make the effort to define and shape their values (see Chapter 7). Most people do not question the values taught them; they accept the values taught in the family, school, and workplace. Indeed, those who are unable to internalize these values are unable to adapt to the mainstream society. Only when these values

---

6 Some psychologists and ethologists who study socioeconomic systems and cultural patterns object to the use of the term *drives* as unobservable and prefer using *behaviors* or *behavior patterns*. In Appendix B, I explain why I use the term *value drives*.

conflict with each other or don't work will most people start thinking about changing their values. Now is such a time for people who have experienced dramatic changes in the workplace. An example of those experiencing change is the group of experts, described in Chapter 4, who must transform hierarchical values that may have worked to gain them their management position, but impede their ability to work effectively on teams.

Value drives are the energized way in which human beings satisfy the strivings that we all share for survival, relatedness, meaning, and various forms of self-expression. How do we determine which are the shared drives that become the values and needs that motivate people at work? Psychologists and psychoanalysts study motivation through experiments and clinical observation. In this book, I try to integrate their findings in the light of my own experience with the emotionally disturbed in my consulting room and with ordinary people at work in many different cultures.

Most psychoanalytic views of motivation are limited by the sample of humanity upon which they are based—the emotionally disturbed, mostly from a common culture and social class, i.e., the white, urban upper-middle class, studied in an artificial setting such as the hospital or the psychoanalyst's office. The psychoanalyst is not likely to study values as they operate in healthy, productive people, but as they are expressed in perverted form, by patients with unconscious conflicts and addictive, irrational needs.

Thus, psychoanalytic theories apply the psychology of illness to healthy situations. These theories assume that attitudes expressed by mature people at work are all formed in early childhood. In contrast, in the tradition of Erich Fromm, David Riesman, and Erik Erikson, I expand psychoanalytic theory to nonpatients and, as an anthropologist, observe the workplace in different countries and social classes. Social character concepts are tools for understanding both health and sickness.

My observation and study of children and adults, the emotionally disturbed and the healthy, peasant farmers and high-tech managers, have challenged me to make sense of similarities and differences in human motivation that are not explained by the existing theories of motivation. At the same time, we all have our own theories of motivation, of what moves people. Usually the explanations are partial man theories (see Chapter 1) that focus on money, power, or status. However, the concepts presented here provide intellectual tools for others to use to develop, critically examine, and refine their own working theories of motivation.

The search for goals and behaviors common to all cultures leads me to group value drives into eight categories: survival, relatedness, pleasure, information, mastery, play, dignity, and meaning. (See Appendix B for a note on how I arrived at these categories.) This is not a hierarchy of values; every person expresses each drive in some form. Furthermore, values may be in conflict. At certain times, one drive will dominate. The value of survival usually takes precedence over the others, but not always. For example, a person may risk death to preserve dignity or freedom, or to protect others; or death may be accepted because it has religious meaning. Some people risk their lives for the pleasure of mastering mountains or winning car races. Paranoiacs sacrifice relationships in their drive for elusive total security; their investment in defense leaves little energy for health, education, and welfare.

Because all eight value drives are what make us human, we cannot rank any of them as necessarily higher versus lower. But each drive can be expressed in values that are either lower — primitive and childlike, or higher — mature and developed. Higher values expand consciousness and inner freedom, increase hope and creative power. Work can be a means for developing our values and becoming more integrated and purposeful, or it can cause a conflict of values, for example between achievement and close family life.

Needs and Drives

In common language, we speak of needs, not value drives to describe the feelings that motivate us. How many times a day do we use the phrase, "I need"? We say, "I need to work," or "I need to eat," not "I am driven to work." But the term *need* refers to both a feeling and to a value; I use the term *value drive* to emphasize that motivating values are felt as needs and to stimulate readers to evaluate their needs. Human needs are never purely physiological; we always express a value when we speak of a need. A need statement can always be transformed into a value statement. If I say, "I need something," ask me what will happen if I don't get it. The answer, "I'll be lonely, less capable, humiliated," describes a value—relatedness, mastery, dignity. Even necessity ("I need it to survive") expresses a universal value of preserving life. We can correlate some common needs with their common values.

Need	Value
Eating, drinking, sex	Survival, pleasure
Dependency, protection, love	Relatedness
Achievement, glory, fame	Mastery, dignity

To evaluate needs, we can distinguish three types: developmental, maintenance, and addictive. These kinds of needs can either strengthen or weaken us, depending on the values they express. *Developmental needs* activate us and increase energy; they include the need to know, to achieve, and to create through art and science. *Maintenance needs* keep us going and maintain a sense of dignity through good habits. They usually refer to necessities for maintaining health. They include eating (in moderation) and sleeping, exercising mind and body. Both developmental and maintenance needs require discipline, and both strengthen us. *Addictive needs* weaken us; they are needs for drugs and also the perverse needs for sadistic power, effortless luxury, narcissistic adulation, and false hopes. When our drives are directed by productive values, we make decisions and practice habits that serve our best interests; we strengthen developmental needs. When we are driven unconsciously by irrational values, we have addictive needs. Even needs that are developmental at one stage of life, like dependence on a good teacher, can later become addictive bonds that sap our initiative and self-confidence.

Feeling Motivated

Normally, we are not particularly conscious of being motivated to work. But when faced with a problem to solve, or an opportunity to exploit, we are suddenly aware of being motivated. Pressure makes us aware of our values as pressing needs to act. Frustration brings out our drives. We are stymied by a problem and feel a need to solve it. We are threatened and feel a determination to prevail. We are insulted and feel a need for self-assertion and dignity. But drives can also be repressed and unconscious. Today, many people repress the fury generated by attacks on their self-esteem. This repression is caused by a conflict of values; for example, the desire to keep your job clashing with a wish to punch the boss in the nose, an impulse which goes underground. The wish does not disappear, but festers into some form of bad-humored resentment.

Workaholics are driven by irrational drives such as the need to gain a parent's approval. Those of us less irrationally motivated express the work ethic in the need to be responsible or to achieve and create. We are most motivated when work satisfies both our developmental (intrinsic motivational) and maintenance (extrinsic motivational) needs. We feel the most productive energy when there is an opportunity to satisfy these needs through a balance of work, leisure, and play. Our energy either is strengthened and focused by these activities, or it is dissipated through addictive needs and frozen by frustration and repression.

The Eight Value Drives in the Workplace

Different situations at work stimulate different drives. Furthermore, different character types are motivated by patterns of value drives, which, as we shall see, have been reinforced by different types of family subcultures. For example, the dominant drive for the expert is mastery; for the helper it is relatedness. The innovator combines play and mastery; the defender combines dignity and mastery, while the self-developer focuses on mastery, information, play, and pleasure. The Value Drives graphic on the next page presents the value drives and the different ways they are expressed in needs that range from the more primitive to the most developed.

The Eight Value Drives Expressed As Needs

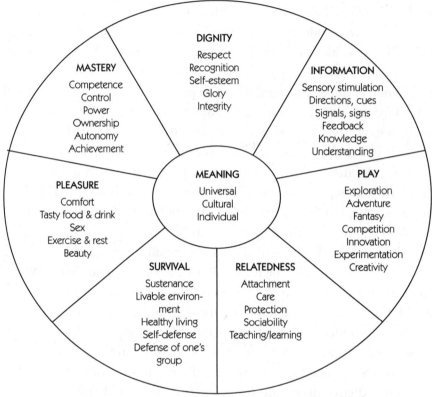

Drive for Survival: This drive results from the need to gain sustenance, nutrition, a livable environment (temperature, air), healthy rhythms of sleep and wakefulness, relief from life-threatening stress, avoidance of danger, and the means of defending oneself or one's family by flight or fight. For many people in a rich society like the United States, worries about survival focus not on getting enough to eat, but on maintaining health through diet, exercise, and relief of stress. Indeed, with affluence, survival becomes a less dominant concern.

But survival remains a powerful drive that can trigger flight or fright. The human organism is quickly mobilized by real and imaginary threats to survival. Indeed, a problem for the organizational careerist is that threats to employment security or even promotion are reacted to with the same rush of endocrines and feeling of fear that Neolithic men and women felt in the face of attack by wild animals. When our survival drive is triggered, emotions of flight or fight and catastrophic images dominate thought and behavior. The possibility of layoffs and unemployment, even uncertainty during reorganizations, alert the survival drive. Crisis produces adrenaline, which first activates but eventually paralyzes the body. Good leadership can calm survival anxieties by presenting a hopeful vision and directing people to act for the common good. The job of the leader throughout history has been to direct survival drives to common goals, to express and defend a vision that infuses followers with hope.

But sometimes it is essential for leaders to break through defenses and mobilize anxiety to save an organization: people must be told that unless they cut costs, produce more, improve quality, the business will go under. This kind of situation is always risky. While survival fear focuses energy, it narrows interest to looking out for "number one." For many employees, especially in large organizations, personal security becomes the overwhelming need; insecurity drives them to unproductive politics, protecting themselves by trying to undermine rivals.

Like the other seven drives, survival can dominate personality. When this occurs, a person is forever oriented to defense. The jungle fighter is the survival-obsessed character who sees the world in terms of threats to survival and organizes other value drives—relatedness, mastery, meaning—around this orientation. Such people need power over others to quiet their fear. The most positive version of the type is the protector, who expands the drive to survive to include others.

In the workplace today, survival is interpreted as employment security. Without it, people learn they will not survive, even though this may be an exaggeration. Each character type emphasizes his or her own style of maintaining a sense of employment security. Traditional craftsmen believe they will maintain security by self-reliance, by controlling nature and the world around them as farmers or builders of needed goods. Modern bureaucratic experts expect to find security in both specialization, expertise, and seniority. Helpers trust in family-type groups like unions where people stick together. Self-developers, brought up in relative affluence, are least worried about employment security, but they are concerned with maintaining and developing their marketable skills. The fear for them, as for the gamesman, is not survival, but of being a loser in the career game, not finding work that engages them. The gamesmen-innovators are unique in that danger triggers their productive motivation. The challenge turns them on.

Drive for Relatedness: This is the drive for attachment, care, protection, communication, sociability, teaching, and learning. Relatedness is essential to sanity. Different modes of relatedness separate illness from health. A neurotic is someone who lives with fantasies more than with people; the totally unrelated individual is psychotic. Psychoanalysis has charted the development of the drive for relatedness. Originally, Freud focused on the individualistic sexual drive, but in his later years, he took more account of the infant's drive for relatedness, when he realized that the child's tie to the mother began long before the Oedipal Stage. Since Freud, other psychologists—for example, Rene Spitz, Margaret Mahler, John Bowlby, and Mary Ainsworth—have studied infants and young children, showing how relatedness develops and describing negative results when the drive is frustrated.[7] William James had earlier observed infantile instincts of imitation, sympathetic response, smiling, and attachment — all beginnings of the drive toward relatedness.[8]

From early childhood, we have all sought to be understood and to be connected with other human beings. The drives for care, protection, and recognition inevitably clash with other more individualistic drives for autonomy, mastery, play, dignity. The resolution of these conflicts depends not only on individual character, but also on the culture and its support for diverse, individual expression. When George Foster and I

---

[7]   Rene A. Spitz, *The First Year of Life* (New York: International Universities Press, 1965). Margaret S. Mahler, Fred Pine, and Anni Bergman, *The Psychological Birth of the Human Infant* (New York: Basic Books, 1974). John Bowlby, *Separation: Anxiety and Anger*, vol. 2 (New York: Basic Books, 1973). Mary D. Ainsworth, "Attachment: Retrospect and Prospect," in *The Place of Attachment in Human Behavior*, eds. C. M. Parkes and J. Stevenson-Hinde (New York: Basic Books, 1982).

[8]   William James, *Principles of Psychology* (Cambridge, Mass.: Harvard University Press, 1983).

studied Mexican villagers, we found one of the most original potters in the village suffered crippling anxiety because he was too original and feared being ostracized by the other villagers.[9] In contrast, our society supports the process of individuation, breaking away from constraining relationships to express the self. At an early age, we already react to "excessive" care as constraining. Paradoxically, we want to be free, but not lonely, so we seek playmates, work partners, or the camaraderie of a team. As we become more individuated, to avoid isolation we must seek others who share our values and support our aims.

The chance to enjoy sociability at work is a significant motivation for many people. It must be considered in the design of a motivating workplace and the selection of people for jobs. In *The Leader*, I reported that many assembly-line workers in the Harman auto parts factory in Bolivar, Tennessee, said that socializing was the most important aspect of their work, and they rejected more challenging jobs that would have isolated them from conversation. When I repeated this to a group of General Mills managers and workers, I was told a story about two women who spent years dropping coupons into cereal boxes coming off the line at a factory. When they were told by a manager that the job was to be automated and that they would be relieved of the monotony, they were disappointed. The manager asked if they liked the job. They told him the job had long ago become automatic, but they had spent the work hours talking to each other about their outside lives. Each knew the other's family intimately. What they would miss were the daily conversations. In Cambridge, Massachusetts, mothers working on computer terminals at home preferred bringing their children to a child-care center at a common workplace where they could talk to each other.

The vision of the electronic cottage industry appeals to expert programmers, telemarketers, and perhaps financial consultants. But the loneliness of the word processor turns off many in the new generation. In 1987, a poll showed that when given a choice between working at

---

[9] Michael Maccoby and George M. Foster, "Methods of Studying Mexican Peasant Personality," *Anthropological Quarterly*, 43 (October 1979), pp. 225-242.

the office or at home by telecommuting, only 7 percent of employees chose to stay at home.[10] Studies at AT&T show this to be somewhat higher today, but the vast majority of employees enjoy face-to-face interaction. What we shall probably see is a larger number of people working part time at home, but maintaining face-to-face relationships at the workplace.

The satisfaction of work relations is not limited to lower levels of organizations. People underestimate the glue of fellowship in organizations, especially at the top. In Los Angeles, marketing managers of a large technology company became independently rich buying and selling real estate. Yet they did not leave the company. The reason: they enjoyed being part of a team and learning about new products. In traditional companies, the father-son mentoring relationships provided deep satisfaction. Among competitive peers, those who have overcome obstacles together feel bonds of affection that facilitate teamwork. Top managers in large corporations have told me that being part of a supportive team and sharing values are among the most satisfying aspects of their work, but they seldom generalize this experience to the design of lower-level work.

Relatedness for helpers includes contact not only with co-workers, but also with customers and clients. When the Communications Workers of America (CWA) organized social workers in New Jersey, Morton Bahr, the union president, noted that a new type of resolution was introduced at meetings. In contrast to expert-type union technicians, who demanded better pay and improved working conditions for themselves, the social workers demanded more help for their clients.

The development of the drive for relatedness requires the ability to question authority and break the chains of dependency. Many who work in organizations, especially the experts and the helpers, fail to achieve a sense of independence. They experience the organization as a protective family, and their drives for security and relatedness merge into powerful transferential feelings toward the leader, inappropriately

---

[10] Study reported in *The Wall Street Journal*, March 30, 1987, p.21.

seen as a parent, feared and loved as though one were still a child. The strong transference motivates one to please the parent. This is why traditional entrepreneurial leaders could motivate subordinates so effectively by expressions of approval. The new character, the self-developer, is more critical of parents and authority, more intent on gaining independence, and therefore less moved by transferential drives that make managers into father figures. Self-developers are less likely to seek mentors, but also less likely to be mentors.

Drive for Pleasure: This is the drive to gain comfort (avoiding discomfort and pain), sexual satisfaction, tasty food and drink, stimulation, novelty, fun, beauty. Physiologically, there are three types of pleasure: appetite, as in sweet taste or sexual arousal; tension reduction, as in orgasm; and activity pleasure, as in the harmonious exercise of mind and body. Pleasure and pain are the infant's first way of learning and they forever influence all value drives. For the adolescent, sexuality is, of course, most demanding, experienced in continual frustration and frequent fantasy. Pleasure is developed aesthetically as good taste, a love of beauty, and a sense of harmony. It is developed ethically as the pleasure of staying within the rules. It is developed creatively as the pleasure in learning, innovating, designing, building, crafting, and helping things grow. However, the drive for pleasure is easily transformed into addictive needs that undermine productive values.

Historically, economic conditions have placed limits on the expression of the pleasure drive. In an era of scarcity, the Puritan Ethic demanded self-restraint, ascetic control, and mastery of the pleasure drive. Of course, today, in an era of relative abundance, such prohibitions are no longer considered necessary by most people. By lifting the limitations placed on private and public pleasure, we fertilize the economy of a society, allowing an infinite number of needs to flower. But we also increase the possibility that addiction to pleasure might undermine drives for mastery and self-control.

What implications does the strengthening of the pleasure values have for the workplace? The liberation of the pleasure drive means that people want and expect work to be more fun. If the workplace fails to fulfill needs for pleasure, workers seek pleasure in ways that divert them from work. Correspondingly, where work is more fun and, as we shall see, playful, people invest more of themselves at work, just as they would in a game.

Drive for Information: This is the drive to gain sensory stimulation, messages (directions, cues, signals), feedback, knowledge, understanding. From early infancy, we seek information in the form of sights and sounds that exercise our faculties, and in messages that reassure us. As we grow older, we need information to orient ourselves to the world we live in and avoid danger, find pleasurable experiences, and master skills. Also, the brain transforms information into memory and uses it to project visions of a desirable future, the hope essential to motivation. This ability to gather information from our environment is necessary to feeling human. Psychologists have found that putting a person into a dark, soundproof room disintegrates the individual's sense of self.

Culture and language shape the drive for information. In different cultures, people attend to and name the world according to their needs and traditions. Peasants notice and react to small differences in crops and animals, information that would not register in the urban mind. In peasant villages, information about neighbors, gossip, is highly valued as a form of social control. In modern organizations, gossip becomes the main source of information when people lose trust in the messages coming down from the top.

All of us seek useful feedback, information that tells us how we are doing and how we are evaluated. People are motivated by the opportunity to get results. They enjoy seeing the score and the chance to improve it. They want to know plans so they can adapt. Lack of information is troubling. Yet some managers tend to hoard information and remain stingy with positive feedback.

As we grow, we acquire, store, and transform information more effectively to adapt to our environment and realize our aspirations. Also, we learn to identify and solve problems and test hypotheses; we transform information into understanding the meaning of information and knowledge, the "knowing how to" use information. With maturity, we develop wisdom, the ability to predict the consequences of our decisions or the exercise of knowledge.

Managements often puzzle over how difficult it is to communicate information to the troops. Yet, when the message is trusted or appreciated, there is no communication problem. In a corporate building with 3,000 employees, the executive in charge worried about improving communications. But he noticed that one winter day when an announcement was made at 2 p.m. that because of blizzard warnings, employees could leave early, the building cleared out within ten minutes. The problem was not in the process of communication but in the credibility of the message.

We are most motivated to acquire information that satisfies our values. Experts scan for information in their areas of expertise that maintain their sense of mastery, and they filter out what they consider irrelevant information, such as human problems. In contrast, helpers like information about people. The ears of defenders perk up when there is information about threats, plots, dangers to their sense of security. Innovators seek information to design new approaches. Self-developers have from childhood sought new experiences and information that expand their horizons, scanning for trends so that they can prepare for an ever-changing future.

There is a reverse side to this need to know: the addiction to information as predigested experience, a cognitive fast food. This is a danger for the new generation, raised on instant knowledge from television and the computer. Members of the new generation need discipline to filter and edit useful information, and beyond this, to develop deeper interest in and understanding of the world and themselves.

Drive for Mastery: This is the drive for competence, control, ownership, autonomy, achievement, power. Mastery is directed not simply toward the external world, but also toward the self. Survival and hope of success demand competence; moderation and discipline of drives require self-mastery. If we are to adapt to the world, maintain dignity, and enjoy life, our drives must be tamed or managed. Children struggle to walk, talk, and manipulate their environment. Watch the frustration of infants when they cannot move around or make themselves understood. Mastery of language skills allows us to participate in a human group. Expertise and craftsmanship are mature expressions of mastery.

The need for achievement strengthens and develops the mastery drive. People are motivated by challenges that stretch but do not exceed their skills. The research of David McClelland, the Harvard psychologist, has shown that people with a strong need for achievement continually push themselves to master new tasks and develop competence.[11] But mastery requires some control over the job. Where the drive for mastery is frustrated at work, it is either expressed elsewhere or perverted. In 1971, an auto worker with strong pride in his skill told me that the fast-moving assembly line blocked any attempt to care about craftsmanship. He and others expressed their sense of mastery in a perverted way by trying to stop the line or sometimes by putting a soda bottle into a gas tank. But when work engages the drive for mastery, then both the company and workers benefit. Today in Fremont, California, at the Nummi plant (New United Motor Manufacturing Inc., General Motors in partnership with Toyota), assembly workers can stop the line at any time if they spot poor workmanship. In 1992, managers and union officials both reported that the gain in quality and motivation is much greater than the loss in downtime on this line.

Control and power are forms of mastery; the corollary of Lord Acton's dictum that "power tends to corrupt and absolute power corrupts absolutely" is the equally certain law that powerlessness perverts as it did in the case of the workers who sabotaged the assembly line. (This concept will be developed further in Chapter 8, during the discussion of Self-Development.) The meanings of power differ for different types. Defenders seek power as an addictive need to dominate or, more positively, to protect themselves and subordinates. Experts want power as authority to do the job in their own ways. Innovators want power to organize new approaches to serve customers better, and to improve the quality of life at work. In the technoservice economy, innovators know that to gain real power, they must create it for others. Unless their subordinates have power to satisfy customers and innovate, their own power will be constrained.

---

11 David G. McClelland, *The Achieving Society* (Glencoe, Ill.: The Free Press, 1967).

Drive to Play: This is the drive to explore, fantasize, find adventure, compete, experiment, innovate, and create. This drive might be grouped with mastery, since play can contribute to mastery by serving as a means of trying out new skills and strategies.[12] However, there is an important difference between play and other forms of mastery. Pure play belongs to the realm of freedom, while other forms of mastery are necessary to cope with the world and accommodate to authority. Play implies self-expression through exploration, experimentation, and invention. Only in its most developed forms, does play merge with mastery to become creative work: the innovation that depends on disciplined technique necessary to express artistic, scientific, and economic intuitions with beauty and elegance. (See Chapter 3 on The Innovator.)

In our society, parents and teachers sometimes make children sacrifice play to mastery. Accommodation and conformity can dampen the spirit of play. When the drive for play is repressed, it does not disappear, but may emerge as mischief, or go underground as fantasy, escape to the canned creations of the media or to an inner, isolated world. As a result, the personality becomes impoverished. Since free play is so individualistic, its development requires teaching that respects the unique individual or a temperament stubborn enough to resist regimentation.

My first experience as a psychotherapist was with children who could not learn, and who, I found, had also lost the capacity to play. They feared both the external world of parents and teachers who judged their work, and the internal one of their own angry fantasies.[13] Play that might express these impulses was felt to be dangerous. Treatment for these children made a game of fearful relationships. I played the roles of feared authorities in such a way that the child could laugh, gain control over impulses, and realize that learning and performance were not matters of life and death. Then the child could tolerate fantasies of terror, anger, and revenge. Through play, the children gained a sense of freedom and a sense of humor that rekindled their self-esteem and hope and allowed them to put energy into mastering schoolwork.

---

12 Jean Piaget, *Play, Dreams and Imitation in Childhood* (London: Heinemann, 1951).

13 Michael Maccoby, "The Game Attitude" (unpublished doctoral dissertation, Harvard University, 1960).

In America, the idea of making work into play has long been the ideal of entrepreneurs. The play spirit is a unique strength in this country. It sparks a spirit of exploration, competition, innovation, and adventure. It provides a sense of fun and meaning to businesspeople who enjoy making deals, marketers who play with product concepts, and researchers who test out hunches. Americans, more than any other nationality, are motivated by the opportunity to perform, to show off, to make work into play. At international management meetings, if asked to present a skit or sing a song, the Americans are the first to respond. (Other nationalities need a few drinks.) Workers in factories that have won awards enjoy performing for visitors. Recently, I visited the AT&T Power Systems factory in Dallas, the first American manufacturing facility to win the Deming Prize, Japan's highest award for quality. The factory of about 4,000 employees has been divided into 39 skilled, empowered teams, which do their own planning, scheduling, and problem solving with minimum supervision from supervisor-coaches. Teams give themselves names — the Top Dockers, The Providers, the A-Team, and also design logos. When I visited, each team was eager to present its story. This was three weeks before Christmas and at lunch, in the cafeteria, a diverse group of employees serenaded us with Christmas carols and popular songs.

In the regimented workplace, people joke and play jokes as a form of rebellion. If this drive is engaged at work, and if there is a sense of game spirit, people easily become motivated. The new generation wants more play at work, or work as play, and management that can provide it, at least some of the time, is rewarded with more motivated employees. People who are most effective with computers have played with them; they feel at ease with the machine as their tool, not their master.

However, the drive to play must be managed. Unbridled play becomes unproductive: the gambling gamesman playing with other people's lives, the expert's infatuation with high tech as an expensive toy instead of a useful tool. Love of play can cause instability and waste. The spirit of play is best engaged at work by the chance to experiment and innovate, to question organizational forms and practices and try out new ones. It is the spirit that founded and built America, a society constructed on the impulse to experiment with new models. It can be harnessed at all levels of organizations.

Drive for Dignity: This is the drive to gain respect, self-esteem, glory, integrity. We must value ourselves to survive; our sense of dignity, self-esteem, and integrity is essential to productive motivation. Notice the response of shame, pain, and anger when a young child is ridiculed. The drive for dignity appears fragile, easily crushed, but this perception is misleading. As adults, we know the pressures to survive or accommodate to a job may cause us to swallow humiliation. But while the drive for dignity may be frustrated, it is not extinguished, and takes another form. It is often perverted into fantasy, revenge, and hatred. This frozen rage of people at work can explode into destructive violence. This has occurred when people have been abruptly fired after years of loyal service.

Despite the dramatic consequences of wounds to dignity, including inner-city murders provoked by feelings of disrespect (being "dissed"), psychologists seldom refer to this drive. When they do, they confuse dignity with narcissism, which is the drive to love thwarted and turned back on the self. Heinz Kohut, a psychoanalytic theorist of the self, portrays narcissism as a normal drive, when, in fact, the patients he describes express narcissistic behavior as a reaction to dignity wounded in early childhood.[14] The drive for dignity is a normal one, common to all societies. It unfolds naturally if a child is lovingly valued. Neglected, unloved children can suffer deep wounds to their dignity. Feeling worthless, they compensate with grandiose narcissistic fantasies of becoming loved by everyone. Oppressed children identify with their oppressors and internalize their guilt, turning their anger against themselves. Thereby, they borrow the dignity of the powerful person. In contrast, overly admired and indulged children have an inflated sense of self-importance, and an exaggerated sense of dignity.

In healthy children, the demand for fairness and justice expresses the drive for dignity. At about age three to six, children recognize that

---

14 Heinz Kohut, *The Restoration of the Self* (New York: International Universities Press, 1977).

others share the same feelings. The family and culture facilitate this emotion through teaching and games. Children learn to curb their egocentric drives and to respect the dignity of others. It is the role of the parent and teachers to shame disrespectful children, not enough to humiliate them, but enough to ensure they learn good manners. Shamed in early childhood by a caring elder, children avoid being shunned later by a community that harshly punishes disrespect for others and the law. Plato and Aristotle argued that the capacity to feel shame made ethical development possible, since shameless people are beyond the reach of the moral community.[15]

Older children may damage their sense of dignity by playing the fool, letting themselves be pushed around, or betraying themselves to avoid a fight or to gain an advantage. These self-betrayals later affect adult behavior in organizations. As I reported in *The Gamesman*, climbers within bureaucracies reveal a sense of self-disgust because they give in too easily to the boss. This loss of integrity is disheartening and dampens motivation at work. Another person can wound my dignity, but the only way I can repair it is by acting with courage and self-respect.

Much human destructiveness results from frustrating the drive for dignity. Gandhi pointed out that people without dignity could not practice his nonviolent *satyagraha* (truth force).[16] We must express our rage and either avenge humiliation or activate a sense of humility through prayer. Gandhi, like Jesus, became a model for maintaining dignity despite poverty, both in teaching and in the practice of a simple, healthy, self-sufficient way of life. Of course, the drive for dignity can dominate the personality. False pride, touchiness, the confusion of dignity with special privilege, the compulsive drive for approval, all these strivings for a sense of dignity undermine relationships and destroy teamwork. In contrast, the positive qualities of the playful gamesmen include the ability to lose without losing face, and

---

[15] Plato, *Laws*, II, 671, trans. B. Jowett (Princeton, N.J.: Bollingen Foundation; Princeton University Press, 1973). Aristotle, *Nicomachean Ethics*, IV, 9 (Indianapolis: Bobbs-Merrill, 1962).

[16] Erik H. Erikson, *Gandhi's Truth* (New York: W. W. Norton and Co. Inc., 1969), pp. 184, 197, 207ff.

to detach themselves from the game while enjoying the play, strategy, and tactics. To gamesmen, joking put-downs and locker-room banter serve as homeopathic doses of humiliation that inoculate against serious loss of self-esteem.

In some people, the drive for dignity is so easily bruised that they compensate by overdefending it. Swedes suppress their spirit of play at work for fear of losing dignity. For the Japanese, dignity is "face" and losing it can make life worthless. Machismo is an unending struggle to maintain an exaggerated sense of dignity. In Latin and Islamic cultures, men express what seems like a caricature of touchy dignity compared to the English-speaking cultures, whose playful and self-critical humor lightens up organizational life. If we can maintain a sense of integrity, then the ability to laugh at our exaggerated need for dignity is a sign of emotional maturity. There is a universal appeal to this shared humor in Charlie Chaplin's silent ballets, which deflate the pompous and create sympathy for the tramp's struggle to maintain dignity at the bottom of the social pyramid, even on the assembly line of the movie, *Modern Times*.

In the United States, a person's sense of dignity and self-esteem depends all too much on repeated success, because being a winner rather than a loser is like an infusion of dignity. To Americans of all social and economic groups, the promise of winning is highly motivating. We admire the competitors in business, the arts, entertainment, science, government, and sports, who gain the glory of the winner's circle. As a culture, we have a strong need to win and an overdose of optimism. Since we expect to win, to be branded a loser by others or oneself is especially humiliating. In the workplace, good management not only respects employees, but also gives them opportunities to win by setting goals they can reach. The effective manager not only rewards success, but also presents employees to their peers as winners. However, the success must be real to be motivating, and the award meaningful to others who recognize and certify one's achievement. Otherwise, awards can backfire and cause disaffection and cynicism.

A manager of telephone operators, a paternalistic expert, described to me his practice of recognizing the operator of the month, an initiative which he believed was motivating. I asked one young woman, the current recipient of the award, about her feelings and if she were motivated by the award. "I'm embarrassed," she said. "All the girls think I'm sleeping with him." In contrast in suburban Chicago and Salt Lake City, AT&T operators began to reward achievements in a different way. They would pin on the bulletin boards photos of fellow workers who were helpful to customers and colleagues, with the result of boosting self-esteem, increasing solidarity, and raising productivity.

Respect for another's sense of dignity is essential to the trust needed for success in the information age. There are degrees of trust, from the willingness to explore mutual interests and agreement, to joint activities, to teamwork, to friendships that make people vulnerable to each other. The beginning of any productive relationship requires trust that the other person will not take advantage of our goodwill. There must be a sense of mutual respect. If people do not feel respected, they will not even begin to develop relationships that can lead to mutual benefits.

In AT&T's Workplace of the Future, cooperation has begun by building trust based on respect for each person. If American managers want workers to take responsibility, they can never discount dignity. Managers must rebuild employees' self-esteem and confidence; they must repair the damage done in autocratic classrooms where working-class children were made to feel stupid, and by jobs where they were told not to think. Bureaucratic factories and offices have further bruised the dignity of workers by emphasizing hierarchical differences, including special privileges for managers. These privileges are now disappearing in places where the goal is to increase productive motivation. At Ford and GM factories, the reserved space for management cars has been replaced by first-come, first-served parking. Everyone eats in the same cafeteria. A greater sense of equality strengthens and helps to create teamwork. By attacking status, these companies also deflate an exaggerated sense of managerial dignity that blocks managers' learning from subordinates and customers. At the height of the bureaucratic-industrial era, during the first part of the 20th Century, organization man gained dignity by being the *paterfamilias*, the breadwinner and boss at home. Today, a renewed spirit of individual rights and dual-wage-earner families affirms dignity in relationships that involve greater equality between men and women. For some people, being a part of a powerful organization, even in a minor role, provides a sense of dignity, but I find increasingly that employees, from the front line to the executive suite, resent submitting to a boss. In recent years, many entrepreneurs in search of dignity as well as fortune have left management positions in large companies.

Everyone wants respect and esteem from others, but each type protects dignity in a characteristic manner. Experts find dignity in autonomy and professional certification that insulate them from bureaucratic indignities or in the role of the salesman, from the humiliation of repeated rejection. Helpers find dignity in being needed and in being a part of a protective family. Defenders gain a sense of dignity through power, and the willingness and ability to fight those who threaten it. The innovator's sense of dignity comes from a freedom to experiment and create, achievement that promises fame and glory. And self-developers consider dignity their right. They expect to be treated with dignity, and if not, are prepared to leave the situation, be it job, marriage, or a business interaction.

Success in the technoservice economy requires careful attention to the dignity of both employees and customers. The American spirit of freedom makes service seem like servility. There is a notable lack of the service spirit in bureaucracies, and the helpers in service jobs feel like second-class citizens. Customers feel lucky to get help. Only if they can play the service role with dignity can we expect service employees to respect the dignity of customers.

Drive for Meaning: This is the drive that integrates the other drives and make sense of each situation by infusing value, seeking reasons, finding hope in religious transcendence. All other needs are eventually shaped by the drive for meaning. It is the strategic drive. Although we may not be conscious of it, we give meaning to all our experiences and impulses. Even when we sleep, the drive toward meaning continues in our dreams. The healthy person finds shared meanings that contribute to growth. The neurotic clings to childish, irrational meanings covered by self-deceiving rationalizations. Without meaning that gives hope, there is no motivation. Emile Durkheim, the French sociologist, observed that extreme economic fluctuations that either wipe out men and women in small businesses and make their struggles and hopes meaningless, or that create equally meaningless windfalls, cause depression and suicide.[17]

Harry Stack Sullivan, the psychiatrist, differentiated three kinds of human meanings: universal, culturally given, and private.[18] Universal meanings are based on shared human experiences such as the sun as a source of light and life. Culturally given meanings are embedded in language and folklore, and learned by all members of a particular culture; thus, in tropical countries, the sun is also a destroyer, but not in Scandinavia. And finally there are private meanings: individual experiences determine whether dogs will be thought of as dangerous or as warm and loyal companions.

All three types of meaning are formed in childhood, but with development, meanings change. Piaget showed that children at age three give meaning to events according to principles of egocentrism. For example, if they disobey parents and then step on a rotten board that breaks, they think this is punishment for misbehavior. Prescientific man imputed meaning in terms of spirits and gods. The growth of our knowledge determines the meanings we give to events, but the meaning we give to our own self integrates cultural messages and experience and forms our sense of identity.

In wartime, work has the meaning of defending the nation: the same boring work that turns off a worker in ordinary times becomes essential during war. In the monopolistic Bell System, the meaning of work for managers was expressed in the spirit of service, of providing all America with the best telephone service in the world. In the competitive marketplace of today, gamesmen at AT&T and the Bell Operating Companies are motivated by the chance to innovate and be winners. But this does not inspire some helpers, who feel the spirit of service has been lost. Because of different meanings, one worker may be motivated

---

[17] Emile Durkheim, *Suicide: A Study in Sociology*, trans. J. Spaulding and G. Simpson (Glencoe, Ill.: The Free Press, 1951).

[18] Harry Stack Sullivan, *The Interpersonal Theory of Psychiatry* (New York: W.W. Norton and Co. Inc., 1953). See pp. 28ff for a discussion of syntaxic (culturally given), prototaxic (universal), and parataxic (private) meanings.

by the same work that turns off another, as in the story of two medieval stonemasons. One was bent over, drained after a day of work, while the other sang to himself. Asked what they had been doing, the first said, "I have been lifting heavy stones all day." The second said, "I have been building a cathedral." Today, there are still bricklayers and stonemasons motivated by working on buildings that serve meaningful functions, and who speak of their pride in buildings that require quality craftsmanship. These same workers speak of being turned off when working on poorly designed buildings or those where the desire for profit results in the use of inferior materials.

Without a powerful shared religion or a common enemy such as communism, meaning has become a problem in our society. The weakening of traditional religion, family ties, and patriotism, leaves us as a nation without common meanings. There is also confusion about the meaning of work, especially for the new generation of self-developers. Most Americans no longer consider work as a means of survival or as the dutiful support of a family. Business leaders explain their own work by such socially meaningful terms as creating wealth for owners and employment for workers, helping customers to succeed, providing the public with needed services, and supporting innovation. But they try to motivate workers by telling them they must work hard to beat the competition and keep their jobs. This motivation is not enough.

When everyone shares a positive meaning at work, the workplace becomes more attractive and intrinsic motivation is strengthened. But character types are differentiated by the different meaning each gives to work: expertise, helping, protecting people, innovating, self-enhancement.

In summary, each of the drives can be expressed in terms of developmental or addictive needs, as the Developmental vs. Addictive Needs graphic summarizes. Developmental needs are active. They are needs *to do* something that increases one's freedom, individuation, and creative power. Developmentally, the survival drive becomes a need to protect others as well as oneself. The drive for relatedness becomes a need to love, to understand and care for others, and to be loved in return. The drive for pleasure becomes a need to experience and create beauty. The drive for information becomes a need to learn and understand.

Developmental vs. Addictive Needs

	DEVELOPMENTAL NEEDS TO:	ADDICTIVE NEEDS FOR:
SURVIVAL	Protect	Security
RELATEDNESS	Love and be loved	Dependency
PLEASURE:	Experience and create beauty	Escape from reality
INFORMATION:	Learn and understand	Novelty and stimulation
MASTERY:	Increase competence	Power over others
PLAY:	Explore and innovate	Freedom without limits
DIGNITY:	Be respected and respect	Praise
MEANING:	Act purposefully	Certainty

The drive for mastery becomes a need to increase competence. The drive for play becomes the need to explore and innovate. The drive for dignity becomes the need to be respected and to respect the dignity of others. And the drive for meaning becomes a need to act purposefully, to give meaning to one's work that in turn adds value for self and others. Satisfying developmental needs creates energy and makes people stronger.

In contrast, addictive needs limit freedom and weaken people. Compulsively driven addictive needs *for* something can never be satisfied. These include needs for total security, dependency, and escape from reality by compulsive consumption of material goods, drugs, and sex. The drive for information becomes the information junky's need for constant novelty and stimulation. The drive for mastery becomes a need for power over another person. And there is never enough power, because the other person wants to be free from oppression. The drive for play becomes the narcissist's need for freedom without limits, and the drive for dignity becomes his or her need for constant praise or adulation. Finally, the drive for meaning becomes a rigid need for certainty that provides the emotional charge for self-righteous ideologies.

We shall learn in the following chapters that each type has positive (developmental) and negative (addictive) motivational potentialities. As we shall discuss in Chapters 8 and 9, which one emerges is a result both of personal development and, to some degree, organizational leadership. In the five chapters that follow, we examine each of the social character types in detail: what motivates them; the meaning they give to their work; their relations with co-workers, managers and subordinates; their strengths and weaknesses; and how their values were formed. We start with the innovators because they were the pioneers in designing the new models of workplace organization.

CHAPTER 3

THE INNOVATOR

While many experts today would like to think of themselves as innovators because technology and competition are forcing them to change organizations, true innovators are a breed apart. Innovators are motivated above all by their visions: they want to change the world. They may do this with a break-through invention or by designing and leading new kinds of organizations. Innovators see the existing organizational forms not as a given, but as part of the technology, a tool to be designed to optimize cost-effective service and increase the motivation of everyone involved. Since they are so intrinsically motivated, so enthusiastic about realizing their visions, innovators want others to feel the same way.

The Values of the Innovator graphic on the next page summarizes the needs that drive innovators at work. The dominant values of innovators combine play and mastery. Innovation is a form of disciplined play, creating visions that work and making it possible to experience the joy of creation. Plato writes that man is closest to God when he is playing. While we may work out of necessity, for survival, play is an expression of freedom. Through play, we discover, express ourselves, and test our visions. The innovator's disciplined play is a form of experimentation and adventure combined with the goal of improving the world and, in the case of innovator managers, infusing the god within them (enthusiasm) into others.

Since many of the innovator's ideas come from understanding what others have achieved and building on these achievements, information for them is always in some way strategic, to be put to good use in the process of innovation. Threats to survival are felt as opportunities to

Values of the Innovator

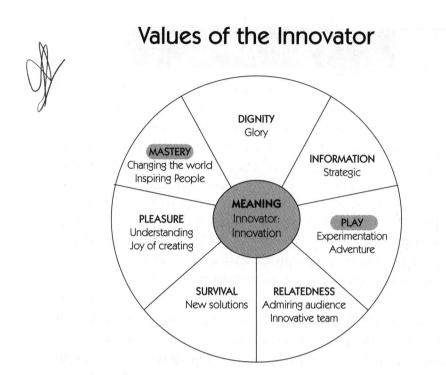

find new solutions, to innovate, although a true innovator may be stimulated by a humanitarian impulse or merely by the inspiration that something might be created. Although Alexander Graham Bell invented the telephone while he was trying to help the hard of hearing, the inventors of integrated circuits at AT&T's Bell Labs were driven by the vision that they could find a better solution than vacuum tubes for the insides of radios and computers. Although innovators are often loners, they are motivated by an admiring audience.

What are the rewards for innovators? Recognition and glory are enjoyed, but they are not the main motivation. As Masuru Ibuku of the Sony Corporation simply phrases it, "I invent because making new things provides one of the biggest joys of my life...." Says John R. Pierce of the Bell Labs, "I do like to see things that wouldn't be there without me." The motivation to innovate is complex. It includes curiosity, challenge, and a spirit of disciplined play. Innovation gains meaning in its significance to human progress. But I suspect that even more, the most creative innovator's satisfaction is in the joy of understanding and creating.

However, as we describe the managerial innovators, the reader should bear in mind that while innovators share motivations with the new-generation self-developers in some ways, there are significant differences. Both are motivated to create an innovative culture and to make work more fun. The differences are that managerial innovators have made the organization of people to create wealth into an art form, a life project. Self-developers seek a more balanced life. Their goal is a sense of measured happiness rather than the wish to change the world, the exhilaration of playing in the big leagues, and the drive for glory.

Innovators will motivate the self-developers as long as they recognize the difference between the latters' values and their own. However, if innovators expect commitment like theirs, they will be disappointed. Self-developers may enjoy the game and share the innovators' results-orientation. But for them, it is not all of life, and they want to leave the game at the office. They prefer to invest energy in relationships, avocations, and entrepreneurial activities that give them a sense of independence from organizations. They want to be involved in an interesting project but not to the point of unhealthy stress. They may be committed to the meaningful goals, but not necessarily committed to the organization. As one self-developer put it, "The hen is involved in your breakfast of eggs and bacon, but the pig is committed. I want to be a hen."

Both the engineering and managerial innovators provide clues for developing all people at work to become more innovative. Innovators pursue their activities out of a sense of freedom. Yet they can work harder, concentrating more intensely, than if they had been forced to work at a task set by someone else. This sense of freedom is rooted in their independent spirit and courage. In general, they were not disciples of mentors like many experts, but rather used good teachers as do the self-developers. Their goal was not to become good students, but rather to become masters. However, this independence has been buttressed by a sense of security, which perhaps was nurtured in childhood, but has been affirmed by supportive institutions.

While the cases presented here suggest ways to strengthen the innovative spirit in organizations, we should also ask: Who wants more innovators? On the one hand, innovation drives progress and creates wealth. On the other hand, innovators threaten the status quo. I was once with a chief executive officer of a large company, who was asked, "How many real innovators do you have in your company?" "I don't know," he answered, "but I'd like to know exactly who they are, so that I can keep my eye on them." Innovators pursue projects that may or may not be useful to a company and may, in fact, tie up resources that could be better employed elsewhere.

In great corporations, innovation must be managed. The trick is to recognize and support the exceptional person, the genius or near genius who sets his own problems while providing the others with a framework for innovative problem solving. Although everyone does not have the systems mind of many innovators, good management can teach people how to see the organization as a system with goals. Everyone can learn the logic of business strategy and the need for organization that supports this strategy. Everyone can be engaged in the process of continuous improvement.

Some Japanese companies have understood this better than most American firms. When I visited Toyota in Nagoya in the late 1980s, I was shown long lists of ideas for improvement suggested by front-line workers. I asked how many ideas each worker offered on the average. The answer: 47, of which 80 percent were adopted. That seemed impossible, almost an idea a week from each worker. A Toyota manager responded. "I have visited your factories," he said, "and you have a different view of ideas from ours. You are pleased when there are no complaints from the workers, but for us, each complaint is a potential idea, an opportunity for improvement."

The improvement of quality, according to W. Edwards Deming a pioneer in quality management, is a combination of innovation and incremental improvements in product and process. These create new value by satisfying needs, creating new tools, lowering costs, and enhancing human life. The companies that succeed in the 21st century will be those best able to make use of innovation, and to continuously improve quality by balancing discipline and freedom, clear goals, high standards and opportunities for innovation — work and play that engage all types of people.

Engineering Innovators

Let us now turn to two kinds of innovators, engineers and managers. In 1991 the editors of *IEEE Spectrum*, the journal of the Institute of Electrical and Electronics Engineers (IEEE) interviewed eight innovative engineers who were picked from a list of nominations made by IEEE fellows. I was invited to provide questions to ask the innovators and to analyze the interviews.[1]

The innovators included: Jacob Rabinow who has 326 patents and sees inventions as an art form; Carver Mead who has both invented dense silicon chips and developed companies to create them and is now working on artificial neural networks, including chips that learn from experience real time; Ibuku who with entrepreneur Akio Morita developed Sony's innovative products like Walkman; John Pierce who came up with the idea for communications satellites, among other inventions; James F. Blinn who has created graphic design for computer animation; Jun-ichi Nishizawa who created the graded-index optical fiber as well as other inventions, and holds 700 patents; Charles H. Townes who invented the maser and the laser, and John Cocke of IBM who created reduced-instruction-set computer (RISC) technology, which has allowed the development of powerful workstations.

The disciplined play of the innovators interviewed by *IEEE Spectrum* editors employs the tools of science to understand how things work and to build on that insight by inventing. As Carver Mead puts it, "Sometimes you can't prove it. You need to do it." In the Platonic sense, these innovators have become God's colleagues in creating the world. As Charles Townes reflected, "I never felt that I really worked at anything. It's all play."

---

[1] Michael Maccoby, "The Innovative Mind at Work," *IEEE Spectrum*, December 1991, pp. 23-25.

Perhaps it would take a different kind of inventor to understand the most gifted innovators fully — to comprehend their psychology and mode of thinking. Doubtless, genetics plays a major role, and so it would seem from their family histories. Jun-ichi Nishizawa's father, now age 98, was dean of the faculty of technology at Tohoku University and his younger brother is now professor of metallurgy there.

Townes' older brother was a well-known entomologist, and his other siblings are teachers and professionals. Rabinow's older brother was also an electrical engineer. Although the interviews do not emphasize childhood experiences, one gets the sense of families that support learning and curiosity. The spirit of play is not stifled by scarcity, fear, or demands that these innovators become early over-achievers.

How do such innovators' minds work? In particular, how do they choose problems to think about? John Pierce said, "I see something that ought to be within my grasp, but it isn't, so it seems worthy of pushing on."

These innovators enjoy grappling with problems, especially in untrodden areas. Townes says that he stays in a field until it is no longer "interesting," meaning it offers nothing new to discover. For Mead, inventions are things that "just had to be done." He admits that "something is bothering me because it isn't understood." He feels "there must be a better way."

A difference between innovators and inventors is that while the latter contrive new devices or methods that may or may not be adopted, the innovator changes things for the better. The most notable innovators choose big problems with large implications. Pierce designed telecommunications satellites; Townes invented the laser. Mead is determined to transform the programming industry, and Nishizawa wants to revolutionize power electronics the way he changed telecommunications with fiber optics.

Innovators need a big ego, a strong vision to maintain their motivation since the bigger the innovation, the more resistance and disbelief it provokes from others. Genius innovators see things in ways that may not make sense even to distinguished colleagues. This is because innovators have a vision of a new *gestalt* or whole, while most people only see one piece at a time. When I studied technical innovators for my book *The Gamesman*, I used the Rorschach test. I found that when asked to describe what they saw in the inkblots, the most innovative engineers and physicists saw the blob first as a whole and then as delineated details. In contrast, most engineers first look for clearly recognizable details and then may try to put them together.

While *Spectrum's* innovators did not take Rorschach tests, most of them said they first try to see the problems as a whole and then work on the details in relation to the whole. This is the process of forming a motivating vision. Masuru Ibuku puts it this way, "I think over the issue I am working on and wait until I get a vision that illuminates its overall nature. Then, I communicate this to my staff and we work together to set a clear direction for its solution. We explore all the various possible alternatives."

Although as children they were tinkerers, as grown-ups the innovators tend to grapple with problems that have broad implications. The meaning of their work has to do with its human implications. These problems are not merely technical, but have to do with enhancing human capability to communicate and create. Nishizawa sees the meaning of his work as improving "the living conditions of every human being." He notes that this mission has developed from a nationalistic drive: "We Japanese do not have many natural resources, even foods, so we Japanese should invent and develop new technologies."

James Blinn invents his high-technology animations in order to teach about science, while Mead connects his inventions to the world of business. For him, creativity includes not only science and technology but also the need to transform the market. Pierce believes that "peace and prosperity depend on communications." He is turned off by the idea of space travel: "I didn't believe man would go up into space and do anything useful, and I don't think they have!"

The innovator has a systems mind, one that sees things in terms of how they relate to each other in producing a result, a new *gestalt* that to some degree changes the world. The goal of the system depends on the breadth of one's thinking. For example, one can think about a car in terms of all its parts working together to make it go. Or one can think of the car as a dynamic element of a transportation system depending also on highways, fuel, and environmental considerations.

In contrast, most engineers are experts who do not think in systems terms. They are concerned about designing a good piece-part, like a clutch. The innovator's system goes beyond the invention to consider its impact on a larger system. Once a new conception begins to develop, the innovators like to try out ideas with students and colleagues. Rabinow likes to "bounce ideas off people." John Cocke speaks of "playing off ideas." Writing it up is important for Pierce. However, they do not necessarily expect immediate agreement or acceptance. Townes relates how his new ideas were disparaged by I. I. Rabi, the Nobel physicist. Nishizawa pointed out that his inventions in fiber optics antedated by 10 years Japan's ability to make use of them. It is significant that although they work in a society known for pressures to reach consensus, the Japanese inventors march to a different drummer. Their motivation is intrinsic and powerful. "I never give up [just] to obtain agreement," states Nishizawa, and Ibuku says much the same: "I do not take any heed to negative opinions. I just go about my work in earnest."

Many people do not learn from negative instances. In fact, failure, or the inability to find confirmation of one's hypotheses, causes an emotional letdown, disappointment. Research shows that in these cases, the information that might be learned is ignored. The innovator, on the other hand, finds disagreement an important stimulus to problem solving and is not put off by failure. Rabinow talks about "the right to fail" without feeling a failure. Cocke says, "It is a pleasure when you are wrong, because that is when you learn something." But to admit one is wrong or does not know is not easy, especially in expert high-technology cultures where status depends on never having to say, "I don't understand." Arno Penzias, vice-president of research for AT&T Bell Laboratories, once told me that one of the major drags on innovation at the labs was the reluctance of people to admit ignorance. For people less gifted and visionary than these innovators, it is essential to create a workplace culture in which there are no stupid questions and in which everyone has an opportunity to suggest improvements.

Managerial Innovators

The managerial innovators presented here were among the first to create a new technoservice workplace, which fits both the needs of customers for customized service and the values of the new generation for teamwork, participation, and personal growth. The earliest models of technoservice organization, like AT&T's American Transtech, Westinghouse Furniture Systems, and Scandinavian Airlines (SAS), were led by managerial innovators who transformed bureaucracies so that employees on the front line were empowered to solve problems for customers. They taught supervisors and middle managers to be facilitators and teachers, and they encouraged innovation, albeit not the breakthroughs of the *IEEE Spectrum* innovators, at all levels. These innovator-entrepreneurs showed that a motivated, empowered front line can be a competitive advantage in the age of information-based service.

Each character type described in this book has innovative potential. The expert-innovator promotes new uses for methods, products, and services. The helper-innovator finds new forms of care. The protector-innovator builds a team of loyal followers and leads them into new territory. Innovative self-developers team up for cooperative entrepreneurial ventures. But only the managerial innovators, like those described here, redesign organizations, inventing new rules, roles, and relationships. The 30 managerial innovators we interviewed in the mid-1980s share behavior patterns. They were organizers, instigators, and strategists. Their vision involved motivating people — not necessarily developing them, but energizing them. In the process, they created power for themselves and others. Other innovators I have worked with in the '90s are no different.

In this chapter, I present three chief executive innovators whom I both observed and interviewed over a period of several years in the early to middle '80s. Unlike most of the individuals described in the following chapters on other character types, these innovators and their companies are identified so that the reader can gain a better understanding of the technoservice organization and how it has been designed. However, the values of these leaders, their approaches to service, management, and work relationships, are similar to those of managerial innovators at all levels of employment.

While innovators at lower levels may become boxed in, this usually is only temporary. They refuse to act like bureaucrats. They either find projects where they can be entrepreneurial, or they leave the organization that does not allow them to innovate. Notably, none of these three is still in his job. Characteristically, they pushed innovation to the limit and beyond. These innovators—Larry Lemasters of AT&T, Russ Nagel of Westinghouse, and Jan Carlzon of SAS, created the models for the information-service workplace, which others have copied. While there are more recent examples, they all include the same elements presented here. As AT&T and Swedbank develop the customer-focused workplace of the '90s, they build on these models. However, there are a number of innovative companies which may not survive for reasons like those that doomed People Express, mentioned later in this chapter. Because of the innovator's enthusiasm and the excitement it generates, many innovations are touted in the business press. However, not all of these last, and even the best must be continually renewed as markets and technology demand change. The three cases presented here are ones I have seen for myself and studied with my associates. We can understand what the innovators did and why they are no longer leading their innovations as lessons to be learned by all those wishing to create a motivating organization.

Larry Lemasters of American Transtech

In 1979, American Transtech was a bureaucratic backwater, the stock and bond transfer division of the Bell System.[2] This division of some

---

[2] Before the breakup of the Bell System, AT&T included about one million employees in its twenty-two operating companies (e.g., New York Bell, Pacific Bell, Ohio Bell, Illinois Bell); the long-distance company, Long Lines; the manufacturing company, Western Electric; the research and development organization, Bell Labs; and the central AT&T headquarters staff, of which Stock & Bond was a part. In 1982, AT&T and the Justice Department settled an antitrust suit by agreeing to separate AT&T, together with Western Electric and the Bell Labs, from seven independent companies formed from the original operating companies (Nynex, Ameritech, Bell South, Bell Atlantic, U.S. West, Pactel, and Southwestern Bell).

600 white-collar employees handled 3.2 million AT&T accounts, issuing stock certificates, transferring them, sending dividend checks, and answering inquiries from stockholders. Many expert managers had passed through the division and built a layered bureaucracy.

The new boss, Larry Lemasters, in his early forties, was an innovator who had shaken up management at Ohio Bell by creating a spirit of teamwork among installers and maintenance workers. When I first met him at Ohio Bell in the late 1970s, Lemasters was disgruntled by the listless, unmotivated workers he observed. He believed the problem was bureaucracy: managers followed regulations and did not like to listen to workers. There was too much monitoring and not enough roadblock removing. He had recently asked Hal Burlingame, a public relations manager at Ohio Bell, to help him by producing a film, *The Death of the Bell System*, a movie with professional actors who played turned-off workers. (One example of dialogue from this film: "Why should I tell them anything? They don't listen anyway.") Then Lemasters brought groups of workers, managers, and union leaders together to watch the film and to respond.

The Death of the Bell System evoked new ideas from the groups, and Lemasters encouraged them to experiment with less monitoring and more self-management. As a result, in Lancaster, Columbus, and Cleveland they accomplished faster turnaround times, made fewer errors, lost less equipment, and had a higher output in fewer hours; and at the same time Ohio Bell saved money. One year in Cleveland alone, Lemasters saved $6 million.

Then in 1979 he was promoted to lead AT&T Stock & Bond when he faced another cynical, turned-off staff. He was convinced that "people could work more efficiently, if only given an opportunity to utilize their pent-up potential." He recruited internal and external consultants and asked them to consider every possibility for improving productivity and morale, including sociotechnical analysis of the computerized system. Lemasters' motivation included personal ambition, boredom with bureaucracy, dislike of inefficiency, and enjoyment of the drama: the game of change, the exercise of power.

He began by raising consciousness of dissatisfaction. Employees distrusted management. They complained of secrecy, disrespect for the lower levels: typical complaints in large bureaucracies. Before Lemasters arrived, these complaints had been shared privately. Now they became public and legitimate. Lemasters was creating the desire for change and giving it meaning in terms of needs for dignity and mastery. He formed diagonal-slice project teams, which included each organizational level but were chosen so that no one was a supervisor or subordinate of a team member. One team interviewed employees about their feelings regarding work and supervision and videotaped some of the responses, which were then viewed by the entire organization. Lemasters led the meetings. Mutual evaluation sessions revealed employee feelings that there was too much control, not enough freedom, and too little training.

After 8 months, I participated at a meeting of the 30 top managers who watched the videotape of employees criticizing them, and explored their own goals and values. I hit on the idea of making values into bipolar dimensions, so they could measure their value gaps. For example, the group felt, "There is too much rivalry and not enough teamwork." So I took teamwork as a value and contrasted it with its opposite, maximizing self-interest. Authority based on knowledge was identified as a value; they agreed that its opposite was authority based on hierarchical position. Innovation was another value; its opposite was conservatism. My strategy was to help them see that the change process had to do with realizing their own values, and in so doing, engaging their intrinsic motivation.

I wrote these values on a blackboard as a scale:

1	2	3	4	5	6	7	8	9	10

- self-interest   vs.   • teamwork

- authority based   vs.   • authority based
  on hierarchy   on knowledge

- conservatism   vs.   • innovation

The group voted on where they would rank the organization on each scale. In each case, the mean vote was about 4. They then defined the task of management *as closing the gaps between the values of their present conservative hierarchical bureaucracy and those of the new innovative team.* This definition included the successful introduction of a redesigned computerized data system to give employees the information and freedom to serve customers and solve problems without having to ask for approval. It included training for managers to become teachers and facilitators rather than monitors and policemen. This scale would probably produce the same results in companies that have not yet transformed themselves for the new workplace.

After the meeting, taskforces were chosen from volunteers. One group visited and reported on innovative participative factories at Hewlett-Packard, Cummins Engine, GM, and the Dana Corporation. Another group designed a ten-question survey, which was eventually called the Barometer Questionnaire (see the next page) for periodic measurement of morale and management effectiveness.

Project Teams

The younger self-developers at Stock & Bond took the lead in implementing the change process. They eagerly volunteered for project teams to visit other companies and administer the Barometer. They tested their skepticism about Lemasters. They spoke out in taped interviews and published the highly critical results of the Barometer. Lemasters pushed the process tirelessly, talking with managers for hours, challenging their expert attitudes, encouraging them to engage their subordinates in the change process, overcoming their disbelief and complacency. After a year and a half, operating costs had been cut by 30 percent. Lemasters eliminated a layer of management and found jobs for the unneeded. People at all levels of Stock & Bond became enthusiastic.

All this was accomplished in the monopoly world. With AT&T's divestiture, Lemasters saw an opportunity to innovate in a growing market, to expand the stock and bond business, serving not only AT&T but also the seven regional Bell companies. The further objective was to gain other corporations as customers. He found himself in a very competitive market. With his managerial team, including new entrepreneurial recruits and consultants, he sized up the competition and

THE BAROMETER QUESTIONNAIRE

1. In my dealings with people at other levels, I am treated courteously.

[ ] [ ]	[ ] [ ]	[ ] [ ]	[ ] [ ]	[ ] [ ]
1 2	3 4	5 6	7 8	9 10
Strongly disagree	Disagree	Neither agree nor disagree	Agree	Strongly agree

2. I am informed about changes that will affect my job.

[ ] [ ]	[ ] [ ]	[ ] [ ]	[ ] [ ]	[ ] [ ]
1 2	3 4	5 6	7 8	9 10
Strongly disagree	Disagree	Neither agree nor disagree	Agree	Strongly agree

3. I am involved in decisions that affect my job.

[ ] [ ]	[ ] [ ]	[ ] [ ]	[ ] [ ]	[ ] [ ]
1 2	3 4	5 6	7 8	9 10
Strongly disagree	Disagree	Neither agree nor disagree	Agree	Strongly agree

4. I get training when I need it.

[ ] [ ]	[ ] [ ]	[ ] [ ]	[ ] [ ]	[ ] [ ]
1 2	3 4	5 6	7 8	9 10
Strongly disagree	Disagree	Neither agree nor disagree	Agree	Strongly agree

5. Overall, how would you rate the morale in your unit?

[ ] [ ]	[ ] [ ]	[ ] [ ]	[ ] [ ]	[ ] [ ]
1 2	3 4	5 6	7 8	9 10
The worst	Getting worse	About the same	Getting better	The best

6. Over the last six months, how would you rate the honesty of communication between you and your supervisor?

[ ] [ ]	[ ] [ ]	[ ] [ ]	[ ] [ ]	[ ] [ ]
1 2	3 4	5 6	7 8	9 10
The worst	Getting worse	About the same	Getting better	The best

7. Over the last six months, how would you rate the recognition people get for a job well done?

[ ] [ ]	[ ] [ ]	[ ] [ ]	[ ] [ ]	[ ] [ ]
1 2	3 4	5 6	7 8	9 10
The worst	Getting worse	About the same	Getting better	The best

8. How would you rate the fairness of the appraisal process?

[ ] [ ]	[ ] [ ]	[ ] [ ]	[ ] [ ]	[ ] [ ]
1 2	3 4	5 6	7 8	9 10
Poor	Fair	Average	Good	Excellent

9. Changes in policies and procedures are well thought out before they are made.

[ ] [ ]	[ ] [ ]	[ ] [ ]	[ ] [ ]	[ ] [ ]
1 2	3 4	5 6	7 8	9 10
Strongly disagree	Disagree	Neither agree nor disagree	Agree	Strongly agree

10. I feel I have a good sense of what is going on at Stock & Bond.

[ ] [ ]	[ ] [ ]	[ ] [ ]	[ ] [ ]	[ ] [ ]
1 2	3 4	5 6	7 8	9 10
Strongly disagree	Disagree	Neither agree nor disagree	Agree	Strongly agree

11. How would you rate your confidence in Stock & Bond's top management?

[ ] [ ]	[ ] [ ]	[ ] [ ]	[ ] [ ]	[ ] [ ]
1 2	3 4	5 6	7 8	9 10
Poor	Fair	Average	Good	Excellent

designed an organization that could do the job at lower cost. In 1983, American Transtech became a fully separate subsidiary owned by AT&T.

Downsizing, including cutting levels of management, was not enough to ensure profitability. The management group met and decided they could not remain in business with their high wage rates. All the Stock & Bond employees were being paid management salaries. By moving to Jacksonville, Florida, in 1983 they situated themselves in an area with lower wage rates and rental costs. Although they knew some people would not move, the group decided that the choice was to move and accept a salary cut, with the promise of profit sharing, or stay and risk losing the business and employment for many of them. Everyone was invited to move and 40 percent accepted.

The average age of American Transtech employees surveyed at that time was 34. They were organized into four levels (Stock & Bond had six), starting at the first level with the front-line workers. This process of re-engineering, accomplished before the term came into use, involved cutting away levels of management that just supervised or checked on the frontline and designing information systems to empower the front-line to do an expanded job of serving customers. These people were divided into participative teams of 20 to 40 people. The teams used new computerized systems to interact directly with customers, set their own schedules, including vacation, and measured themselves weekly in terms of their profitability. They knew the costs and charges for each type of transaction billed to the customer companies. Transactions included giving information (How many shares do I have? Was my dividend check sent? Can I reinvest my dividend automatically?), making stock transfers, and drafting letters explaining company policy to be signed and sent by corporate officers. Other first-level teams dealt with telemarketing, financial record keeping, data security, printing, and mailing. Front-line workers were trained to rotate to different teams, to learn the whole business and avoid forming exclusive groups. Their salaries were based on skill ("pay for knowledge").

At the next level were facilitators, on call to provide training in technical and group problem-solving skills, trained to counsel workers and be supportive ("catch people doing things right"), and also to sniff out problems before they caused trouble. This arrangement appealed to the self-developers, who want responsibility for the whole job and prefer unobtrusive managers who are available to them only if needed. Meetings were called by managers or team members to resolve operations' problems or communicate new policy. Team members were encouraged to innovate, even to try out new services, if customers were willing to pay for them.

The third-level managers ran the lines of service and staff departments (public relations, advertising, organizational development and training, strategic planning) and had the entrepreneurial role of finding new customers, companies looking for high-quality, low-cost information services and direct mailing.

At the top, Lemasters was chief executive and leader of the strategy team. The whole company of 2,000 employees (1,000 full-time and 1,000 part-time) met quarterly and received the financial reports, customer evaluations, Barometer results, and reports on the state of the business. Yearly bonuses were given, based on profitability and customer satisfaction.

A Systemic Vision

Lemasters started the process of innovation believing, on the basis of experience, that the people doing the work could help design more effective processes and in so doing become more enthusiastic and involved. He used everyone who could help him. As he moved along, his vision became more systemic, including competitive service and supportive organizational roles, measurements and rewards. Unlike that of an expert, his vision was not of becoming the big brain that knows and controls the pyramid from the top, but of using the skill and knowledge of all the brains to build a business, of developing each individual's potential. In this sense, he combined the entrepreneurial approach of the helper-developer with that of the innovator. The pure helper might build teams to increase cooperation, but not think of redesigning the organization to be more competitive. Employees responded to Lemasters by accepting a sense of ownership, by feeling that they represented the company to customers. They considered themselves business people, not bureaucrats. This is the kind of motivation that provides a competitive advantage for service organizations. Lemasters recognized that the enterprise needed spirit, and he saw his main task as creating a culture in which all members feel involved, where all employees understand that they make a difference, and where contributions are recognized and rewarded. American Transtech became a model for financial services with streams of visitors from other companies coming to learn about the company's culture throughout the '80s.

Lemasters left Transtech to take another executive job at AT&T. Subsequent to his leaving, there were a series of CEOs who expanded the telemarketing business. One CEO sold off the original stock and bond services division which had developed partnerships with its customers, and with that gone, Transtech became a rather different place, with many part-time employees. It also became a bone of contention with the Communications Workers union, which tried unsuccessfully to organize Transtech with resistance from local management. The union argued that because it was supporting the Workplace of the Future in the core of AT&T's business, management should be neutral if not positive about its organizing activities at Transtech. Those AT&T managers who were the beneficiaries of the union's support, tended to agree with this but hesitated to make decisions for local management, which believed a unionized company might be less competitive. There were also other AT&T managers, particularly in newly acquired companies that were not unionized who felt the company should not make it easy for unions to organize. Thus, Lemaster's bold experiment had become an irritant to union-management partnership and from the point of view of some managers in the core business, of dubious value to AT&T.

Jan Carlzon of Scandinavian Airlines

The second case, that of SAS, has been the model for international airline service. Until 1993, Jan Carlzon was chief executive of SAS, a consortium formed in 1946 by three joint ventures between government and private companies in Denmark, Norway, and Sweden to take care of their intercontinental air traffic. The mission was extended in

1950 to include both European and domestic business. SAS also has managed hotels, catering services, restaurants, tour agencies, and other entrepreneurial service companies.

Carlzon became chief executive of SAS in 1981, at age 40. The group, with 28,000 employees, had been losing money due to a stagnant market, rising oil prices, deregulation, and increased competition in the airline industry. Carlzon was brought in because he had been a successful CEO at Linjeflyg, a domestic Swedish airline, where he used innovative pricing to make a losing company profitable. He started his career as a tour guide while studying at the Stockholm School of Economics, Sweden's business school. In 1969, he went to work as production manager at Vingressor/Club 33, Sweden's largest tour agency. In 1971, when Vingressor became a wholly owned subsidiary of SAS, he was appointed director of marketing, and in 1974 became managing director, at age 33. In his first year as head of Vingressor, he turned a $1.9 million loss into a $3.8 million profit.

Up until 1978, the company was managed by engineers, experts who took the market for granted and concentrated on safety, technical excellence, and cost cutting, what Jan Carlzon called the cheese-slicer approach to acceptable profit. But international competition as well as costs were eroding profits. In 1978, a new CEO was hired who believed that profitability and motivation could be increased by decentralization. He set up project teams, but little happened. His approach was too piecemeal and experimental. Uncertainty provoked resistance from those threatened by change. In 1980, for the first time, SAS reported a loss.

Focus on Satisfied Customers

Then came Carlzon; he analyzed the business problem and proposed a systemic solution, using consultants to examine what other airlines were doing and to survey customers. He changed the question from how to cut costs to "What generates revenue?" His short answer: "Satisfied customers," was at that time an idea that woke people up. Carlzon said that "the place to begin was to understand what the customers wanted and then determine how to transform that need into a profitable business." From market studies, he found the strategic segment to be the business traveler. If SAS could attract more business passengers traveling to and from Scandinavia and paying full coach fare, the tourists and first-class passengers would be gravy, and the company would become profitable. Surveys and interviews showed that businesspeople wanted reliability, punctuality, and comfort. They resented standing in long check-in lines with tours and families, all on supersavers, while they paid full price.

This understanding was the basis for innovation. Carlzon designed an organizational strategy to gain the business customer. It included investment in the hub airport of Kastrup in Copenhagen to improve punctuality. A new "business class" was devised, with more comfortable seats on the plane, free lounges, and special check-in counters. This innovation has been copied by most international airlines. But Carlzon believed that for this strategy to work, everyone had to share a radically different vision of the business. Everyone must understand that the assets are satisfied customers, not technology. With these assets, it is easy to get technology; without them, technology is worthless. Today, this may seem like common knowledge, but then it was a radical departure from business strategy.

Like Lemasters, Carlzon saw potential power in what he called "the front line," where cabin attendants and ticket takers meet the customer in the "moment of truth," the some 50 million encounters per year (10 million passengers with an average of 5 interactions each) that determined satisfaction or dissatisfaction at that time. Carlzon's vision demanded that all employees understand the business and recognize that they are needed to make it work. It meant freeing the front line from bureaucratic controls and policing supervision, as well as developing new training that made room for initiative and response to customer needs. He invited his managers to propose change within the framework of his vision, to change systems so they measured profitability and customer satisfaction, rather than internalized budgetary accounting. Wherever possible, cost centers were made into profit centers. Maintenance was told to sell its services to operations, and urged to find new customers from other airlines. Administrators were encouraged to be entrepreneurs.

Principles of the SAS Philosophy

Carlzon sold this vision as a whole, first to the board, then to the unions, then to countless groups within the company where he preached the new SAS philosophy based on the following principles:

1.   The most important thing for a person to know is that he or she is needed.

2.   Satisfied customers and employees are more valuable than billions of dollars worth of aircraft.

3.   Everyone — each customer and employee alike — wants and deserves to be treated as an individual. That is what good service means: living up to customer and employee needs and expectations at every contact.

4.   To free employees from rigorous control by instructions, policies, and orders, to give those people freedom to take responsibility for their own ideas, decisions, and actions, is to release hidden resources, which would otherwise remain inaccessible to both the individual and the company.

5.   An individual cannot take responsibility without information. An individual who has information cannot avoid taking responsibility.

In the summer of 1984, Carlzon described his job to me in terms of two phases: innovation and implementation. In the first stage he defined the problem, strategized, and offered a systemic solution. In the second, he picked executives, taught, monitored, and developed the corporate culture. This approach meant delegating responsibility to interpret the grand strategy, while he took the role of preacher spreading the gospel within and outside the company.

Carlzon vigorously defended his views against criticism from all sides: expert-engineers claimed his marketing emphasis undervalued safety; expert-cabin attendants feared that by satisfying the customer they would lose autonomy and integrity. (One cabin attendant complained in a letter to a newspaper that the new course was sexually suggestive because it taught cabin attendants how to gently control amorous drunks. Carlzon defended the course and asked why she had not voiced her criticism directly to management.)

Carlzon wanted believers. He demanded participation. Before he announced his vision publicly, he wanted his managers to criticize it. He said, "If you are responsible for the company, you get a little scared. Even if you know you are right, you want to check up. By listening to people, getting their confirmation, you are on the right track. Actually, in a positive way, you hook people. It is impossible for them to say later, 'I think you made the wrong analysis.'" However, with approval by his board in his hand, it was not easy for managers to criticize him openly. Carlzon contrasted participation with democracy. He described democracy as an arena for a clash of interests. However, a company is owned by stockholders who invest wealth to create wealth. The chief executive is delegated by the board of directors to run the company for this purpose. Those who join the enterprise, and none is forced to join, must accept this goal and follow the rules. He considered participation and delegation to be management tools.

Carlzon said, "Many people make the mistake of thinking that this kind of distributed responsibility is some kind of undefined democracy. It is not. I think that getting the right people and giving them total freedom is the incentive to get many, many more things to happen within the company than if you try to steer it from a central point." This "total freedom" was liberating and with the new spirit, motivating. However, it also caused some anarchy (see Chapter 9), as people tried out all kinds of ideas.

As do most innovators, Carlzon had an intuitive sense of timing about when to risk decisions. According to Carlzon, "A wrong decision can always be corrected. Lost time you can never get back. If you enter an organization like I have done, the crisis is your resource, you have to use it. It is better to do ten things and two are wrong, than to do one thing which you are absolutely sure is the right thing to do."

He wanted his managers to be daring. Carlzon explained:

> Many times people say, "I want to go through this
> wall," and they start walking towards the wall and
> they are two meters away when they tell themselves

that it will not work. The authorities will not let us, or the management will not let us. I tell them that the Civil Aviation Board [like the Federal Aviation Administration in the U.S.] has 6,000 employees, and they get their salaries to tell us where the wall is. You should not take their work upon your shoulders. If you come to the wall, two times out of ten it gives way, and you get through. Then you have the middle managers; and that is a more complicated and interesting situation. When you move into a decentralized situation, a lot of people have to become strategists and preachers. They get insecure because they are not used to it. We are talking about that in our education of 2,500 middle managers; we are teaching them the new management philosophy.

What motivated Carlzon, like Lemasters, was not only the power and excitement of the business game, which he loved, but also the pleasure in seeing people respond and grow. He said:

There is no doubt that I like this role very much, coming into the organization, trying to grasp the situation, making the overall decisions, and having it achieved through education, information, and the new organization. I like to feel people respond to responsibility, how people come to life or grow in this process. My personal reward is to see people get enthusiastic and act on their own and reach goals.

He likened the workplace to a circus, where the brave and competent have a chance to perform on the high wire, risk themselves for glory. In his circus, ideally, everyone should have a moment under the spotlight, and there should be a safety net for those who fall.

Carlzon maintained he did not care about personal power. In this, he was still in the culture of the '60s and '70s. *Power* became a dirty word in the 20th century, something for dictators. In fact, CEOs in Sweden particularly were expected to disclaim interest in power. But when I asked Carlzon, "Don't you want the power to change things?", he responded, "I think I am honest to myself if I say that I am very results-oriented. I don't get any reward from power as such. I think I can prove that. I very seldom act as having power. I don't think power comes from position. I think that power comes from the results you achieve." This is a different kind of power from that of the CEO who gives orders to people and expects them to jump. In the new workplace, such power is limited. You cannot order people to be true believers or make good decisions. Carlzon like all innovators wanted the power to change the world, a kind of power which can be gained only by empowering others (see Chapter 9).

To gain this type of power, leaders must be able to give up formal power, let go of the controls. They cannot be experts in everything. Carlzon's example of a bad decision was the time he personally gave orders to improve the freight business and so set the company back a year. Carlzon's favorite book is Erich Fromm's *To Have Or to Be*,[3] which contrasts power *over* and power *to*, having formal power as opposed to being a leader who is respected, trusted, and followed. In *The Leader*, I described an innovative foreman in a Tennessee factory who taught his subordinates how to take over many of his functions. When asked by an executive from New York whether he was not wounded about losing his authority, he answered, "Since I started giving it away I never had so much authority." His subordinates trusted him and wanted to follow him because he was teaching and trusting them.

However, I remain skeptical about Carlzon's idealistic view of power. Although he created a customer-responsive frontline, it remained dependent on his inspiration and personal involvement. When he turned away to new strategic initiatives, such as creating a consortium of European airlines, SAS tended to revert to the traditional hierarchy, and the spirit of innovation was lost. In 1989, Carlzon invited me to meet with his top executives in Oslo, and I found them unconvinced about his organizational innovations. After Carlzon reviewed his

---

[3] Erich Fromm, *To Have or to Be* (New York: Harper & Row, 1976).

concepts, one vice-president, a former pilot, said, "I still think the military organization is best." "Of course,", said Carlzon, "that's right, if your goal is to shoot the customers." But that witty reply was no substitute for persuasion. Perhaps, if Carlzon had concentrated on developing the organization, aligning measurements and rewards, rather than focusing on new initiatives, he might have used his power to transform the behavior of the experts who never bought into his vision. In 1993, with the airline again losing money owing to overexpansion and failure to cut costs, Carlzon was replaced by a more traditional expert.[4]

However, Carlzon's vision and personality have had an impact beyond SAS, on the whole of Swedish society. His concept of organization and style of management have challenged the traditional Swedish industrial bureaucracies, and have become a model for innovators in business and government. His transformation of customer service became the model for transportation and telecommunication companies in Western Europe and the United States.

Russell Nagel of Westinghouse Furniture Systems

The third innovator whom I studied showed that in the new workplace even traditional manufacturing is more successful when it becomes a form of service. Under Russell A. Nagel, Westinghouse Furniture Systems was transformed from a failing industrial bureaucracy to a model of technoservice that integrated office and factory to meet the needs of demanding business customers. Nagel employed the concepts of total quality management and re-engineering before these were popular. Before Nagel's direction, first as operations manager, then as general manager, the factory in Grand Rapids, Michigan, lost money cranking out office equipment according to the goal of quantity rather than quality. Under Nagel, it became a profitable and exciting "living laboratory" for 700 people, and the third-largest global company for a

---

4 For an analysis of some of SAS's problems, see A. Edström and J. E. Rendahl, "Scandinavian Airlines System (SAS): Strategic Reorientation and Social Change," in *Sweden At the Edge*, ed. Michael Maccoby (Philadelphia: University of Pennsylvania Press), 1991, pp.77-109.

growing international market of customers who wanted to replace the bullpen-type office of rows of desks with more private office modules. Westinghouse office employees played a continual role in designing new products and collaborating with customers and every major producer of electronic and computerized office equipment. Factory workers participated in designing production methods, while marketers tried out glitzy multimedia approaches on the whole staff. Nagel somehow put together two disparate cultures, the marketing world of hype, games, and fun and the production world of craft, care, and quality. After he left in the early '90s, his innovations were discarded and the company again lost millions.

In the late '80s, Nagel's team proudly stated:

> We don't think of the Westinghouse workplace as "the office of the future." That is an engineering vision where people are replaced by computers. This is a continually evolving workplace where people continually find better ways of using new technology to satisfy customers. More accurately, it represents a living, working example of the future of the office.

"Our business is service" was Nagel's philosophy; "Our product is not an end in itself but a means to help businesses operate more productively." And he tried to involve everyone in thinking about how to increase office productivity. He believed the key to success is "total quality," and not just in the product, but in every function: relations among people, processes, product design, and sales calls.

When Nagel was general manager, Westinghouse Furniture Systems made 15,000 different products: tables, desks, chairs, office modules equipped for lighting, and electronic equipment. At the high-tech office in Grand Rapids, employees worked with customers to try out products with computer-aided design (CAD) systems. As one of them said, "It is like putting together the largest Lego set in the world." Nagel, then in his late 40s, was an innovator and developer of organizations and people, a teacher and helper with strong values of dignity and productivity. Before joining Westinghouse, he taught math, architectural drawing, and industrial arts at Bedford (Ohio) High School. Starting in 1961 as a junior industrial engineer, he moved up the Westinghouse corporate ladder, holding 25 different positions in manufacturing, including general plant manager, before he arrived at the office furniture factory in 1981. After leaving a plant where union and management fights had sparked violence, he took over another Westinghouse factory with poor labor relations, and engaged the union (the United Steelworkers) in a successful Quality of Worklife, employee-participation program. Nagel sees this experience as his years in the trenches.

He was sent to Grand Rapids to evaluate the factory's potential. Relations with the carpenters' union were faltering, productivity was low, but Nagel liked the people. He felt they had a strong work ethic, but needed leadership. Indeed, nearby competitors Steelcase and Herman Miller were both extremely well-run companies.[5] Nagel believed that productivity depends on self-esteem, that people feel motivated by pride of identification with a winner. In fact, he created that kind of motivation and much more. His winning workplace supported mastery and play, quality production and innovation. He hired bright young people and enjoyed competing with them for new ideas. In the "future of the office" were both traditional and new-generation types, unionists and individualists, men and women, black and white, but these differences did not impede an easy relationship between factory, sales, and executive offices; workers were, in fact, promoted into the office.

Involving Employees

Like Lemasters, Nagel started the change process by getting people involved, inviting them not just to solve problems but to understand the causes. He said, "If we can understand a problem, we can solve it." Sixty percent of employees were involved in problem-solving teams. He supported the team atmosphere with parties and picnics. There was

---

5 Max De Pree, the former CEO of Herman Miller, who wrote *Leadership is an Art*, (East Lansing, Mich.: Michigan State University Press, 1987.) was a more paternalistic example of an innovator in the tradition of Thomas Watson of IBM and Bill Hewlett and Dave Packard of H-P.

also a wellness program, which reduced health costs through non-smoking training, aerobics, and weight control. Factory employees met monthly to hear reports on results of productivity, new orders, shipping objectives, absenteeism, financial results, quality results, and goals. Questions were encouraged and answered. Every month, Nagel also hosted a union-management roundtable to discuss strategy and listen to union concerns.

The progress justified investment by Westinghouse in new products and technology. After three years, the new technoservice concept jelled and became an organizing principle for new products, processes, systems. Factory productivity rose 50 percent, resulting partly from quality improvements and automated processes. White-collar productivity improved one-third. Nagel believed that 40 percent of these gains was the result of motivation, "People began to believe we were a high-quality provider and acted that way."

Everyone was invited to improve quality and service, and productivity continued to grow. Methods experts interviewed customers and redesigned order forms so they became easier to use and allowed the office to keep better track of orders. On-time deliveries jumped from 65 to 95 percent. Westinghouse experts trained major dealers to install the furniture systems. Once installers were certified, Westinghouse took responsibility for their work. Field representatives with video cameras recorded the products as soon as they were installed, and sent the information to Grand Rapids for review. Not everyone was fully satisfied. On the one hand, many employees wanted even more participation, more opportunity to improve methods. On the other hand, some middle managers were uneasy about the challenge to their authority. Union leaders tolerated the process. After all, their members wanted it. But they feared an erosion of union power.

Components of Change

Nagel was not surprised that change caused conflict. He felt that change requires debate, that innovation flows from dissatisfaction. He was pleased by the whole process and with his role of the innovator-coach motivating a winning team into world markets. He kept searching for the best resources he could find, for he believed that quality is the key to success. He contracted with German ergonomics experts to make the furniture more comfortable and, therefore, more productive for the customer. He scanned the world for designers to create stylish fabrics, colors, and configurations. He hired young managers, including a Rhodes Scholar and an Olympic athlete. Nagel said, "I love to be around young people. They keep you young. They have energy. They keep me on my toes." He laughed, "But they won't get ahead of me. I play the game."

Nagel seemed a contradiction of styles: down-to-earth and in the stars; competitive yet comfortable and supportive; humorously self-effacing yet grand; gamesman and helper. When the newly renovated plant was inaugurated, Nagel invited President Ronald Reagan, who brought with him Gerald Ford, formerly a congressman from Grand Rapids before he became Vice-President and President. Reagan not only gave a speech emphasizing revitalizing American industry; he also handed out awards to workers.

In the new plant, visitors rode around on a futuristic customer trans-portation vehicle and watched a lively film on the future of the office. But the technology did not overpower the people. Westinghouse Furniture Systems did not try to automate everything. People still made furniture. The ideal was not an automated plant cared for by experts, but an orga-nization of people using the best possible tools to satisfy customers while having a good time doing it. Nagel created a model for making an aging industry competitive by transforming manufacturing into technoservice.

Despite his appeal to his own organization and customers, Nagel was not fully appreciated by Westinghouse. Customers like Texas Instru-ments and Chrysler's new technical center testified about Westinghouse Furniture Systems responsiveness to them. However, when I joined him in presenting his strategy to corporate planners at Westinghouse's Pitts-burgh headquarters, known as "the tower of power," there was little enthusiasm. Yet, without the value added of Nagel's approach of not just meeting the customer's expectations but helping the customer to succeed, many products like office furniture became commodities, subject to competition by price alone.

Like other innovators, Nagel focused on expanding his business in Europe and Japan and made acquisitions in the early '90s. Westinghouse acquired Knoll, a slightly bigger office furniture company with a different philosophy based on superior design. With the backing of top management at Westinghouse, the Knoll experts took control of the company and were contemptuous of Nagel's quality efforts. In a meeting, one said, "If I hear that ... word quality one more time, I'll throw up." Finally Nagel could take it no longer and decided to leave. He had other offers in Westinghouse, but he opted to remain in the Grand Rapids area and became president and chief operating officer of Batts, Inc., a family-owned company in Zeeland and the largest producer of coat hangers in the world. There he applied the same quality principles he had pioneered at Westinghouse Furniture Systems. When I spoke to him in early 1995, Sears, his biggest customer, was in the plant for their first visit to discuss how Batts might better serve their needs.

And what happened to the innovations at Westinghouse Furniture Systems? No longer do dealers and customers consider themselves partners. Employee participation has faded. Nagel's innovations are no more. From an operating profit of 10 percent when Nagel was in charge, the company lost 66 million dollars in 1994.

Government Innovators

In 1995, as the Clinton administration attempts to reinvent government, they can learn from earlier attempts by innovators who showed what was possible to do, but who finally gave up because their efforts were not appreciated and changes in their political masters undermined their efforts. There are few innovators in the bureaucracy, and these few are frequently frustrated because there is little opportunity to transform the industrial-type bureaucracy of expert specialization, rigid hierarchy, and turfism into a customer-focused team organization. Without a market mechanism, there is no compelling reason to do so. Without understanding and support from political leadership, innovation is a risk with little chance of reward. Federal innovators sometimes achieve remarkable results in reorganizing a particular function, such as auditing, or transforming an office, such as the Passport Office at the State Department. But all too often they give up and move to private industry. Even when political leaders like Clinton and Al Gore sincerely seek to transform government, they have a relatively brief period to change institutions that have been entrenched for decades and respond to the commands of Congress as well as the White House.

In the '80s, we found innovators in the Departments of State and Commerce, the Federal Aviation Administration, the Veterans' Administration, ACTION, and the National Park Service. These women and men were results-oriented and disliked bureaucratic routine. They viewed problems from a systemic point of view, emphasizing how their work fit into the big picture. They were among the first government employees to make use of information and telecommunications technology. They were quick to grasp how it could be used to improve productivity, cut away layers of hierarchy, and make work more exciting by decentralizing information and decision making.

Our study within the government included Paul Pepper (a pseudonym), age 48, an innovator, a manager of auditors, who defined his role as making government work better:

> While the function of auditing is to save the government money, I really view my function as seeing that systems work better. This would result in not wasting money. We have all sorts of ways to come up with dollar savings. Cutting waste is one. But improving something is a cost-avoidance type thing where you would have had to spend more money if it hadn't been improved on.
>
> To me, you look at it like a house with cracks in the wall. Most managers want to know if there is a crack and if I get time, I'll fix it up. But I'm not going to let the cracks worry me if the termites are eating away at the foundation. I'm more interested in the structural weakness. If there are too many cracks, you will

develop a structural weakness. A lot of auditors don't think in those terms. That's the problem. They've got to think systems or they are out there talking about peanuts when we ought to be up here talking about watermelons.

Experts view the audit as a review by the rules. They assess whether there has been compliance with appropriate regulations. An expert in Pepper's organization said, "An audit is simply a review to see that what management has stated is correct as can be told by various tests performed. An audit to me is just a probe—to find something adverse, but there are possibilities of finding something good, too. You use whatever authority you have—regulations, handbooks, laws—to represent what is good and bad."

In contrast, a helper in Pepper's group described auditing as:

> ...Dealing with people, sometimes you get satisfaction that you are helping. For auditors, it is hard to get that because most people see you coming, and it looks like it is a downer to most folks. The way I do it is that I approach the person, and we talk about any problems they have and I let them know that I am here just to do the audit and not to criticize on a personal basis. I want to go by the guide and the restrictions of the contract that they signed, so they can improve their organization, and to make sure that they are doing the right things, so that they can prosper and get the contract renewed.
>
> I don't want to be a policeman. If I wanted to be a policeman, I would be one. I want the auditees to feel the way I would want to feel, so they can treat me accordingly. I like to get a good working relationship because you can't work with people when they are tense and are not sure what you are doing. So I try to explain it fully so that they can be confident that I am there to help and not to hinder what they have done.

A defender in Pepper's organization also used the policeman analogy, but he liked the idea of protecting honest people from "thieves." "I think that the reason for some of the rules and regulations was this moral ethic that we have. And I think it was to keep people from going astray. As a result, I feel it's important that people follow the regulations. I believe some of the regulations have just been overdone. I'd rather not see them." He added, "But I do believe that there should be a policeman around to make sure that people do the right thing. If there weren't, there would just be a world full of thieves who do all the things they are not supposed to do, and laugh at everybody else."

In a previous government job, Pepper developed for a whole industry an early-warning financial-analysis system that was important for national security. He collected information from all over the country, put it into a computer, analyzed it, and fed back the indicators. He discovered indicators that give early warnings of financial disaster for their companies. Like other innovators, Pepper was not satisfied just by having a position of authority. He wanted real power to improve situations, as he said, "to make good things happen." Early on, he left one government job because he had a weak boss:

> I felt he had no clout. First of all, he was frightened, I also perceived him as having very little clout with the assistant secretary. And if he had no clout, I had no clout. And if I had no clout, there was only so much I could do. And there were a lot of things I wanted to get done. I had strategies to get them done. But if he understood them, he didn't have the guts or the determination to try to make them happen. I just don't think he really understood what I was trying to tell him. Consequently, he was afraid to do anything, because he wasn't sure if it was right or wrong.

When he became manager of auditors, with the support of a stronger assistant secretary, he saw his task as improving the effectiveness of both internal and external audits (of government contracts and grants). He said of his goal, "Can we make it work more effectively, efficiently, enjoy it more, deliver the system better?"

To improve effectiveness, he realized he needed to educate the experts to expand their views of the mission and their roles. He recognized the resistance of experts who want unambiguous rules:

> I'd like to be able to communicate a management philosophy on what is out there and how all these things kind of fit together and how they really don't. You have to learn to live with ambiguity. Most people don't want to do that. Ambiguity runs people down and they dissipate their energies instead of learning how to live with it. I think that's because they have no conceptual image of how things fit into the whole. I think if they could just begin to recognize that, then I think they could begin to deal with it.

With the help of a consultant, he organized team meetings where experts, helpers, and defenders discussed their preferred approaches and agreed to allocate audits according to their respective interests and strengths. Defenders took the suspicious-looking cases. Helpers were assigned audits of internal department operations and those minority-owned businesses that needed help in setting up financial systems. In group meetings, auditors learned from each other. Pepper kept pushing the experts to take on different types of audits, to risk making mistakes and learning from them. This participative approach to fitting responsibilities to intrinsic motivation has been replicated in many parts of the government, in large part because Pepper's experience was widely communicated within the auditing community.

Pepper became an evangelist for a new approach to auditing. He said:

> You've got to instill a different kind of philosophy, a different kind of feel, a different kind of perception of the world. Just because you are an auditor, that doesn't make you God Almighty. Just because you are an auditor, that doesn't mean that you are 100 percent right. Just because you're an auditor doesn't

mean that you can't be flexible. Because you're an auditor doesn't mean that you're the only one with the solution.

You must deal with the fact that there are no magic answers. You know, you deal with each situation within certain parameters, and you make a decision, and some you make right and some you make wrong, and if you make it wrong there's no sense crying about it, because that's not going to make it right. There are some things that you just have to learn to live with, and if you blow one, you blow it and move on. I think auditors generally want to be so right, and if they're ever wrong, it's just like their whole world falls in on them.

The audit group in his agency became more effective and more lively. Pepper encouraged challenge and debate rare in bureaucracy. He was promoted and moved to another agency, where he continued his innovative leadership another four years before leaving the federal government in the mid-'80s. Pepper said he was tired of fighting the bureaucracy, where the experts drag you down. What kind of management did he most appreciate during his government career? Pepper enjoyed innovators like himself, but he also appreciated the expert civil servants and political leaders he considered smart and secure enough to let him innovate. He said:

I don't like dumb bosses, because I think dumb bosses get frightened. I like a bright boss. I like them to be straightforward. Not mealy-mouthed. If they're bright, they're straightforward. They give you room, and they're willing to talk about challenges. That's what matters. The four or five bright ones I've met in my total career have been those kinds of people. They're generally dynamic themselves. They want to get something done.

I had a boss — I was hired to replace him. They said he was going out in four or five years. I wanted to learn as much as I could, and he was bright. Now, he wasn't going to do anything, but I could learn one helluva lot from him. He was a very bright guy. And you should see him work with the industry. He knew how to handle people. He knew how to keep himself out of problems and he knew how to keep the agency out of problems. I learned an awful lot from him. He wasn't going to initiate new things. He let me. He didn't stand in my way. Like when I'd say, "Hey, you know, I've got this idea, what do you think of this?" he'd say, "Go ahead, try it," So even though he wasn't dynamic in that respect, he wasn't going to stand in my way. When he thought you were wrong he said you were wrong. And I could live with that kind of guy. The kind of guy that I can't live with is the kind of guy who really doesn't want to make anything happen and won't let you make anything happen.

Although there will never be enough bosses like this in government, the process of reinventing government is never ending. Where feasible, government functions should be spun off into the private sector, so that innovators like Pepper are not subject to changing political appointees. Where this does not make sense, as in policing functions, foreign and military service, effective organization will depend on how well leaders are able to create the motivating organizations as described in Chapters 9 & 10.

Character Formation: Innovators as Gamesmen

Let's step back and consider the character of the innovator and how it develops. In *The Gamesman* and *The Leader*, I described managerial innovators as gamesmen, driven by a spirit of play, motivated to be winners. The term *gamesman* causes an emotional reaction, partly because it is not clearly understood. There is no precise translation in most languages. Words like *gambler* (Swedish, *spelaren*) or *player* (French, *le joueur*) were used to translate the title *The Gamesman*. Some people confused the gamesman with Stephen Potter's manipulative character, who is expert in the art of winning without actually cheating.[6] When I have asked groups of high-tech managers whether they consider it positive or negative to be a gamesman, the response is usually fifty-fifty. The bureaucratic experts are generally most negative, focusing on the manipulative, superficial, egocentric, and threatening aspects of the gamesman, while entrepreneurs and self-developers tend to identify with his daring spirit.

Gamesmen do enjoy risk taking, but the best are innovators, like Lemasters, Carlzon, and Nagel. They create power not only for themselves but for a whole organization. Less attractive are the paper entrepreneurs, the speculators, gamblers whose goal is limited to personal gain and glory, without much regard for the effects of their deals on other people. Although these two types, innovator and gambler, share the game language and a certain antibureaucratic informal style, there are significant differences. Both express the play spirit at work, but the innovator's approach is more developed. It is more in the tradition of Johann Huizinga's *Homo Ludens*, the innovator who throughout history has created new forms of organization out of a spirit of play.[7]

The great Swiss psychologist Jean Piaget traced the development of the play drive by observing children's games.[8] My doctoral research built on his discoveries to show the relationship between the development of play and learning.[9] The infant first plays with his body, then plays repetitively with objects, rolling a ball, pushing an object on a string: play for mastery over body and external objects. Freud described how very young children play peek-a-boo with parents as a way of

---

6 Stephen Potter, *The Theory and Practice of Gamesmanship: The Art of Winning Without Actually Cheating* (New York: Holt, 1948).

7 Johann Huizinga, *Homo Ludens* (Boston: The Beacon Press, 1955).

8 Jean Piaget, *The Moral Judgment of the Child* (Glencoe, Ill.: The Free Press, 1955).

9 Michael Maccoby, "The Game Attitude." Doctoral dissertation, Department of Social Relations, Harvard University, 1960.

mastering the trauma of their sudden disappearances, turning power-lessness into a game.[10] At the age of four or five, children begin to play seriously with each other, but there is little cooperation. Each tries to impose his will on the other. Gradually, through experience of conflict and education in games, children develop a cooperative play relation-ship. But to do so, they must free themselves from their awe of and unquestioning belief in the authority of grown-ups. They must develop a critical attitude so that they can think for themselves and accept or reject ideas on their merits. This is something innovators achieve more than experts and helpers. For experts to become more like innovators, they must free themselves from internalized authority.

In the United States, the United Kingdom, Australia, Sweden and other Western industrial democracies, this development is fostered in games like hide-and-seek, ringalevio, or Red Rover, played between the ages of six and eight. These games encourage cooperation, banding together against the central person, the symbolic authority, to home-free all one's fellows. In the traditional, conformist Mexican village, this type of game is not played. There, central-person games teach the message that the individual cannot escape a punishing authority.[11] In the game *cuero quemado* (burnt leather), the "it" wields a leather belt and can strike anyone he catches. In a version of hide-and-seek, the "it" is the deviant who tries to escape while everyone searches for him. These games are mostly played by boys. The village girls' central-person games have descended from medieval Spanish roundelays, where a circle is formed around a virgin, and the symbolic male predator, the wolf, tries to break through and rob her.

By the age of 10 or 11, in the United States as in Piaget's Switzerland, the more independent children develop a spirit of reciprocity. Neither adult pronouncements nor the rules of the game are blindly accepted as God-given truths. Children evaluate rules in terms of making the game

---

[10] Sigmund Freud, *Beyond the Pleasure Principle* (1920) (London: The Holgarth Press, 1950).

[11] Michael Maccoby, Nancy Modiano and Patricia Lander, "Games and Social Char-acter in a Mexican Village," *Psychiatry*, 26, 1964, pp. 150-162.

fair and fun. They are able to put themselves in another person's place. While the younger egocentric children must win or feel humiliated, reciprocal gamesmen enjoy the contest for its own sake: the interaction, strategy and tactics, the exercise of skill, and the sense of freedom. Innovative gamesmen conceive of the whole game as a system that can be better organized with improved roles, rules, and technology. This is why innovative gamesmen are more likely than other types to strategize systemically. They have learned not only to play the game, but to make better games.

The innovators we interviewed and those interviewed by the editors of *Spectrum* came from families where they felt valued, supported, and encouraged to explore their own paths. As children, they combined a sense of freedom with discipline and love of challenge. The engineering innovators began tinkering as children. The managerial innovators were involved in entrepreneurial activities in school, developing their skills and gaining financial independence from parents. Lemasters, Nagel, and Carlzon were entrepreneurs and leaders in college. Most have far surpassed their fathers in terms of career. Carlzon's father was a chauffeur for a government official, Lemasters' and Nagel's were supervisors in service companies, Pepper's was a merchant seaman.

Any analysis of the psychology of innovators must focus not only on cognitive style, but also character. The innovator is confident he can solve a problem if he sticks to it. Thomas Edison is said to have stated that genius is 1 percent inspiration and 99 percent perspiration. What this leaves out is the courage to innovate, to invest one's time in an idea and affirm it against resistance. It is not necessarily the case that if one invents a better mousetrap, the world will beat a path to your door. Even IBM took 10 years to adopt the RISC or reduced-instruction-set computer technology, an innovation created by one of its own employees.

Not only are new ideas doubted, but also they threaten those who profit from older ideas. Carver Mead, the California Institute of Technology innovator, speaks about "the huge amount of negativism" he has experienced. "Looking back," he says, "it was clear that in that case the reason there was negativism was that people did not want systems designers designing silicon, because it was an entrenched industry with a vested interest." He recalls, "I had known the early semiconductor industries. They were the most innovative places that I had ever been. What I had not realized was that they had aged and had gotten entrenched, and they had a vested interest now. Whereas when I knew them," he says, "they were trying to break in, now they were entrenched and they didn't want anyone breaking in on them." The innovations of the past become the home of today's change-resisting experts.

Weaknesses of Innovators

However, the character of the innovators, their vision and determination can also lead them in the wrong direction. In the early '80s, Donald Burr, founder of People Express, was written about as a model innovator until his company collapsed. He built a one-billion-dollar airline on a vision of low-cost air travel produced by a highly motivated team. At People Express, before it was bought by Continental Airlines, everyone except contracted-out baggage handlers and plane reservation clerks (non-People people) was a manager, and each person, even the pilots, who were called "flight managers," did a regularly scheduled turn at everyone else's work. Everyone owned stock. Burr's vision did not inspire some of the pilots, who felt they had paid their dues in Vietnam and deserved the special status and salary pilots have at American and United. The pilots pointed out that while they could do the other managers' work, the others could not do theirs. Some pilots at People Express tried to organize a union. Burr saw them as the bad guys who were destroying the vision.[12] Today, while People Express is no more, Southwestern Airlines, considered among the ten most innovative companies in the U.S. by *Business Week* (Feb 13, 1995), boasts of union-management cooperation.

Some innovators have no patience with people who refuse to accept a vision they believe to be both economically positive and expressive of higher values of cooperation, individual development, and public service. They become too attached to the games they have designed.

---

[12] Interviewed in *INC*, August 1985, p.27.

They fall in love with their creations. They risk seeing people as chess pieces, not human beings. Innovators miss the differences in goal and meaning for different types. Speaking of Pepper, an expert-au litor said:

> I think out of the directors we've had in this office, I think he's the best by far. But technically, he's probably near the bottom in knowing the office. He doesn't really project to me that he knows the people in the office. You know he has something in mind and this is his goal, and he's going to have everybody work for it rather than finding out what he's got to work with and then finding ways to go.

Experts, helpers, defenders, and self-developers may love the innovator's enthusiasm, and be captivated by the vision, but they resent the hype, the manipulation. Innovators do admit that when they get going, they "run over people," "lose their tolerance."

Other types also bridle at the innovator's drive for glory, what they feel as egomania, hogging center stage. A Swedish manager, an expert, said, "Jan Carlzon acts like he did it himself. He is always taking the credit. He did a good job, but I get tired of seeing him." A Swedish small businesswoman, also an expert, said, "I am rather fed up with Jan Carlzon. He has overacted, as I see it, but I am sure he is a very good leader because he gets people to work. I see him as a very good motivator." An Ohio Bell expert manager commented, "Larry Lemasters achieved results, but a lot of people distrust his motives. He always seems to be at the center of everything." (In 1987, Lemasters left AT&T, where his innovative pushing was not universally appreciated.) The big egos of innovators, which allow them to swim against the current are also likely to rub people the wrong way, particularly if the innovator is no longer a charismatic winner.

From a psychoanalytic point of view, the danger for innovators is narcissism. Freud proposed three psychological types. One type that he called the obsessive corresponds in many respects to the expert. A second type that he named the erotic is more like the helper. The third type that he called the narcissist is closest to the innovator.[13] Freud saw the narcissist as the prototypical leadership type, capable of transcending conventional and consensual thinking, able to sustain a vision in the face of disbelief. However, when the narcissist becomes too isolated from others or too grandiose, he is likely to blunder. The very success of his leadership can increase narcissism, particularly if he is idolized. Then he feels that all his intuitions must be right. He has become like a god, and he stops listening to those in the organization who might criticize him or provide information that would contradict his views. Jan Carlzon became a national hero, but he also distanced himself from the organization. He did not develop his vision or solve the productivity problems. Russ Nagel did work with his organization, but he lacked the power to fully implement his vision in an expanded company.

The managerial innovators described here created organizations that depended on their enthusiasm and charisma. When they left, the organizations became more traditional, the magic went with them. Other celebrated innovators, like Ken Olson of Digital Equipment and Ed Land of Polaroid, were unable to adapt their visions to changing business environments. They built companies that for a time were considered models, but ultimately they refused to listen to others in the organization and were then faced with disastrous results.

However, there are many more balanced leaders who have learned lessons from innovators and are creating customer-focused participative organizations that do not depend so much on a single individual (see Chapters 9 & 10). They have instituted processes, measurements, and reward systems that support quality. For example, AT&T has adopted many of the lessons learned from Lemasters and Carlzon about service management in its quality management training and Workplace of the Future activities.

---

[13] Sigmund Freud, "Libidinal Types," *Collected Papers*, Volume 5 (London: Hogarth Press, 1953), pp 247-51. Freud writes, "People of this type impress others as being 'personalities,' it is on them that their fellow-men are especially likely to lean; they readily assume the role of leader, give a fresh stimulus to cultural development or break down existing conditions." p. 249.

In the next chapter we meet the expert, the more traditional social character who fit so well the roles of the industrial bureaucracy. While experts have resisted the innovators, they are coming to recognize that continual change is inevitable. The technoservice age is a reality, and the experts must learn to adapt to it. By learning from pioneering innovators like Lemasters, Carlzon, Nagel, and Pepper and using the 4Rs of Chapter 9, they can help to build the motivating organizations that do not require charismatic innovators, but are, because of that, more likely to last.

CHAPTER 4

THE EXPERT

The expert, who dominated the industrial bureaucracies still accounts for half of the workforce and an even greater percentage of top management. Experts are motivated by opportunities to demonstrate their knowledge, master challenges and gain recognition. In the information-age service (technoservice) workplace many of their traditional strengths become weaknesses, and unless they develop new attitudes and values, experts resist the changes needed for efficiency and customer focus.

The Expert Circle graphic on the next page summarizes the expert's values at work, which have become motivating needs. At the center of the graphic is the need for excellence, or as has become popular, its synonym, quality. The dominant value for the expert is mastery, including needs for achievement and advancement. The expert's sense of self-esteem and employment security is achieved by gaining status and professional respect. Experts find pleasure at work in their craftsmanship and recognition by their peers and superiors. They have a strong need for autonomy. At their best, experts stand for high standards of service and scientifically proven knowledge. They value professionalism, a term with roots in the Calvinist concept of professing a calling to serve. However, at their worst, experts are prototypically inflexible, rules-driven or know-it-alls. They are rooted in a system of master and apprentice, where knowledge is based on experience, at a time when knowledge is quickly out of date and competence depends on continual learning. Thus the expert's character can be a major roadblock to creating effective technoservice. Experts want control over their functions

Values of the Expert

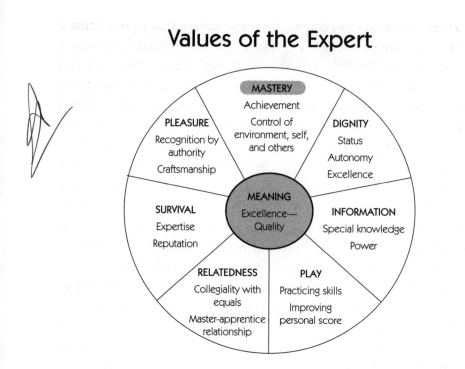

and they resist the empowerment of others, which they see as loss of control. They relate well only with bosses, peers, or younger high-potential apprentices who share their values. To them, the innovator's vision often feels like anarchy, and the new generation's drive for independence seems arrogant.

Approach to Service

As defined by *Webster's New International Dictionary*, an expert is "an experienced person...one who has a special skill or knowledge in a particular subject, as a science or art...." *Expert* comes from the Latin *expertus*, meaning tried, experienced. Over 75 percent of the employees surveyed identify with this definition as describing them very well. This assumption makes sense. Expert knowledge is essential for good service. For about half those surveyed, becoming an expert is the most important meaning of work. People with this goal have dominated American organizations. They represent a social character adapted to the industrial bureaucracies.

Experts are driven to *perform*. They find satisfaction in mastering a challenge. For them, service is performance, achievement, meeting a standard of excellence rather than helping people. They are less concerned about the customer than about measuring up to standards. A 35-year-old expert accountant at one of the major auditing firms bridles at the very idea that it is her job to help customers. She says, "Helping is a bad, crummy word. 'Help me' is like saying you can't do it yourself. You're not free. Advice is not helping. You don't go to a doctor to help you. You go to have him cure you. You help an old lady across the street, that's help. But helping isn't tax advice you pay thousands of dollars for." Yet, at the top level of the same company, managers tell me that the accountants who do more than give advice, who strive to help customers solve their problems and implement business strategy, get the business. So it goes for banks, telecommunications, and other information services.

The dreams of experts show how they are driven to perform, and how they fear not measuring up. These dreams are often about solving problems and taking tests. "I had a nightmare," said a research director. "I was trying to get a key program through and I could not convince management." An air traffic controller has nightmares of being unable to "get the words out to warn the pilots, and they hit." He says, "Every time there is a bad situation, I can count on dreaming about it. Sometimes I drink a lot that night to knock myself out." In addition, lawyer-experts work through cases in their dreams.

The ideal job for an expert is one that allows the exercise of independent judgment and personal control. But it is difficult for a group of individualistic experts to work interdependently. Experts want control, as the following case illustrates. A woman psychiatrist in a mental health center at a county health department says, "As I see it, they hire you for your expertise. They are very interested in your qualifications. They really want to be sure what you are talking about, and then they spend all their time arranging not to listen." She maintains control where she can, "I medicate patients sent by the nonmedical psychotherapists. But never do I medicate anybody where the psychotherapy is done badly. If you want me on your case, you'll do it the way I think is good."

Character Formation

The expert orientation has developed in the traditional father-dominated family and has been reinforced in school and in the bureaucracy. Typically, a child, boy or girl, sought to be like and gain the approval of an expert-oriented father who became the model for a productive relationship outside the family. The mother managed the support system for the father and children. Father's work determined where the family would live and its standard of living. Father interpreted the world of work and the values essential to success and esteem. Over and over again, in many ways, he would say, "You must work hard for success. No one can do it for you. You and you alone must take the tests. Those who succeed are the ones who accept responsibility." The child's dominant drive became mastery of self and schoolwork, successful performance that was rewarded by paternal approval. The school programmed meritocratic hierarchy into the tender young psyche. Grades were the measure of achievement. People were classified as As, Bs, Cs, Ds, and Fs.

Part of this pattern is changing, due to the dual-wage earning family or single parents. Schools still classify by merit and give grades. But children are learning, as we shall see in Chapter 7, that to get ahead, they must also learn cooperative, interpersonal skills. It is not enough to please the authorities. To gain self-esteem and confidence, they must also have support of their peers.

The typical experts are still adapted to the traditional family, which characterized more than one-half of the homes when managers now in their 30s were children, and about 75 percent of families of those (mostly men) now in the top management jobs of major corporations. Consciously, experts value autonomy, freedom to do things their way. Unconsciously, this striving for autonomy conflicts with the wish for approval from paternal figures. The result is ambivalence to authority. On the one hand, experts resent oppressive control that limits freedom. On the other, they yearn for the caring father, who provides support and recognizes a job well done.

Most experts, both men and women, say they most admire their fathers or father figures who are models of fairness and hard work. A corporate executive sums it up, "I admired my father, who taught me to be myself and do a good job. I admire my boss. He is thoughtful and supportive, and leaves me alone. He gives me autonomy." I asked, "What about your mother?" "Dad was strong. She was beautiful," he answered. "She treated all the children alike. My dad represented the outside world. She lived for the family."

Experts do not want to be controlled, but neither do they want to be so independent that they leave the system of measurable achievement, comfortable rewards, and expressions of approval. The most mature experts grow into the good-father-teacher role and take responsibility for development of subordinates. The less mature experts remain overly impressed by and dependent on authorities, and correspondingly, they remain stuck in an egocentric view of the world. Oppressed by autocratic fathers, these people are motivated to seek security and a sense of dignity by controlling their space and maximizing their power. Although they want autonomy for themselves, they believe their freedom and effectiveness depend on controlling subordinates. When you ask them what would make their job most satisfying, they say, "Give me more authority. Get the boss off my back." When you ask about their subordinates, they say, "I need more control there." It is difficult for them to work interdependently with peers who are competitors or customers, and who are seen neither as bosses to be obeyed nor subordinates to be directed. Despite their wish for autonomy, the expert's most important relationship at work is with the boss whose approval is so motivating.

The genius of Franz Kafka was to describe the ambivalent strivings of expert bureaucrats, one moment servile, the next stubborn and proud. The bank clerk of *The Trial* and the surveyor of *The Castle* struggle to maintain autonomy and dignity as they climb the corporate ladder. This challenge is still the psychic struggle for expert-bureaucrats.

Challenge and Recognition

Experts mention two kinds of motivating factors: external recognition (extrinsic) and inner satisfaction based on meeting challenges (intrinsic). Experts love medals, plaques, and awards, but payment and promotion are the highest forms of recognition. In companies where there is little chance for promotion, experts become extremely frustrated. But it is also important for them to be respected as professionals. A typical expert says, "I would like to be treated professionally, to have my decisions and opinions valued." The inner reward comes from mastering a challenge, demonstrating competence. Some experts tend to seek the same challenge in sports.

A computer technician says, "I like most that my work is challenging; it's something new every day. I think that people should be given variety, but only after they have mastered the job." He reports that his "main satisfactions outside of work are boating, water skiing, scuba diving, hang gliding." These are challenging, individualistic sports. Many expert-executives love golf, a game in which one can continually measure one's response to challenge. Experts say they play not against another person but against the course. Competitive experts want not only to win, but also to measure their superiority as precisely as possible. Executive teams of experts are often like golf teams, where each member tries to produce the best score with the hope that the combined scores will produce a winning team. In practice, what is required in the technoservice workplace is something like basketball teams, where all team members share responsibility for the score.

Another computer technician says, "Besides the money, the rewards I get from work are the fact that I have done a good job, and being smarter than the computer. It's a challenge to try to beat the system to get something done that the program says you can't do. I like having the freedom to do it. My boss is lenient, so we do things that aren't set up in the instructions."

For experts, all challenges are tests and there is satisfaction in getting a good grade. A policeman comments, "The police profession gives me a chance to deal with all types of people, mostly in time of extreme sorrow, rage, or difficulty. This tests me and my ability to handle people and I enjoy the challenge." A helper would have mentioned his satisfaction in helping people.

Experts like to see the finished job and know it has been well done. The computer program worked, the audit finding fit regulations, the patient got the right treatment, the sale was made, the case was won.

"You like to see the dollar value of your job," says an expert-accountant. In contrast, the helpers measure their work in terms of its human impact, and the self-developers use both the customers' improved operation and what they have learned as yardsticks of work success.

The Expert's Ideal Boss

It follows from their own needs and values that experts have an ideal of the kind of boss they find motivating. Good bosses make their goals clear, have high standards, delegate, give you a lot of freedom, treat you with respect, listen to you, are there if you need help, and recognize accomplishment. But they are not around too much. An explanation for the success of the business best-seller *The One-Minute Manager*[1] was that it described in dreamlike caricature the expert's model of minimal paternal management. The one-minute manager gives one minute's worth of directions and feedback, one minute's praising, and one minute's rebuke, all done respectfully and in such a way as to limit oppressive control. The image of the unexcitable one-minute manager sitting in his office, smoking his pipe, is like the good father the experts unconsciously yearn for.

Here are some verbatim descriptions of what experts want from managers:

The accountant from the big-6 firm says, "My ideal manager would just leave me alone and (here she begins to talk to the interviewer transferentially as though he were her ideal father-manager) I'll get the work done, and you should be there if I need you. You should recognize my accomplishments."

The air traffic controller says, "He gives us guidance when it is needed, otherwise leaves us alone."

A telephone company pricing and billing clerk describes her ideal, "A good supervisor should be seen and not heard except when necessary. You can't do without them, but they shouldn't stand over your shoulder."

Experts criticize managers who are either oppressive or weak, but they want managers who delegate responsibility to them. Although

---

1 Kenneth Blanchard and Spencer Johnson, *The One-Minute Manager* (New York: Berkley Books, 1984).

experts want this autonomy, they also want to control their own subordinates so they can feel they have mastery over ultimate performance. The problem is that autonomy for me and control over my subordinates produce an organization with emotional gridlock, each person struggling to control his or her turf. A police officer complains about such overcontrol:

> You know that to leave a 20-by-20-block area, I have to ask two supervisors! They entrust to me a $10,000 car but I can't drive it beyond a particular block. I can arrest, take away a person's civil rights, or use a handgun, but when it requires going to a particular part of the city, I can't. I can tie up a helicopter, two canines, seven officers, and eight police cars for any length of time (yesterday I did that for one and one-half hours), but to make a $2 phone call, I have to get the permission of a lieutenant, fill out a form, call through a district operator, and then wait five minutes for her to call me back while she puts the call through, even if the call is two minutes. Yesterday, it took one hour to arrest and process a burglar, and three hours to fill out all the paperwork.

Once expert-police officers become managers, they are sticklers for "complete, neat, and accurate" forms, and they see their challenge as getting subordinates to use the forms, follow the rules. Experts, as subordinate patrol officers, experience control systems as limiting their performance. As managers, they believe these same control systems *express* their performance.

Experts resent managers who do not respect their expertise, and wound their sense of dignity. A nurse administrator of a county health facility says, "The thing that is really the hardest for me to take is that nurses were administrators of the health centers for years. And we know that they can do it. Now, what top management has done is brought in physicians as administrators. Their salaries are considerably higher and there is a tremendous amount of money spent on physicians' salaries, which could be saved."

Although experts resent overcontrol, they are even more critical of managers who are uncertain, whose delegation expresses *laissez-faire* incompetence, and who lack goals and objectives. Experts are also uncomfortable with matrix management, which requires them to report to managers in different departments. They want to know: Who is my boss? What does he or she want from me? When experts have a relationship with a boss who is like a good father, they do not ask for formal feedback. One manager with this kind of relationship said, "It is clear what he thinks about my work. We understand each other." Where this relationship does not exist, the expert feels frustrated about the lack of paternal response and recognition, and wants a formal evaluation. Experts also want the boss to hear their views, but they do not demand participation in decision making. An auditor at the General Accounting Office says:

> I like leaders to tell me what they want accomplished, and what they want done. I don't want them to tell me how to do it. I like for them to be receptive to my questions of why. I want them to listen to me, and to listen with reason. And then after the decision is made, regardless of what the decision is, I will do it. Whoever is the boss is the boss, and I'll do it the way they want to do it.

Experts do want a manager to consult them about their particular area of expertise. For them, this is participation enough. It indicates respect and efficiency. But a boss who asks everyone to share in making decisions is seen as a weakling who is afraid to take responsibility.

The Expert as Manager

Expert-managers are motivated to take charge. They believe in setting clear goals, letting competent subordinates do their thing, and following up to make sure things are done according to the plan. A vice-president of a large company says:

> This is what I believe about people. I believe people want to contribute and feel good about real contributions. I believe people like to win; they need wins.

People like to be recognized. That doesn't come naturally to me. I have to push myself. People will rally to
confident leadership that is competent and knowledgeable. People need to respect leaders to function
well. People need to know what to expect.

This expert and others try to select subordinates who are like themselves and who understand what to expect from them. Many experts
have to push themselves to take the paternal role, because they, themselves, are too concerned about pleasing their own bosses. It is difficult
for expert-managers to give recognition, when they are themselves still
unconsciously good children, seeking approval from a higher level.
Others, including subordinates, may be seen as sibling-competitors.
Only those experts who accept the paternal role can comfortably give
the recognition subordinates need.

Expert-managers try to get rid of people who do not share their
goals and are not good performers. They believe in giving everyone an
opportunity, but they do not invest time in developing those who fail
to measure up by themselves, who do not know how to be an apprentice. For example, a medical administrator says:

How do I get my staff to accomplish their goals? I
have chosen a staff, to the extent that I was able to
have anything to do with the choice. I have pushed,
prodded, and otherwise led people to have goals like
mine when they didn't want them. We talk about
quality patient care and quality of this and that quite
a lot. Most of them share my goals. I had hoped that
the others would leave, and I have done things so
they might more likely make that choice.

It is well recognized that expert-managers tend to decide quickly
whether people are good or bad in terms of whether or not they are
similar to them. Subordinates who need more care, coaching, or
development complain they are ignored. In fact, reflective expert-
managers admit they sometimes write people off too quickly.

Expert-managers feel they should know everything their subordinates know. Furthermore, they want to take responsibility for every-

thing that happens in their organizations, and they hate making mistakes. So even though they might want to delegate and give people freedom, they constantly demand to know everything and tend to second-guess, undermining subordinates' need for autonomy.

However, smart managers realize they cannot know everything and control everything by themselves. They must gain consensus and trust subordinates to make decisions. But when experts confront this reality, it makes them uncomfortable. "I've just come out of one of those damned Japanese-style management meetings," an expert-bank president told me. "I wish I didn't have to waste time listening to a lot of stupid opinions, but that is what my subordinates want."

Relating to Others

Expert-managers don't realize that their style drives away competent people of the new generation. Such was one plant manager I visited in California. He was proud of his technology and work organization. He told me he had enriched the jobs and motivated his workforce. He was surprised when I asked if I could interview the workers. "What will you learn from that?" he asked. I said I would like to hear their views of work at the factory. He reluctantly agreed and suggested we meet afterward. The workers told me they were frustrated. The younger ones were angry because the plant manager never asked for their views. Many had ideas for cutting costs, improving processes, but they had given up. Back in the manager's office, he asked me what I thought of the factory. I said he had a problem. "What is that?" he asked. I said, "It's a communication problem." "You got that right," he said. "I keep trying to communicate the best ways to do things and they don't hear me." I said, "I mean two ways." "Of course I use two ways," he said. "I give speeches and I write memos."

Expert-executives like this plant manager have a hard time understanding the self-developers, who do not believe they must know everything or spend hours at home reading everything. In one large company in the early '80s, a vice-president who was an early self-developer spent his time with subordinates creating a common strategy and delegating assignments. He seldom took work home. His results were always excellent, but the experts at the top of the company were skeptical of him. The self-developer manager didn't know the answer to every question so they believed he must be superficial. Today at this company, managers realize that their subordinates will always know more about their own jobs than they do and their role is to be strategists and integrators, not big brain know-it-alls.

Still many experts believe they can learn any new style, meet any challenge, exploit any new opportunity. All they need is a good book or a course in how to do it. But they can't learn something if they are not aware that they need to change their values. Experts do not know how deeply rooted are their unexamined assumptions that only people like themselves are reliable and effective. Nor do they realize how the expert mind is programmed. Unlike the innovator, who treats organization as a tool that can be shaped differently to perform different tasks, the expert does not question the need for a hierarchial structure. When the expert decides that modifications are needed to increase managerial motivation, these are seen in terms of decentralization, which results in changing the number of pyramids but not the shape of the organizational pyramid. If a big pyramid decentralizes into little pyramids, the only beneficiaries may be those at the various peaks who gain autonomy, but even then there is a new problem of integrating all the pyramids.

It is difficult for the expert to adapt to the requirements of the new workplace: interactive planning, front-line empowerment, no "one best way." Experts want to hold on to control at the top. Experts are reluctant team players. As one expert-manager said, "I prefer to work alone, because I prefer to do the work myself and be responsible for (read: have control over) my own work." Another, forced to work on a team said, "My job was easier when I didn't get so much help." Knowledge gives experts power and they do not share it easily. When they do share it, they may make it hard for others to participate. On teams, they may try to dominate discussions and particularly when they are knowledgeable, other people tend to keep quiet.

Expert-Managers and the New Technology

The design of organizations by experts often clashes with requirements of new technology. A study published by the International Institute of Applied Systems Analysis describes the same human cause of two
major technical failures: the nuclear core overheat at the Pennsylvania
Three Mile Island nuclear power plant in 1979, and the North Sea Platform Bravo oil drilling platform blowout in 1977. In each case, people
close to the problem lacked the authority to close a valve and prevent a
calamitous chain of events. The systems were organized by experts who
retained authority at the top. The National Transportation Safety Board
reports the same causes for the collapse of the mobile offshore drilling
platform that took 80 lives in 1981.[2] A similar situation, in the sense
that those who knew most about the danger of the brittle O-rings that
cracked in the cold lacked authority to cancel the flight, contributed to
the ill-advised launching of the space shuttle *Challenger* in 1986, resulting in the deaths of seven astronauts. In 1991, the same causes resulted
in loss of power for the telephone system in New York City.

The expert orientation also causes conflict with management and
increased stress for air traffic controllers. One expert says, "You can't
manage a controller's work. I'm there with a mike and a button. I do it
the way I think is best. If I'm messing up, they're going to pull me out
of there. That's the only management I need." However, the supervisors feel it is the controllers who are uncooperative. What explains the
conflict and the stress is that both controllers and supervisors are
experts, and supervisors are trying to control the controllers. With a
simpler technology and fewer flights, the individualistic orientation
functioned well enough. These observations are reinforced by a MITRE
Corporation study that describes the history of the controller-supervi-
sor conflict. According to Glen C. Kinney, "A macho culture of hard-

---

2 "Lessons from Major Accidents: A Comparison of the Three Mile Island Nuclear
Core Overheat and the North Sea Platform Bravo Blowout," Executive Report 6, based on
the work done by David W. Fischer of the International Institute of Applied Systems
Analysis (IIASA), A2361, Laxenburg, Austria, 1981. National Transportation Safety Board,
"Marine Accident Report: Capsizing and Sinking of the U.S. Mobile Offshore Drilling Unit
OCEAN RANGER," Washington, D.C., 1983, pp. 47-50, 69-72.

drinking, risk-taking experts was formed. New controller recruits who didn't fit were rejected by the group. The union reinforced the controllers' rights."[3]

As the air traffic system becomes more complex, it requires a service orientation. Easy and clear communication between controllers, managers, pilots, and centers lubricates the system. An airline executive said to me, "One trouble is their name. Air traffic 'controllers.' They believe they control the air. They should be renamed something like air traffic facilitators or pilot helpers. That would describe their real function." In 1993, a senior administrator at the FAA told me that information technology is taking over the traditional functions of the controllers, and only the role of facilitator remains, requiring communication skills more than technical knowledge.

As organizations attempt to empower front-line employees, expert managers are the main roadblock. Not only are they overcontrolling, but their paternalism provokes sibling rivalry among subordinates, further undermining any impulse to cooperate. They try to solve organizational problems by increasing management control or offering individual incentives, not by redesigning processes and developing supportive relationships.

As designers of technology, they seek prestige and awards by impressing other experts, rather than focusing on ease of manufacture and customer usability. Arno Penzias, vice-president of research at AT&T's Bell Laboratories, writes that his major task has been reorienting the experts so that they stop paying "more attention to the plaudits from their colleagues than to the real needs of non-expert users."[4]

---

[3] Glenn C. Kinney et al, *The Human Element in Air Traffic Control* (McLean, VA.: MITRE Corporation, April 1983), pp. 4-21.

[4] Arno Penzias, *Harmony*, (New York: HarperCollins, 1995), p.12. Penzias writes, "Recasting first-level management roles has proved the most challenging undertaking. Experienced researchers themselves, managers had worked hard to ensure the best possible research in their organizations. But 'best' as they defined it: the world's most powerful laser diode; a record-breaking transmission experiment; the 'best paper' award at a major professional conference.... Since the researchers saw themselves as guardians of traditional excellence, they naturally regarded new criteria as a lowering of standards. But over time, the new ideas took hold. Building a manufacturable record-breaking laser presents a far greater challenge than building one that just works long enough to get a paper published, after all" (p.72).

Some experts recognize they must learn to understand people better. They talk about taking courses to improve their "people skills," so they can communicate better. An AT&T middle manager says, "My biggest problem is communicating and getting along with people. I want to have a more open mind, understand people's ideas more. I'm too much 'My way is right and there isn't any other way.'" More and more technoservice companies present techniques of listening courses which generally emphasize skill in explaining and rephrasing. These courses try to sensitize the expert to recognize emotions that get in the way of rational analysis. However, even those experts who take the courses find it difficult to overcome their dislike of having to listen to other people's problems, of being forced into a messy world of emotions rather than the comfortable world of measurable facts.

The difficulty experts have with people stems in large part from their drive to master and control. To control another person's behavior, one must limit that person's autonomy, narrow his or her job. However, most experts are not hardhearted. Beneath the armor of control, many are softies. When they treat people as predictable objects, they do so because they do not want to have to deal with feelings. Furthermore, while bosses may be able to control behavior, they cannot control another person's feelings.

Some experts admit that people make them uncomfortable. The expert-government accountant says, "Don't tell me about the secretary's personal life, because I don't want to hear about it." Expert-policemen have no patience with the problems of people and little sympathy with those who have lost control. A policeman says, "I won't bullshit you. I'll tell you that when a citizen stops me and asks routine questions, he starts to become a pain in the ass."

The computer technician comments, "I most dislike the politics about my work, having to be friendly to nasty people. A supervisor told me, 'Be sociable, learn to read the sports section.' This is a bunch of bull. Why should I try to snow someone? My work speaks for itself. If you don't like my results, let's discuss it. I will not be a yes-man just to get ahead."

Development of Expert-Managers

When companies emphasize relationships, the experts get uneasy. Their confidence evaporates. They feel insecure. But development of experts is possible with good leadership and new organizational systems. In the U.S.A., everyone, even the experts, shares an underlying suspicion of experts and an irreverence toward authority, or at least anyone else's authority. If they feel their knowledge is respected, many experts can become team players like the Hewlett-Packard engineer-salesmen who as early as the 1960s went out to their customers and learned what they needed. At Westinghouse, Russ Nagel, the innovator, put experts to work finding ways to improve customer order forms, on-time delivery, and quality. However, experts must be taught that interdisciplinary project work and teaching are part of the expertise needed by organizations. The definition of expertise must include process as well as substance, teaching and facilitation as well as in-depth knowledge.

An element in the success of Japanese management is the redefinition of performance for experts. When Japanese middle managers are asked whether their work includes helping people, they are puzzled by the question. For them, the definition of work is helping co-workers, superiors, and subordinates. That is how they are evaluated. They are cooperative not out of idealism or free choice, but because an authoritarian system demands cooperation and shared responsibility. Japanese experts must balance intense individual ambition against responsibility to the company and to their demanding superiors. They are expected to tell the truth, share information, and challenge authority in the interest of the company; listen carefully to each other yet gracefully subjugate themselves to the decisions made by authority.

This requirement for balance causes intense stress, but it produces successful results for the Japanese corporation. Experts can learn a participative approach to management, but the road may be rocky. In the mid-'80s, the president of a well-known technology company introduced me to his vice-presidents in the following way:

Lately, I have been reading a lot of psychology. Participative management is good humanly, and it also makes an organization more effective. That may be hard for most of you to understand. Like you, I was trained to be an engineer, and I know how rigidly you think. Why, you squareheads don't even know that without self-esteem, you can't be productive. Some of you may not want to work humanistically. You may be happier somewhere else. But here, we are going to participate. I'm sorry I can't stay to answer questions, but Dr. Maccoby will explain this approach and what it means.

With that statement he left the room. I asked the V-Ps to wait a minute and rushed after the president. I found him outside and said, "What you just did was a contradiction. You spoke about participation and self-esteem, but you did not let them participate and you put them all down as rigid experts. Will you go back and talk about it?" He said, "I can't. I've got to go to another meeting." I said, "If I go back in that room, I'll have to tell them that I don't want to cause you trouble, but there is no way to create trust without facing the contradiction. Should I continue or leave now?" "OK," he said. "You can tell them."

I was not invited back again, but later I heard from one of the V-Ps that although angry at me, he tried to change his style, to listen to others, and to fully support participative management in his company.

Let me emphasize the point that expertise is not the problem; it is the expert value system. Leaders need to broaden their concept of expertise so that it includes managing relationships and learning how to be educators, as well as knowing about strategy and technology.

Donald A. Schön, an educator at MIT, describes how an expert can develop into a "reflective practitioner" who can teach and learn with others.[5] Part of this development requires seeking connections to the

---

5 Donald A. Schön, *The Reflective Practitioner: How Professionals Think in Action* (New York: Basic Books, 1983), pp. 300-302.

client's (or subordinate's) thoughts and feelings. Part is finding a sense of freedom, as a consequence of no longer needing to maintain a professional facade of omniscience. Schön adds that the experts will be more moved to change when clients (subordinates) renounce the comfort and danger of being treated as children for the satisfaction and the anxiety of becoming active participants in a process of shared inquiry.

In the past, the expert approach worked well enough for highly functionalized industrial bureaucracies. At each level, managers coordinated work done by individuals on a lower level down to the highly formatted production jobs. Little horizontal communication was required.

New Approach to Management

Today, different behaviors and attitudes are required for the kinds of teams that must strategize together, design products, and manage complex companies. Even on the front line, empowered people should share information they learn about customers. The corporate game has become more like basketball than golf. Team members must support each other. They must pass as well as dribble and shoot. They need to agree on plays, react quickly to competitors, and share responsibility for diving after loose balls. Therefore, a key problem for the corporation is to transform individualistic experts into team players.

Corporate measurements and rewards can help. If you reward basketball players on the basis of scoring alone, they will be less likely to pass the ball than if rewards are also based on numbers of assists. But is it enough to design measurement and reward systems that reward teamwork? Will this approach cause corporate managers to listen and understand the needs of people they should support? Will it produce among experts the behavior needed to create good teamwork? Will it replace a win-lose view of interpersonal relations with a win-win attitude? I doubt it.

Expert attitudes are too ingrained. Learned in family and school, these mindsets are hardwired in the expert psyche. This is particularly the case for managers raised in families headed by a sole male wage earner and educated in schools where they have been graded according to a normal curve. For traditional corporate executives to become good team players, incentives are not enough. Nor are exercises in teamwork, even though these can demonstrate what impedes teamwork. Experts must want to improve themselves. And they need tools to work with, good concepts and practices they can use to facilitate personal change.

The 7 Habits of Highly Effective People by Stephen R. Covey[6] appeals to many expert-managers. Three and one-half million copies of *7 Habits* have been sold, and the book has remained on *The New York Times* best-seller list for more than 145 weeks. Covey and his disciples have given lectures and workshops to managers throughout the country and have certified official trainers within companies. Some companies, such as AT&T, have invited employees to bring their spouses to the workshops, since Covey's habits are meant to develop effectiveness in family as well as in worklife. What does this book say, and how well does it achieve its purpose?

The first habit is to *be proactive.* This means taking responsibility for one's fate as opposed to being reactive and blaming circumstances or other people. No one will change habits unless he or she feels free to take the initiative and believes it is in one's interest to do so.

The second habit is to *begin with the end in mind.* Stated simply, Covey's point is to envision the goal before starting the journey. This is usually good advice, especially for managers, since it helps strategic thinking. Creative scientists might argue, however, that this is not always an effective habit. Creativity sometimes involves playing with hunches and intuitions without a clear-cut end in mind. The late physicist Leo Szilard once confessed that he applied for grants by proposing research he had already completed so that he could use the money to explore half-formed hypotheses, which would never get funding. This

---

6 Stephen R. Covey, *The 7 Habits of Highly Effective People* (New York: Simon & Schuster, Fireside Edition, 1990).

worked until a National Science Foundation grant-making committee rejected a proposal on the grounds that the proposal was impossible to do. Szilard was so taken aback that he admitted he had already performed the research successfully. Covey speaks pointedly to the typical technical expert by emphasizing that we should envisage *who* we want to *be* as well as *what* we want to *do* or produce. What kind of person are we trying to become? The ability to create trust depends on being a person who can be trusting, and this means acting according to principle rather than short-term expediency.

The third habit Covey puts forth is to *put first things first*. This means more than prioritizing. Covey offers worksheets and diagrams to focus the managerial mind not on just meeting deadlines and fighting fires, but on organizing, delegating, and avoiding problems.

The fourth habit is to *think win/win*, which really requires the fifth habit, to *seek first to understand, then to be understood*. Win/win thinking requires an individual to listen in such a way as to understand the other person's position. Covey writes that when another person speaks, we are seldom trying to understand what he/she is saying. Experts in particular often listen only enough to formulate their own position, especially when they are thinking win/lose. But as Covey argues, empathic listening combined with win/win thinking makes one more effective in closing deals, leading others, and getting along with spouse and children. He might have added that there are times when one must fight for good principles and the principle of integrity calls for win/lose, as is the case with the whistleblowers in Chapter 6.

The sixth habit — *synergize* — follows logically from win-win. Synergy results from people sharing their knowledge. The team can be more effective and creative than any single individual, particularly if it is a heterarchy, in which leadership shifts according to the situation to the person with the relevant knowledge. This arrangement calls for the expert to frustrate the desire to be the know-it-all.

I had an experience with a group of executive experts that illustrates the dangers of expert style leadership. There is an exercise called "Desert Survival" (published by Human Synergistic) that I sometimes use with management teams to demonstrate problems in team decision making. It presents a team of five or six people with a crisis. They have crashed in the Arizona desert and must decide together how to survive. Their main task is to prioritize 15 items saved from the wreck, such as water, a mirror, a blanket, etc., and decide which ones are most useful to survive in the desert? Before they prioritize as a group, each member does so individually. The score of a good team will be at least as good as that of the best individual, because the team will share its collective knowledge and learn from the most expert among them. Their scores are then compared to the prioritizing done by the experts in desert survival.

Once I used the exercise with an executive team, headed by a CEO who had not yet learned to listen to his vice-presidents. In this exercise, he insisted on a strategy that, according to the experts, would have meant probably not surviving in the desert. One of his vice-presidents had an excellent individual score, but the CEO would not listen to him, and the others went along with the boss. However, I have also witnessed a situation in which a top executive had a good solution, but listened to and followed an erroneous team consensus.

Listening empathically may be essential to win/win synergies, but without knowledge and courage, it can cause lose/lose agreement. Agreement and feeling good about it does not make an idea or conclusion a good one, a point missing from *7 Habits*.

Finally, we reach Covey's Habit 7, *sharpen the saw*, meaning we should continually renew ourselves. According to Covey, we should spend a minimum of one hour a day working on our physical, spiritual, and mental dimensions. For those employees who are victims or in fear of corporate downsizing, Covey has a direct message: "Your economic security does not lie in your job; it lies in your own power to produce—to think, to learn, to create, to adapt. That's true financial independence. It's not having wealth; it's having the power to produce wealth. It's intrinsic." In terms of this book, Covey is trying to move the experts to become more like the innovators and self-developers who already understand this message.

According to *Business Week* (December 6, 1993), these principles work very well for Covey. He and his Leadership Center in Provo, Utah, take in about $50 million annually for speeches, sales of videotapes, and a newsletter. However, *Business Week* takes a somewhat cynical tone in describing Covey as "Dr. Feelgood" and telling us, "In truth, the Covey message isn't much more than recycled clichés, translated into business-speak and updated with charts, tables, and illustrations."

Although Covey's seven habits are not based on new research on what effective people do, and Covey does not claim they are so, I believe they include mostly useful counsel, well stated with fresh illustrations. And once one understands how important it is for organizations to develop experts so they meet the needs of technoservice, Covey's message becomes even more valuable and strategic.

Business Week dismisses Covey's ideas as "rooted in religious teachings—he is a devout Mormon with nine children." Does this negate the value of Covey's message? Whether or not one shares Covey's religious beliefs, I think it is possible to derive his principles from observation and analysis rather than revealed truth. Covey's principles are consistent with the message of the great religions: We are born with free will, and we gain a sense of harmony and fulfillment by taking responsibility for ourselves and overcoming our egocentrism to care about others. Furthermore, good habits and rituals keep us on a path that strengthens our will to live according to our best ideals.

The *7 Habits* book does not appeal to everyone. Helpers and some self-developers find that the Covey message and illustrations tend to be paternalistic. The prototypic Covey manager is male. In stories he relates about his family, Stephen Covey is the breadwinner, while wife Sandra runs the household and serves as a volunteer for good causes. It is inevitable that lessons for good living express the character and culture of the teacher. This is what differentiates psychology from the hard sciences. When evaluating the advice of *7 Habits*, readers will find it helpful to understand the Mormon family influences that have formed Covey. While this book is not the last word on the personal development required by the information age, the habits or principles (the concepts are not sharply differentiated) seem especially useful for the technical experts, brought up in the male-dominated hierarchical organization, who need to adapt their social character to the information age. This book can be useful for other types as well. We should be proactive and decide what in it is useful to us.

In summary, the experts remain a significant group in the new workplace. Furthermore, many experts are to be found in leadership roles. They bring with them values of quality and excellence, but unless they learn to understand what motivates them and others, they will impede rather than facilitate change. In the next chapter, we meet the other, traditional type, the helpers, who have, in the industrial bureaucracies, balanced the experts.

CHAPTER 5

THE HELPER

Helpers are motivated by the opportunity to care for other people. In the traditional workplace they play the maternal role to the expert's paternal role. They balance the expert, so to speak, often softening the industrial bureaucratic world.

The Values of the Helper graphic on the next page summarizes the needs of helpers and how they express their values at work. Relatedness is highlighted because it is the most important value for helpers. Their dominant value is caring for people, and mastery for them is effective helping. Dignity comes from feeling needed and respected, being heard at work. Pleasure comes from conviviality at work and playful sociability. It also comes from feeling appreciated. Helpers enjoy sharing gossip; they need to satisfy their never-satiated interest in people. In addition, their needs for relatedness are satisfied by caring people and mutual support. Their ultimate sense of security lies in being a part of a family or community, possibly a union.

Helpers, both women and men, have taken on what is traditionally thought of as the maternal role in the bureaucratic world. They tend the wounded, smooth conflicts, and build relationships. Without helpers, the autonomy-seeking experts would make organizational life unbearable for all but the winners. Helpers care about people, especially those in need. They like to give assistance and support, and they try to bring a family spirit into the workplace. The best helpers respond to others' needs with useful information and caring attention. The worst are well-meaning incompetents or smothering do-gooders. In business, competent helpers satisfy or gain clients by developing trusting relationships; for example, the successful telecommunications software

Values of the Helper

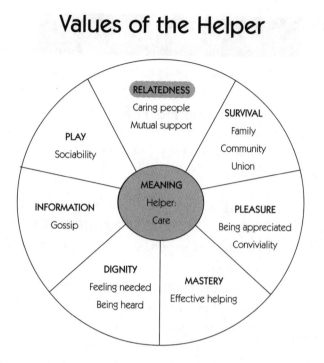

company president who is considered like a mother by her clients, who call on her to solve their personal as well as business problems. Or the union official who mans a hot line to help solve the problems of AT&T employees who have taken jobs at a distance from their families in order to maintain employment in the company. Sometimes, helpers like this just satisfy the need for someone to talk with on a lonely evening.

Helpers are a significant minority in the service sector. Combining the two kinds of helpers (those for whom helping people is most important — about 15 percent — and those whose first priority is helping the leaders of organizations —about 5 percent), one sees that one-fifth of service employees are helpers. The so-called "helping professions" of nursing and teaching have a much higher percentage — 40 or 50 percent. But helpers can also be air traffic controllers, policemen, computer technicians, salespeople, even IRS agents.

Approach To Service

For helpers, the meaning of service is care. As doctors, helpers care about the patient as a whole person, not merely about solving the medical problem with medicine or surgery. Caring police officers prefer to prevent crime rather than apprehend criminals.

One helper-police officer describes how he dealt with a disorderly, partially-dressed man: (Helpers tend to be descriptive. They like to tell the interviewer the whole story.)

> When we got there, the fellow was in the middle of the street with his shorts and T-shirt on. We advised the dispatcher what we had and that there was no need for a scout car and an official to come. We would handle the case. Going through my mind was "What could be wrong with this fellow?" We departed the cruiser to approach the fellow and advise him who we were. [The officers were in plain clothes.] The subject appeared to be intoxicated; he started crying and I wondered why. I advised him there was no need to cry. I asked him if he would step back to the car so everyone wouldn't see him without clothes. I gave him my jacket and we went back to the car. I asked the man what he was doing and told him he shouldn't be undressed. He expressed his anger and humiliation because his wife scolded him for drinking. My partner and I escorted the man up to his apartment and knocked on his door. His wife came to the door. We told her we were policemen and she asked us in, along with her husband.

> We sent him to put some clothes on while we talked to his wife. I explained to her his feelings. She began to tell me of the bills and things and how much they needed money, too much for him to be drinking it away. I then stopped her before she started crying. I

told her some sad stories that happened to others in the same manner. Then I told her that she and her husband should talk things over, or maybe go to a bank and discuss it with them; they might help with a loan. She agreed; I then found he had gone to sleep. I told the wife that when he awakened don't try to talk with him about money and try to take my advice. She agreed and thanked me for being so kind. I gave her my name and number at the office, and told her if I can be of more service to give me a call. We departed and advised the dispatcher of no report other than saying the subject had family problems, along with being intoxicated, and was now sleeping it off. We went back to patrolling.

Rather than being interested in the man or trying to help, the expert in this situation would have likely arrested the man for drunkenness and indecent exposure, and in the process, gotten credit for an arrest.

Unlike experts, helpers focus on people rather than results or procedures. Secretaries or staff assistants who are helpers to leaders speak about doing things for the bosses to "lighten their workloads." Helping IRS agents want to give the taxpayer a break, and when they audit, they explain the tax laws. As an IRS agent says, "My job is negative because I play the heavy, but if the taxpayers cooperate with me, I work to make it as painless as possible." In contrast, expert-auditors monitor by the book and the more aggressive defender-auditors do not mind making the audited uncomfortable to provoke admissions of guilt.

A head nurse sums up the helper's view of service as "having to do with caring for other people." She continues, "You can't be a good manager if you don't really care for other people: caring what happens to them, helping them to get better from an illness. Medicine is too technical and scientific. Many of the physicians have become technical experts."

Helpers Versus Experts

The typical helper dislikes the experts and their world of hierarchy, status, and measurable performance. They even use the term "expert" as a negative. For example, one helper-auditor says, "The experts are report-oriented and like to work with paper. I like to interact with people. They say the report is the most important thing, but it is very frustrating for me." This helper-auditor continues, "*Professionalism* is a word that means a lot to them. For me, it is a nothing word. For most of them, it is doing a job, not getting emotionally involved. It has a snobbish feel to me, like it's a code word for 'white collar,' not a ditch digger or something like that. I don't like the word."

Of course, all doctors are not extreme experts, and all nurses are not helpers. A helper-pediatrician speaks out against the medical model of expert control of health care. She says:

> I think we've created excuses when we set up the medical model. I remember an argument with a nurse at the pediatric hospital. We had a core team and a nurse was describing the job for her child-health nurses, as she called them. And she said certain things were beneath the level of a nurse. And I said, 'That's silly.' As a physician, I don't think anything is beneath my level if it helps the patient. If a child spits up in the room while I'm examining her, I'll wipe it up. I don't call some other person to do it. It's part of my job description to be a helping person.

This helper emphasizes the sense of equality and teamwork among co-workers. She speaks of learning from others, including those lower in job status.

Experts are threatened when subordinates know more than they do. Helpers are opposed not to expertise, but to what they consider the expert mentality. They feel with considerable justification that experts are overly concerned with status and control, and that this impedes them from giving people the care they need.

Character Formation

To understand the motivation of helpers, we must understand their histories. Helpers often come from mother-oriented families, and in a sense, they try to re-create these families in the workplace. The traditional paternal demand is for performance, and the maternal value is unconditional care for all members of the family. The helper's ideal is acceptance that is based on common humanity within the extended family, rather than on performance. The mother-oriented approach provides an ameliorating haven from the hierarchial corporate world of the experts with its admiration of success and a contempt for losers.

The backgrounds of helpers suggest two different dynamics, one from a childhood of scarcity, and the other from a background of abundance. Many helpers come from a poor background, one in which the father was absent or did not achieve and the mother and grandmother kept the family together. These families survived and members got ahead because they helped each other. Often there was a strong religious belief in doing for others what you would have others do for you. In the affluent family, helpers feel they should give to others what has been given to them.

Helpers have typically identified with helping maternal figures and want to be like them. The helper-auditor expresses his admiration for the maternal values of his mother:

> She is super, an incredible person, and the women in my life — daughter, wife, mother, sister, and grandmother — those five women have had so much impact on my life. Mother is at the intersection of it all. She will do anything for anybody. I talk to my mother every day. She never interferes but will do anything she can.

He expresses his orientation to work, "I feel others give me so much, and it's not material things necessarily. I want to give them so much because they have given me so much." This man is going to graduate school evenings, taking advanced courses in psychology, and does volunteer work with the elderly.

Helpers from well-off families with values of service have often been influenced by strong, liberated mothers. A staff assistant to the head of a government agency comes from such a family. She typically admires "Eleanor Roosevelt, not only because she was a risk taker and an innovator, but also because she cared about people. She had loyalty and honesty that I like, I'm like that. She really stuck by Franklin through a lot of stuff." This government worker continues, "My mother was the greatest influence on my life. She's a saint, an enabler. She empowered other people to bring out the best. She set high standards, but never by withdrawing love or approval."

Helpers admire those helpers whom they have known personally, as well as public figures like Martin Luther King, Jr., Gandhi, Mother Teresa, Abraham Lincoln (for freeing the slaves), John F. Kennedy ("for his call to service," " for his attitude that problems could be resolved," "for his belief you could make the world better just by putting in a lot of effort and caring").

Work Relationships

Helpers are personally motivated by relationships at work. The auditor says:

> Even if the work is boring, if you get along with people and help each other out, it makes it better. I place more importance on the people and relationships than on the work itself. When I worked in a warehouse and when I really didn't feel too well and they had to cover for me, they knew that on other days I would cover for them. You need help and understanding and compassion for people.

Helpers want to work with people who are lively, enthusiastic, and caring. They want to be with cooperative, trusting, loyal people who are "warm, outgoing, dependable, with an accepting attitude," and who are not "supercompetitive." The negative of this is that helpers sometimes spend too much time chatting or "schmoozing" with co-workers and clients. Relationships at work can get in the way of productive service.

In fact, helpers are often frustrated by management systems, which they feel are made by and for experts. Police officers and auditors who are helpers complain that the system rewards performance in quantitative, not qualitative, terms. The government auditors who are helpers complain that they are rated on the number of errors or examples of criminal cheating they catch. If they try to help someone who gets in trouble later on, they are blamed. And they gain no credit if their help is effective.

A social worker claims that an agency encourages caseworkers to push welfare clients into jobs to get credit for a case, when in fact they know the person is unskilled and untrained, and likely to lose the job. This helper does not want to force someone into a situation where he or she will soon be back needing help from the agency, and will likely fall into deeper despair.

One of the helper-police officers points out that not only is it difficult to measure helping, but helping can actually hurt your job rating. He says:

> According to the general orders of the police department, the most important purpose of every member of the police department is the prevention of crime. A policeman standing on the corner may or may not be preventing a crime at any given moment. This is something that is unmeasurable. In other words, there is no way of telling if a policeman is fulfilling his most important function. A policeman is usually judged by the number of good arrests he makes. But if a man is diligent in his coverage of an assigned beat, crime will be low and his chance for an arrest will be lessened. Therefore he will go down in the eyes of his superiors.

Another police officer says:

> Patrolmen are under the constant strain of 'quotas' in apprehending law violators, competing with other officers for top evaluations to achieve promotions,

which are accompanied by substantial monetary and status increases. One possible solution would be to lessen the salary differences between the ranks, thereby eliminating officers who are looking only to monetary gain. Many times the officer must compromise his own ideals and standards, possibly severing a good working relationship with his follow officers, in following a course of action designed to please his superiors. Current supervisor requirements consist of memorizing department rules and regulations and obtaining a good evaluation from supervisors who have obtained their ranks through the same process. Both requirements overlook the most essential elements in supervisory personnel, the ability to help and work with subordinates and to inspire people to do quality work and not just what is required.

A third police officer says:

> Once I had a partner who was a great talker. He really liked people and had received many commendations from various community groups. He received an award from the chief of police for collecting the most money for the Police Boys' Club. This man just had a great personality. He made few arrests, and generally tried to talk to people about the law violation or situation. But in serious criminal situations he knew what had to be done and he did it. When he took the promotional test for sergeant he was among the 21 men to pass the written test. But he was given a very low efficiency rating. He appealed and was told that he just did not make enough cases. This officer retired a private.

Thus, helpers see their strengths, which benefit people, unrewarded by bureaucracies. The experts design objective, measurable standards that do not reward helping, even when it achieves the organizational goals.

Rewards From Work

The intrinsic reward of being able to help is extremely motivating for helpers, even if they are frustrated by the extrinsic rewards designed for and by the experts. Helpers feel that good relationships and the opportunity to see people benefit and grow at work are rewards in themselves. They feel more motivated and rewarded by being needed and appreciated than by receiving money and promotions. A corporate secretary says, "Money is not the reward. I consider myself well paid. I am fortunate and pleased; for what I do I am overpaid." She continues, "My father in construction doesn't make that much. My reward is self-satisfaction, of doing a job well, and knowing that I am helping. I enjoy contact with people."

One of the police officers says, "It is a reward to know you have helped someone. If I can prevent one juvenile from becoming involved with drugs, I feel I have done a good job that day." Note again that he is more likely to be rewarded for arresting a drug seller than for preventing sales from taking place.

However, despite such personal rewards, helpers often feel unappreciated and frustrated at work. The pediatrician says, "I just want to be a good pediatrician. Nobody knows me and I don't care. When I leave the office, I don't care if people know I'm a doctor. But I do know that the children I took care of and their parents know that I did a good job." Sometimes she complains that people do not appreciate the help she gives, "You don't get feedback from the administration. You don't get very many strokes in what you're doing. You get complaints. Compared to private-practice medicine, you seldom get good feedback. And the parents don't say, 'Thank you' when you help their child get healthy. A thank-you would be enough."

Because they are not appreciated, some helpers turn off at work. In one government office, expert-managers asked me to help them deal with a secretary who, they said, was unmotivated and unproductive. They suspected she was incapable of doing the job, but because she was Afro-American, they were hesitant to confront her. They were afraid she would accuse them of racism. It turned out that she was a competent helper to the needy, a leader of her church, but an employee who felt demeaned at the office. With little respect or appreciation from managers, she did the minimum. Many helpers, frustrated by their paid work, express themselves in volunteer work. Another government secretary says, "I'm involved in church activities and do lots of missionary work, visit the sick, shut-ins, those confined to a hospital. There's hardly a week when I don't make a hospital visit." She speaks of one person she helped, "I oversee a woman who is 104 years old. I make sure that her basic needs are met. She gets food stamps and groceries. I am also president of the deaconesses and I work with the Board of Education for Sunday school teachers." This helpful enthusiasm could find expression at work if managers respected and encouraged it. This woman would be motivated if she were appreciated for providing help. Instead her bosses expected her to do her job as a duty. They did not develop a personal relationship with her, much less show her any appreciation.

One helper in a large company is resentful of unappreciative management and her low status. She says:

> A clerk's job is largely helping. Managers delegate the detail work. It is necessary to have workers, so how can it be demeaning to be one? Sure, everybody would like to make a hundred grand, but who is going to carry out the trash? Our society says, "Oh, couldn't you get a better job than that?" What happened to the days when a guy was proud to be a streetcar conductor and supported his family that way? America needs to reprioritize its values. How can I be proud of what I contribute if no one really values helping?

At AT&T, half the operators I surveyed in the 1980s saw themselves as helpers. A generation ago, operators took pride in helping people complete calls. Then advances in technology replaced most operators and made many who remained feel like appendages. The company has tried to reinterpret their jobs so that they have more freedom to help customers complete calls that contribute to profitability. Through the Quality of Worklife projects, operators initiated projects to help elderly or disabled people who could not get to the phone easily. The operators called in regularly and made calls for these customers. Of course, when these employees feel they are helping people in need, work becomes more meaningful for them and they are more motivated to help the company succeed. Today, AT&T and other telecommunications companies still need people who help customers, but at AT&T in the '90s, managers teach operators and customer service representatives what kinds of help are profitable.

Helpers And Management

As employees, helpers want managers who care about them, their growth and sense of dignity, and who listen to their ideas. They resent the expert-managers who don't help. A 28-year-old telephone company clerk complains, "The supervisors are not helpful; they're worthless. I don't like the tiers, the class structure." Her frustration is obvious, "My current manager sees us as a temporary bother! There is no warmth or communication. You either feel stupid and awkward, or you get discouraged. It becomes boring and you get apathetic, but as long as you spend a third of your life working, why not make it fun and helpful?"

As managers, the best helpers are teachers and developers. Weaker helpers fail as managers because they can't deal with conflict. They want to be liked and appreciated, and hesitate to give unpleasant feedback. They want people to succeed and are slow to discipline. The best helper-managers practice individualized coaching. One manager of information services comments:

> I had an employee once who wasn't showing up for work and whose work quality was poor. The supervisor said he was incompetent and didn't know what to do with him. When I talked with him, he said his supervisor was the problem. I worked with him defining the problem, how he saw it, and developed a way to let the employee make more decisions. I worked with the supervisor, too, to develop a software package and some training for this employee, and things

improved. I heard of another case of a woman who just wasn't turning up for work, but did good work when she came in. The supervisor took the time to talk to her and find out what was wrong. It turned out she was an ex-actress who was really suffering from having to do 'ordinary' work. The supervisor was sympathetic, helped her get involved with a community theater group, and her attendance improved immediately. But that kind of attention goes even beyond work, and it takes the commitment of the supervisor to sit down and talk with the person to find out the real reasons for what is going on.

Expert-managers would likely not solve these motivational problems because they lack the helper's interest in understanding people. One of the most respected leaders in the Foreign Service was an ambassador who was a strong helper, an institutional helper, and a developer of people and policy. She combined qualities of helping, institutional loyalty, and expertise. She saw her strength as creating openness and developing people so that she could delegate responsibility. She observed:

As an ambassador, you have to create relationships to be sure you are not cut off. I did a series of things. I was a regular at the Marine House Friday-night parties. I found that over a beer, people would bring up things that were bothering them. Along with three secretaries, I was a member of a pinball team. I maintained a very close relationship with the deputy chief of mission (DCM) and administrative counselor. I encouraged my secretary to be receptive to complaints or opposing views and not to be afraid to bring them to me. I told her to do this unless she was personally uncomfortable in that role, and she became the regular spokesperson for different points of view. I encouraged the DCM to be visible through-out the mission. I couldn't have done my job without the DCM. He visited everyone in the mission regularly to sound out their opinions, and I occasionally dropped in.

She added, "I have an enormous respect for institutions and for structure. I prefer the risk of openness to the loneliness of singleness. I want to have fun and have others share in my work." Like the best helpers, she emphasizes values of integrity and honesty as essential to creating the trust fundamental to an open embassy. "We are not playing a game," she said, with an implied rebuke to the gamesmen of diplomacy. "Our work and careers are not a game. We must do a good job. I want and value good character."

The Foreign Service is often considered the elite of government, where the dominant style is that of elegant experts whose highest value is expertise at political analysis, crafting a cable to Washington, and negotiating a treaty. Helpers in the Federal Government are more likely to thrive in the helping agencies, like ACTION, which includes the Peace Corps, VISTA (Volunteers in Service to America, the domestic Peace Corps), and volunteer programs for the elderly. In 1993, ACTION became part of the Corporation for National and Community Service.

In a Midwestern city, a woman in her early 50s ran the ACTION Agency's volunteer programs to help unemployed youth and senior citizens. A survey of ACTION employees named her one of the three most effective managers in the agency. She was a helper with enough of the defender in her that she is a strong team builder and a developer of both institutions and people. For her, that means helping, mothering, and protecting. One of the earliest examples of her helper effectiveness occurred when she went to the Deep South at the height of the civil rights movement there and founded the Congress of Racial Equality chapter in her city. Her mother was a "very religious, churchy lady," but she moved away from the church when the pastor did not support civil rights work. Later, this ACTION leader went back to college, got a degree in community organizing, and worked with a union. Eventually, she got into government work at ACTION, where she tried to hire other helpers.

She described her approach:

> First I look for someone who has been a volunteer, and not just a formal volunteer, but someone who has done something in their community. It could be a mother who has tried to do something in the schools. Secondly, I would look for some interpersonal skills, people who don't take themselves too seriously, are not pompous, and don't get upset at what the community says about them. They have to enjoy seeing other people grow, and not be too materialistic. They don't have to agree with people, but they have to like them.

Her management philosophy expresses the helper's emphasis on building one-on-one relationships, and understanding the strengths and weaknesses of individuals:

> I have to treat employees all the same, but different. My philosophy is that people can do, if you help them and keep a positive attitude. I have to know them as people, and how they work. Gary is a hard worker, but he is still learning, so I have to go by and give him a few strokes rather regularly to keep him going. Norma is meticulous. I have to push her to keep doing the bigger things. I have to slow Domingo down. He really likes to work hard, and is always out in the field rushing around. I sometimes have to give him some detailed desk work to get him to slow down or remind him to take some time off and take a vacation with his family. Cathy is hypertensive and very nervous. Sometimes I have to let her blow and then say, "Okay, let's look at what's happened and try to put the pieces back together." Dennis is new and is not very aggressive. I have to put him on training VISTA volunteers to help him learn to be more outgoing. That's the way I treat my employees differently.

Working with people is the thing I like most about my work. I really like seeing people grow, not only the staff, but also people in the projects. For example, before my people do a site visit, we talk. We go over the problems and discuss a possible approach. Then when they come back, they have a debriefing with me, Then they write up the site visit report. I try to get them to make a recommendation. That's hard. They would rather that I did it. They don't want to have to make the hard decisions like terminating a project or getting rid of a supervisor. If we have to make those kinds of decisions, I write the letter and sign it. This puts them in a position where they can negotiate and they don't have to take all the heat.

It happens that the two outstanding helper-developers quoted here are women. This would appear to confirm the findings of Carol Gilligan, a psychologist, that women, more than men, think of moral issues in terms of relationships rather than abstract principles, and envision an ideal of community rather than of autonomy.[1] This viewpoint has had wide currency in diversity-training workshops.

However, the differences between men and women are more characteristic of the generation raised in single-wage earning families than they are for that raised in the dual-wage earning family. Gilligan is describing the traditional dichotomy between the male expert orientation and the female helper. As both men and women become self-developers, these differences disappear. As we shall see in Chapter 7, the idea of service translates into value-added services that people pay for and that can perhaps be converted into products rather than help, which is personal and requires appreciation.

Weaknesses Of Helpers

The strength of helpers, both women and men, lies in their care for people, idealism, and cooperative spirit. Their weaknesses stem from

---

[1] Carol Gilligan, *In a Different Voice: Psychological Theories and Women's Development* (Cambridge, Mass.: Harvard University Press, 1982).

overestimation of their ability to help, their need for gratitude, and their reluctance to defend their views when they are challenged. Some helpers recognize that they run the danger of making people dependent on them. Trying to help without sufficient understanding and knowledge about people, their motives and capabilities, can weaken the client or patient. The impulse to help can foster dependency, and can become oppressive rather than developmental.

A California social worker understands the dangers of causing dependency. She says of her clients:

> They get dependent on me because I tend to take over and do things for them. You cannot spoon feed everyone and expect them to feed themselves if you do not teach them. I think many of us, and I am from the old school, are more likely to do for people. I think this is necessary, but in addition you must do with people. With all the diagnoses and follow-ups, you keep doing for the patient. You make arrangements with them for going to Dr. Jones, for going for laboratory tests; you find out how they can get money to pay for it, you arrange for the transportation, you do all this for them.
>
> In a way, many of us enjoy doing it because you have a sense of accomplishment — like I said earlier, I am appreciated, I am needed, I have done something. But from a larger perspective, if you keep on doing for Mrs. Smith all these things, Mrs. Smith will never learn; Mrs. Smith will expect this to be done. So I am saying that sharing the responsibility is important. Like, "Mrs. Smith, I know you have no transportation, do you have anyone at home?" "Well, maybe my brother-in-law.", "Well, ask him. Instead of me calling someone, you call your brother-in-law." Or, "Do you know what to do if Johnny has a temperature? Will you get a thermometer? Go out and buy it today so next time when you need it you'll have it."

Sometimes the person has to learn gradually to take responsibility. I think this is one of my frustrations with the social system. We do for people. For a certain segment of our population, we have to do it because they have not been taught; they do not know, but by and large, people should do things for themselves.

Helpers also suffer from gullibility. They want to believe people are good. They think they can get along with everybody. They also expect gratitude for those they help, and when disappointed, they become disillusioned. Some burn out or become hard.

Helpers suffer from being too soft-hearted or becoming bleeding hearts. They try to avoid conflict and that tendency keeps them from standing up for their principles, or protecting the people they are trying to help, or improving service by resolving conflicts within an organization. One helper, a government manager, was pushed into a role that demanded telling people to change what they were doing. He was uncomfortable and felt incompetent. "I'm a very human-oriented type of person, as you can tell," he commented. "Management above me made it necessary for me to be the typical authoritarian manager. Whatever I tried to do to humanize the situation even a little turned out to be a disaster, and I mean a disaster. I don't have the skills to do that. I was constantly forced into an adversary role. I don't do well in an adversary role. It was terrible; I don't even want to talk about it."

Another helper who is appreciated for his help is also criticized by his subordinates because he doesn't enjoy fighting. One of the subordinates says, "He has clarity of communication, but a reluctance to enter the fray, avoiding the unpleasant side of management such as criticizing people." Another comments, "He is too much for the underdog. It's hard for him to be tough. He lets people get away with too much, gives them too many chances." When told how his subordinates saw him, he was defensive, "If those bastards are too dumb to understand, forget it."

Some helper-managers naively believe that if they institute a form of participatory management, a consensus of good ideas will emerge.

They pay insufficient attention to conflicting interests. They underestimate the need for tough-minded analysis, and they lack the courage to attempt new organizational approaches and to defend them.

A helpful manager at ACTION said, "My husband and I have a personal philosophy — you never do anything to hurt anyone. But people hurt us all the time. I don't know why. Am I a sissy, do I have no backbone to stand up to people?" She continued, "Often supervisors must protect employees, and I don't mean in a mothering way, but I know I need to stand up to my boss when he takes away space or moves people without asking first." But she lacked the courage to do so.

Adapting To The New Workplace

In summary, helpers try to humanize the system, to create a team, even a family, within a bureaucracy. They may make the narrow roles of the industrial bureaucracy bearable by humanizing relationships, but in the era of technoservice, this is insufficient. Helpers concentrate on dyadic, one-to-one relationships, rather than questioning whether the organization's existing structures and systems might be redesigned into empowered teams. Their approach does not develop and motivate other types of employees. For helpers, morale and motivation result from caring relationships. In contrast, new-generation self-developers, who share the helper's dislike of bureaucracy, enjoy the give and take of teamwork and a more businesslike, less emotionally involved approach. As information-age managers or union leaders, helpers must balance coaching and care with expertise about strategy and organization. This is exactly what is happening in the educational programs sponsored by AT&T's Workplace of the Future.

Fortunately, many helpers welcome the opportunity to learn new skills and also recognize their own shortcomings. They welcome leadership that develops their skills and balances customer, shareholder, and employee satisfaction.

CHAPTER 6

THE DEFENDER

Defenders are motivated by opportunities to establish justice, protect people from wrongdoing, and right wrongs. Overall, only a small percentage of employees sees the most important meaning of their work as defending against those who do not respect the law, who do harm, or who undermine values necessary to good organization. Although few people are pure defenders, they play an important role in work organizations. At one extreme, defenders are whistleblowers or union leaders. At the other end of the spectrum, they are entrepreneurs who create industries.

The graphic, Values of the Defender on the next page, summarizes the way in which the defender expresses values at work. The defender's dominant value is dignity, which is highlighted on the graphic. This value is experienced by defenders as a strong need for justice and respect. Typically defenders have grown up in a world where the weak were crushed or humiliated by the strong. For these defenders, survival depends most of all on solidarity with a loyal group. The defender either sticks to his or her family or tries to build new ones. Outsiders are rarely trusted. Mastery for the defender is personal power over others, and the defender's competency is in methods of control, including the use of threats and rewards. Defenders seek information that alerts them to threats or gives them strategic advantage. Without power, defenders feel they are vulnerable to oppression by those who do have the power.

For the defender, work is a form of warfare. This can be war against competitors or within organizations, against rivals. For union leaders who fight for "justice," the war may be against management. At their best, defenders protect people by enforcing values of respect and justice,

Values of the Defender

and in so doing they strengthen organizations, since any social system breaks down when no one takes responsibility for defending values against the few who flout them.

Among the defenders we interviewed are social workers who defend the poor, the handicapped, and the victims of injustice; whistleblowers outraged at the excessive harm, cost, or poor quality produced by people who squander the taxpayers' dollars; union officials organizing exploited workers; and policemen and prosecutors in search of criminals. These defenders are angry and indignant with the cheaters, contemptuous of the expert-bureaucrats, who remain detached and objective, and impatient with the peace-loving helpers, who do not confront injustice and protect people.

However, defenders can polarize people into "us" and "them." Unless they are in charge, they may act like loose cannons on the organizational deck. As long as they feel they are the only ones who represent justice, they make life difficult for everyone else, by taking it upon themselves to criticize those who cut corners or bend rules.

Americans are ambivalent about defenders. In fact, the new generation of self-developers, oriented to tolerance and positive experience, dislikes taking the role of policeman or protector. In my 1986 survey, none of the people — mostly in their 30s and selected as Young Leaders by the Kellogg Foundation funded by the cereal company — checked the defender as best representing their approach to work, and only 9 percent considered that the defender type described them very well. When I asked them why, they said things like: "I don't want to be a cop." "I don't like to judge people." "Why should I defend institutional values, when I had no say in forming them?" In 1985, while surveying engineering managers in their late 30s and early 40s, I found the same pattern. In the 1990s, I still find that the defender is the type least identified with by managers. However, unless other types accept responsibility for organizational values, defenders will often take top leadership roles and block the teamwork and delegation essential to productive technoservice organization.

We studied 40 cases of defenders to understand what motivated them in their work: responsibilities, relationships with clients, managers, subordinates, and co-workers, the rewards they sought in their work, and the reasons they found compelling for their behavior at work. We also explored the development of their character in childhood, since by describing their early experiences, we gain a better understanding of their view of service.

The Approach to Service

Defenders define service in two ways. One is advocacy for customers, clients, or subordinates, including defense and protection. The other is the defense of larger institutions, companies, and nations from cheats, subversives, and enemies. The defender-helper, the tough institutional helper who can be called a protector, is perhaps the only bureaucrat who is portrayed favorably by the media and is the hero of many novels and movies: Bumper, the cop on the beat, in Joseph Wambaugh's *The Blue Knight*; Georges Simenon's Inspector Jules Maigret of the Paris police; the Swedish detective Martin Beck in the novels of Maj Sjöwall and Per Wahlöö; and countless others. Maigret is the prototypic protector; suspicious of authority, but a fatherly coach to his assistants; contemptuous of the snobbish, sympathetic to the victims of society, even to the criminals he so relentlessly pursues. Bumper and Beck fit the same mold. However, this model is the exception, not the rule. Most policemen are, in fact, experts, and defenders can be found in all kinds of jobs, not just in the police department. Disproportionately, defenders move to the top, especially in organizations where there is little trust, because they build loyal teams, are effective bureaucratic jungle fighters, and protect their people.

Here are some defenders describing what motivates them about their jobs:

A California social welfare worker says, "I went to bat with the idea that the deserving should be helped, and those that cheated should get kicked off the rolls. It's a fair and square system and should be defended. I wanted to save the taxpayers of California money. I wanted to protect little children from abusive parents and protect the welfare system from clients who would take advantage of it." Here she mentions both defending values from cheats and protecting the helpless children from abusive parents.

A manager of volunteer programs for the elderly says, "What I like most about my work is the fact that I'm dealing with older people. I feel I'm an advocate, a friend. I'm helping people, a quarter of a million older people." How did he become interested in the elderly? "I became interested in forced retirement and ageism. People talk about racism and sexism; there's ageism, too. Old people need defenders." Here the emphasis is on protection, but there is the implication that old people are being exploited by someone.

A telephone company secretary and union shop steward sees herself as defending and helping fellow employees. In this way she gains power and a rewarding experience. She helped form a committee that trains a team to innovate and solve problems. She says:

> I have a deep commitment to what I believe in. I'd go
> to bat for anyone who is overlooked. I love this
> committee. I fought so much for the girls. We are

one. We are together. I've often thought, if I went to my grave today, what would I want people to say about me? I'd like them to say, "If it wouldn't have been for Cheryl, I wouldn't be able to do this, or be where I am today."

Some defenders emphasize the defense of institutions and laws rather than people. An Internal Revenue Service (IRS) agent says, "We serve by enforcing against the people who don't pay their taxes. We serve the many by enforcing against the few. We don't serve the people we enforce against." In a similar manner, a U.S. Commerce Department auditor says, "We are fighting program people, fighting contractors. The auditor is the enemy of those who cheat."

A civil rights prosecutor for the U.S. Justice Department sees himself defending a system of laws in a way that necessarily causes pain for some people:

> I'm not sure I'm serving the public, because my work goes against the mainstream of the public, the majority's view. But by doing that, I'm serving the public in a way they don't appreciate, because my work fosters a system that permits the tremendous freedom we have. By championing the minority view, making the system available to everyone, there's a benefit to the public, although they don't necessarily perceive it as that.
>
> What I do causes certain individuals a lot of pain and hardship. They could lose their jobs or be incarcerated if convicted. And sometimes, investigating unpopular things, forcing people to be witnesses, causes hardship to them. For example, they can lose their jobs or be ostracized by the community or their peer association. But there's no solution to a problem without sacrifice.

These defenders see themselves as defending principles, organizations, and the general public rather than the individual. A medical administrator states, "I owe it to the Health Department to see that it's getting something for the money it's putting out. I believe that. You know, I'm responsible to them, for those management things. I would not let them get cheated. If it weren't going well, it would be my job to do something about it or let people know."

The goal of these defenders is an ideal of truth, exposing fraud and deception. An administrator who also publishes a whistle-blowing newsletter says, "I feel I'm helping to inform the taxpayers by exposing waste and mismanagement." A Nuclear Regulatory Commission (NRC) engineer who blew the whistle about safety problems, hidden from the public, sees his service as bringing "truth in government." He testified to Congress, "The agency [the NRC] has forced us into widespread deception of the public, and that includes Congress."

These defenders are unwilling to let go or ease up once they have gotten their teeth into something they consider rotten. An auditor who sees himself as the "taxpayer's watchdog" examined a government-funded training program for the disadvantaged. He says:

> They decided they wanted us to take a look at the program, actually go out and interview some of the people being trained. And I was finding out it was a lot of fiction. They were taking people, putting them on a payroll, and giving them a nothing job to do until the money ran out and then they let them go. And I started reporting this. I said, "It's a whitewash." Back in Washington, top management put the best face on it and said, "Well, they made their best efforts." I wouldn't accept that. And I fought and I fought and I said, "Dammit, you've got to address the issue."

Character Formation

How do defenders such as these become so motivated to right wrongs and protect people? The central theme in the childhood of defenders is the struggle for justice — to be treated with respect and to triumph over humiliation. We can distinguish two variations of defender backgrounds, although they may also be combined. One is the child who is unjustly picked on because he or she is weaker or different, and who reacts with courage and becomes acutely sensitive to humiliation and injustice. The second is the child from an intact family with strong standards, one which has struggled against adversity, poverty, or prejudice.

Some defenders lost their fathers when they were young. The father of one defender we interviewed had a mental and physical breakdown. Another's father was an alcoholic. They both felt unprotected. They see themselves as people who are weak, vulnerable to humiliation, or at a disadvantage, but who became strong because they fought back. The strongest defenders seem to have had mothers who taught them to fight for their dignity.

This is the pattern for some of our recent presidents. The role of President of the United States calls for someone who, if not dominantly a defender — FDR and JFK were gamesmen-defenders — must at least have a strong identification with that orientation. The President takes an oath to defend the Constitution of the United States. Some recent Presidents, Lyndon Johnson, Richard Nixon, and Ronald Reagan, all shared some of the family dynamics we find in the defenders we interviewed: a strong mother who emphasized pride and self-respect; a family where the father was ethical but not a success; a mother-generated drive to rise above failure, yet a touchiness about wounded dignity.[1] Defenders are quick to see slights and insults, and in a profound way, an attack on their dignity is felt as a threat to survival.[2]

Defenders feel they would rather be bloodied than oppressed and humiliated without a fight. They seek those who share their values. The self-developers are not comfortable with the defender's intense view of relationships demanding total loyalty and ideological agreement.

---

[1] Doris Kearns, *Lyndon Johnson and the American Dream* (New York: Harper & Row, 1976). Garry Wills, *Nixon Agonistes: The Crisis of the Self-Made Man* (Boston: Houghton Mifflin, 1970.) Laurence Leamer, "Make-Believe: The Story of Nancy and Ronald Reagan," *The Ambassador* (TWA in-flight magazine), January 1985, p. 54.

[2] Bill Clinton is more of a helper-self-developer, brought up by a mother who was a nurse. He has been criticized for a lack of defender qualities, a certain softness about people. George Bush is more of an expert-company man, with close relations to peers and a tendency to father-son relationships, as in his choice of Dan Quayle for vice-president.

Reagan's attractive style, the professional actor's detachment, a graceful sense of humor, and profound optimism mitigated his defender qualities of aggressive self-righteousness disliked by the new generation.

In poor families where there is a strong father and mother, we find defenders like the consumer advocate Ralph Nader, whose parents were Lebanese immigrants in a predominantly white, Anglo-Saxon, Protestant town in Connecticut. Some of the defenders we studied recall being outcasts because they were from immigrant families, or families with religious or cultural backgrounds different from the majority, usually white Protestant. These children became alert to attacks on their dignity. They were constantly challenged to prove their worth. This experience, of course, has also been the situation for many African-American families.

It is also true for some poor white families. The government auditor says:

> People talk about ghettos and all that. I lived in one, too, in Albany, New York. We were looked on as outcasts. We didn't have much. And we worked to get it. My mother was tough. She was a wheeler-dealer. She knew exactly what direction she wanted me to go. She pushed me. I knew what I wanted. We lived on a farm for a while behind the university, and I knew damn well I wasn't going to the public high school. I was going to prep, and then I was going to the university. Mother told me, "We can't pay for it, we don't have the money." I said, "I'll get it, I'll work for it." I said, "I don't need any help from anybody. I can do it." And she and my father told me, "Well, as long as you are going to school, you get free room and board, but you are going to have to do the rest of it on your own." So from the time I was 12 years old, every piece of clothing on my back and all the tuition I spent for school was paid for by me. You name it, I did it. I was delivering milk 40 hours a week when I was 10. Delivering newspapers, door-to-door salesman....

A State Department official who is known as a defender of ethics and a protector of those who share his standards says, "It was the Depression years when I was growing up, in the '30s. We had no money, had to scramble for every speck of education. Our background was not only ethical, but there was a sense that you could rise above it and manage." This defender is contemptuous of Foreign Service officers from affluent backgrounds, who do not appreciate the opportunities given them by their jobs, do not support the best in each other, and do not protect the integrity of the service.

Defenders like these are typically survivors who have toughened themselves to cope with and rise above threats to their life, livelihood, and dignity. They look with dismay at people who do not share their values. The State Department official says, "The Depression experience was topped off by going into war for four years. By the time you get through combat, with friends wounded and killed, you have your values redistilled; your character is molded. You either go to pot or you don't. I tell my wife we are the last of the nineteenth century. After us came the Pill and everything else."

Defenders admire heroic qualities: courage, bravery, integrity. In contrast to experts, who admire father figures who are teachers or models of competence, defenders admire models of courage and ethics. Some of the same people a helper would cite for their care, a defender admires for their moral strength. Many admire Winston Churchill (for his tenacity and courage), Abraham Lincoln, and Martin Luther King, Jr. (for their bravery and determination, and because they stood for human dignity).

Some admire the tenacity and courage of parents, such as a social worker in her 40s whose mother was a migrant worker, grew up traveling in camps in California, and had five stepfathers. She never knew her father, but thinks he was a gambler. She married a soldier, had a son, and says, "He left me with all the bills." She became a country-western singer, then married a well-off manufacturer who agreed to support her schooling. "I wanted to be a social worker, because I remember they were the only ones who came out in the fields and cared about us. Coming from where I did, it's sometimes hard to realize that not everyone is as strong inside as I am." She admires her mother because "she never gave up and still hasn't."

Some admire people they consider direct models for their own behavior. A federal government manager says:

> I like Ralph Nader, but I think he's a bit too radical at times. I admire him because he really took on a big task and didn't buckle under the pressures; and I admire the courage, I guess, and the fact that he was trying to fight for something that wasn't very popular. In most cases he was right. I think after he got there, he was a little bit more extreme than I expected him to be. Not everything has to do with people getting cheated. Yet probably you need somebody who is fanatical about what he is doing to get the attention.

In describing the kind of people admired by defenders, I believe it is worth adding a quote from an interview with Dan Burt, the tough lawyer who took on the CBS news network in defense of General William Westmoreland, the Commander of U.S. forces in the Viet Nam war. Burt's ideal is Captain Carpenter, a mythical superdefender in a John Crowe Ransom poem. He explains:

> If you went and looked up "Captain Carpenter," you'd get a better sense of what I respect. It's an allegory. Captain Carpenter is a Don Quixote type. He goes out day after day over the course of some unspecified span, apparently it's his life. And he keeps meeting with various evils, and they keep beating the hell out of him, 'til finally they've cut off his arms and legs and he still goes rolling on. Finally they cut off his head and as his head rolls down the road in the dust and gravel and pebbles and mud and dirt, his tongue is still going. He's still fighting; he's still doing what he thinks is right. With a measure of spirit and a measure of élan.[3]

---

[3] John A. Justice, "The Right Tough," *The Ambassador* (TWA in-flight magazine), January 1985, p.54.

Motivated to defend and protect, defenders feel they need these qualities to prevail at their work. It follows, then, that the rewards most important to defenders are those having to do with getting results, seeing their efforts make a difference, and achieving a sense of justice and triumph over enemies.

The auditor for the Commerce Department says, "One joy is seeing someone take my finished product, and I'm not looking for praise. In fact, if they accept it, and take action, and it works, that to me is a joy. I don't want a reward for it. That's my reward — the action taken."

Defenders consider money and promotion as their right, not as a reward. They demand what they believe they deserve. Defenders want to be treated with dignity and to be heard. If this does not occur, they feel exploited, and they get angry. To achieve these goals, defenders know power is important, and they think about it more than do other types, with the exception of innovators. While for defenders power means direct control, for innovators power is the ability to create wealth by organizing and motivating people. Defenders gain power by developing loyal relationships.

But some defenders see all relationships in terms of power. A union leader and activist for the American Federation of State, County, and Municipal Employees says, "You must recognize that everything is done on the basis of power. There are other things too, of course. Power does not necessarily mean competition and things like that, but if you are dealing with two people, you are dealing with influence. Therefore, you're dealing with power of one over the other." This defender is so addicted to power that he does not believe in cooperative, trusting relationships, even within his own team.

Defenders and Management

In their relationships with management, defenders want courageous bosses they can trust to defend principles and display a sense of dignity. These managers motivate them. Defenders dislike those they consider unjust, weak, and detached, and are not motivated to follow these people. An IRS defender describes an ideal manager: "They all [subordinates] respected him. Some didn't like him, because he was very hard, but he was kind of fair, too. Very fair, a very just person."

A social worker in San Francisco complains about weak, unsupportive management that turns him off. He caught a welfare mother with a man's clothes in her closet (a clear violation of the welfare laws), but he lost the case in court. He explains, "I had her, I took her to court. In court she got her pastor and neighbors to testify for her that the man didn't live there. I was put through the third degree in court and lost the case. What bothered me was that I didn't get any backup from my superiors. They said it wasn't worth tying up the courts. It costs money."

Union leaders who are defenders also want to deal with strong managers they can trust. One says, "I want to be able to sit down with my boss and discuss the solution of problems. At the same time, it has to be a guy with a strong backbone, who can pound his fist on the table when needed. It must be someone with whom you can discuss something, and who sticks to his word. Then we can trust each other."

Defenders are more indignant than other types about being ill-used or exploited by managers. The Justice Department prosecutor says, "My manager uses me when he sees he has the opportunity, and kicks my ass when he has the opportunity to do so." These defenders are not motivated to help their bosses. They will go their own way, seeking challenges that engage their values.

Typically, defenders have strong feelings about what they consider bad management, and they use strong language to express themselves. The chief medical officer is angry that top management doesn't listen to her, and declares, "Yes, I don't want them to get a ... thing from me. What can I say? No, they never used me fully. But they're using me even less fully than they were. All they had to do was listen."

No one likes managers who are not just. But defenders are more outspoken than other types against those who play favorites, such as the manager who "places value on people who defer to him, particularly to anyone who plays up to him. So with him they are considered good employees worthy of praise."

More than other types, defenders refuse to cooperate with managers they consider unethical. A defender working for a real estate firm explains: "They [managers] found their costs were going to go up. They wanted me to try to talk people into pulling out on their contracts. In order to do that, I had to lie. I wouldn't do it. My boss fired me because I wouldn't obey."

Since defenders demand the truth and push management to confront risky or politically delicate issues, they often become pariahs. The whistleblower says, "They don't really trust me. They withhold routine information; they hold meetings without including me. But I insist on having the information."

As managers, the best defenders, in fact, do express the philosophy and behavior that defenders look for in a manager. A manager at IRS says, "I have a keen sense of respecting the dignity and worth of somebody else." The nursing supervisor describes her management philosophy: "First, the dignity of the individual." And these defender-managers want subordinates who share their values.

The State Department official describes his management philosophy: "A few simple rules. Try to use common sense, try to delegate, and trust the people who work for you, always back them up." How does he bring his principles into his managerial philosophy? "I look for a reflection of my own priorities and principles in the people who work for me. People who are not straight, or are self-serving, apple-polishing — I help them get another job. If you are trying to build a team, you need people in whom you have confidence. Else it's not a compatible team of your own."

Do his subordinates understand principles? "It's hard to speak about people, but I think they do. I've had the feeling that the guys who work for me know I want honesty, fairness — that I don't like and wouldn't approve apple-polishing, slyness, deviousness. I have the feeling this fundamental attitude is recognized at the office level."

His subordinates recognize these values and respect the boss. It's been said that when then Secretary of State Henry A. Kissinger asked this same official to be his spokesman, he refused, saying, "I can't take the job, Mr. Secretary, because I don't trust you to tell the truth." When I asked him about the story, he confirmed it and said he had expected to be fired, but Kissinger promoted him — a move which testified to the former Secretary's intelligence.

Defenders also demand openness from subordinates. Just as they want the truth from superiors, they allow no secrets to be kept from them. The supervisor of nurses talks about staff problems that preceded her arrival:

> Anyway, staff members were unhappy, and so they did the whispering and they decided they were going to have a meeting without the supervisor, and they did that. And when I came, they were still having meetings from which the supervisors were barred. Staff-nurse meetings once a month. Well, to me that's totally useless. Even if you are angry as hell at me, how in the hell am I going to do anything about it if you're going to sit back there in the room and talk about what a bitch I am? Somebody's got to tell me. So I eliminated these meetings.

Defenders make tough bosses. They demand compliance and loyalty, and they run a tight ship. Though they boast that they care about their people, they are the type least bothered by firing those who don't measure up, especially if they are not loyal. They feel justified. Even in government, where this is exceptionally hard to do, they do not hesitate to bite the bullet. While most government managers fear firing subordinates and facing the possibility of a time-consuming court case, a manager at ACTION, the Federal agency that includes the Peace Corps, says: "I guarantee I can fire any employee in four months if he doesn't continue to perform and refuses to do so. You set up the criteria. What is required is that the senior manager know how to do that. You write everything as if for a court record." He continues, "There is just enough flexibility built into bureaucracy that the extraordinary needs are manageable. It means you have to spend a little time fighting the good fight." He believes there would not be such a need to reinvent government if there were more defenders in the civil service.

Defenders believe, with Harry S. Truman, who made his reputation as chairman of a Senate committee investigating war profiteers, "If you can't stand the heat, stay out of the kitchen." Defenders are willing to stay in there to fight for what they believe in.

Weaknesses of Defenders

The most effective defenders are the entrepreneurial builders and the courageous institutional loyalists, protectors of people and principles. But even the more productive defenders can cause conflict in organizations by dividing people into loyal friends and potential enemies. The we-they mentality overpersonalizes and fragments an organizational network.

Because they find it so hard to trust people, defenders sometimes sacrifice effectiveness for loyalty. A Commerce Department manager claims that he will become more effective by creating a loyal team, "You must believe in your staff, but more important, you must support your people down to the lowest working level, because without them you would be nowhere. I insist upon loyalty, but I believe you must earn their loyalty." This manager thinks of effectiveness more in terms of maintaining power than of cost-effective service, and, in fact, he supports incompetents who are loyal to him. Those who are trying to reinvent government should take note. For the less productive defenders, legitimate organizational conflicts can become power-driven jungle fighting; the demand for loyalty can become oppressive domination; the demand for trust and openness can become paranoid suspiciousness. Defense of dignity can become a touchy unwillingness to accept criticism or admit mistakes, resulting in carelessness about the dignity of others. A zeal for justice can become identification of self with the law.

In speaking of defenders, a police officer says, "A man can be driven by the pressures of police work from enforcing the law to being the law. He will accept this as natural and there will be no remorse for his actions. He has accepted a new reality, the type that he has tried to prevent in others."

The suspiciousness of the defender can turn into paranoia when possibilities of attack are treated as though they were probabilities. Explaining his suspiciousness, a Justice Department defender says, "I'm not a do-gooder. I'm not a bleeding heart. I don't immediately trust people. I don't just give them an open hand and say, 'I like you.' I'm suspicious—that's my nature. I think it's healthy." This is a common personality trait of defenders, and it makes it harder to create trust when they are members of teams.

Paranoia is the extreme of distrust. It is fed by anger and hostility, which are projected onto others. Others then respond angrily to the hostility and thus confirm the paranoid suspicions. A patient once asked me if the fact that he had put four locks on his door indicated that he was paranoid. Half-jokingly, I said, "Even paranoids have enemies." "Especially paranoids," he said. This process of actually causing what one fears is expressed in a recurring dream of the civil rights prosecutor. He said he dreamed "about a black pick-up truck with wooden side panels, an old truck, which would run me over in the dreams." He was very explicit in his description of the dreams, "In some, I'd cross a street and it would run me over. In others, I'd be trying to do something so it wouldn't run me over, even running up a wall of a building, but it would run me over. There was a man driving the truck, a male; it was like an albatross to me." This man is always expecting that his enemies are out to get him. But he continually creates enemies so that his fear will not make him feel crazy.

A telecommunications marketer, a defender who criticizes his boss as unjust and weak, says, "I've had nightmares related to my ratings. I'd be doing very bad things to my boss. I couldn't sleep. In one, I was driving out somewhere and came upon him on the road. He was in need of help. I tried to hit him." Here we see how the defender turns his feelings of being treated unjustly into hard-hearted revenge.

The danger for defenders is that their strong defense against the hardships, slights, and injustices of childhood begins to dominate their personalities, that their anger, suspicion, and self-righteousness isolate them and make them ineffectual.

Adapting to the New Workplace

When I was hired in 1978 as a consultant to improve work in the Commerce Department, I held a series of meetings with top managers. One, a defender, aggressively challenged my credentials, assumptions, ideas. I took him aside after a meeting and asked him why he was so hostile. He said it was true that he was testing and baiting me. He explained, "The question is: Can I trust you? You are entering a family

I care about — to change people I care for." Yet, he was the least cooperative of the bunch. He was unwilling to delegate to his own staff, who were frightened of him. He was not a protector but a bully who thought of himself as a defender. But he had made a career by persuading insecure political appointees that he could get results.

Union leaders typically express a combination of defender and helper values. They are elected because they promise to defend and protect their members from abuses by authority. These qualities tend to make them adversarial to management. In 1990, the Communications Workers of America (CWA) surveyed their members about what they wanted from union leadership. The response was a wish for leaders who *both* defended their interests vigorously *and* cooperated with management in creating a more participative workplace. One result of this survey was that in 1992 the union agreed to cooperate with AT&T's Workplace of the Future and Bell South's Quality Program, both of which are cooperative efforts to improve customer service, productivity, and employee participation in decisions that affect their work.

Some union leaders, especially those with strong helper and self-developer values, have cooperated in developing participation in teams that improve processes. Others who are extreme defenders cooperate only minimally. They are distrustful and quick to react to inevitable mistakes by management, even when it is clear to others that these managers mean well and are trying to change the relationship with the union. For these defenders, their dominant values limit their competencies. As their members experience the benefits of participation, they will be less likely to elect union officers who only defend and do not help or facilitate development at work.

An example of how a defender can change her behavior without changing her values is the testimony of Laura Unger, a militant CWA local president from New York City. Before she agreed to participate in Workplace of the Future, Unger had pushed for total noncooperation with AT&T at CWA meetings and at their national convention. She had fought AT&T in the regulatory area and led a demonstration at the home of Bob Allen, AT&T's CEO. Through Workplace of the Future, she has come to believe that she can better represent the people who elected her by participating in the process of change in the information-age workplace. In February, 1995, at a meeting of union and management at AT&T, Unger said:

> We have to become experts in things we never wanted to become experts in. I sit on a Workplace of the Future Committee where I have to discuss job design. What did I know about job design? I could talk about some basic issues of what I think constitutes a good job and what doesn't and that's a good start. But if I have a responsibility to learn more than that — I have to study the issue, listen to the company and their consultants, learn to read the flow charts, talk to my members, talk to people I know who have worked on the issue from a union perspective. I don't want to be some kind of mosquito, buzzing around the head of management and periodically reminding them of workers' issues. If I am going to participate in decision making I have a responsibility to put in the time and thought and develop some expertise — not to learn to be like management, but to develop a serious union perspective on these issues that meet the needs of my members and the marketplace.

Unger has not changed her goals. She has recognized that the well-being and employment security of the employees she represents depend on a successful company, and she is taking full advantage of the opportunity to influence change. However, companies that restructure their operations without consideration for the needs of employees, or respect for their years of service, can expect workers to elect defenders who are motivated to punish managers they consider unjust. And if AT&T were to turn backwards, Unger is prepared to resume an adversarial stance.

Defenders do not easily adapt to the information-age workplace. The greater the incidence of injustice in an organization, the more likely that defenders will take positions of leadership either because they are elected or because they develop a loyal team. In impersonal hierarchies, where people are treated as a mass, people without power seek protectors. When people in organizations are respected and are empowered, there is less need for defenders, because everyone has reason to defend organizational values. The self-developers say they will not defend these values unless they have been involved in developing them. The implication is clear. Participation in developing and implementing values makes it more likely that these values will be defended by everyone and there will be no constituency for paranoid-style defenders.

At the top, organizations will always need leaders with the courage to defend the organization against its enemies. There will always be a place for principled institutional loyalists to support leaders and stand up for organizational values. But as we will discuss in Chapter 10, those leaders will best inspire others to follow them, when they balance the values of the defender with expertise, care, and innovation.

CHAPTER 7

THE SELF-DEVELOPER

More than those of any other type, the values of self-developers fit the demands of the information-age workplace for customer focus, teamwork, and empowerment. Self-developers are motivated by opportunities to learn, to develop their competence, and to maintain employability, so they do not have to depend on paternalistic management. They have been raised to expect the uncertainty and flux of the new workplace. They are less fearful of taking risks, because they are prepared to find another job, if they are not treated well. They want to participate in designing jobs to be challenging and processes to be efficient. Skeptical of authority, they have learned to value people for their competence. The Values of Self-Developers graphic on the next page describes how self-developers are motivated by needs rooted in all of the eight value drives, so each is highlighted in the graphic. Self-developers value self-development to maintain a sense of authority, self-esteem, and security by upgrading their marketable skills, mastering technology, facilitating effective teams, and understanding customer needs. Brought up in an environment of change, they have learned to adapt to new people and situations, and to trust their own abilities, rather than parents or institutions. They also are able to form supportive networks. Independence gives them a sense of freedom and self-esteem. They try to stay in competitive condition, physically as well as mentally, and enjoy life to the fullest. They are motivated by opportunities for new experiences. Their weakness is the reverse of their strength: detachment, reluctance to commit themselves, self-marketing, as well as a hesitancy to take parental-type leadership roles.

Values of the Self-Developer

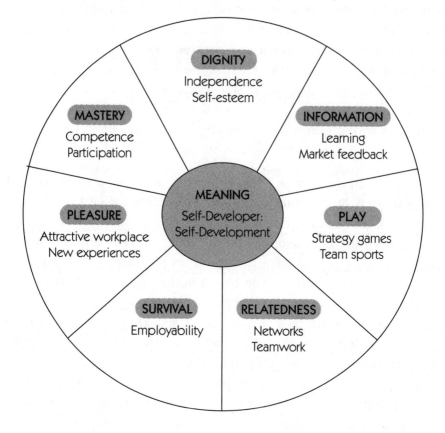

Self-developers dislike bureaucracies. They want organization based on shared responsibility, reciprocity, and continual learning. Unlike the traditionally raised father-oriented experts, they are not motivated to please the boss in order to get promoted. Unlike helpers, they do not value relationships for their own sake. Unlike defenders, they are not driven to protect people or uphold justice against cheaters and bullies. Self-developers want to be business people, not bureaucrats. They look for work that develops business and social skills, but if the job does not meet their needs, they express themselves outside of work. Some establish entrepreneurial businesses on the side, reinforcing their sense of independence within the workplace where they are employed.

Self-development is a traditional American value reinterpreted by each generation and social character. America's founding fathers believed that representative democracy requires a commitment to public education so that people can participate in government and understand their larger common self-interest. Benjamin Franklin, spokesman for the American craft ethic, preached self-development as a means toward prosperity and a rich cultural life. Ralph Waldo Emerson and Henry David Thoreau described the goal of self-development in terms of a strong independent character. In the age of Horatio Alger, such personal development became oriented to making money. In the twentieth century, it focused on moving up the corporate hierarchy through training in administrative expertise and in how to win friends and influence people.

Each of the social character types — except defenders, who rarely express the need — has a partial vision of self-development. Experts speak of "increasing intellectual knowledge and becoming an expert in my field," and "improving skills that management says need improvement." Helpers speak of "learning to help people more effectively," and "growing" in confidence. Innovators talk about self-development in terms of new careers, finding new challenges, experimenting, risk taking. (A gameswoman comments, "I love risk taking because that's where the fun and excitement come from.") For people like her, self-development means testing themselves and breaking boundaries.

For the new generation, all these definitions are attractive but incomplete. Self-developers want competence and knowledge so they can progress in their careers. They like helping people do things better, not because they want to form a relationship, but because it is good business, or because teaching is a good way of learning. They enjoy new people, experiences, and challenges because learning is fun and expands their sense of competence.

Self-developers are appearing in Western Europe as well as the U.S. The French call the self-developers *le personnaliste*, the individual who focuses on the self and its development. Such self-developers are searching for meaning beyond success, or success beyond money and status, and this search includes the meaning of self-development itself. They seek a sense of wholeness and balance at work, home, and play. Self-development includes learning to get along with different kinds of people and to understand them. It includes, as one explains, "developing the ability to be content with what I have." Self-developers engage in a search for a center, by learning to listen to oneself, to concentrate on one thing, to gain control over one's body in order to look and feel good. It includes courage to become more independent. A 20-year-old secretary with a high school education said, "I'd like to be a more independent person, to accept, learn, and realize the uniqueness and differences in all kinds of people. And not be stifled by social traditions and trappings. There are a lot of things I don't do because it's not done. I'd like to grow around that." She admits, "I know I'm young and inexperienced. It will take time and patience; it will take initiative and guts to go out there and live."

Approach to Service

Self-developers are motivated by service work that satisfies their needs for personal growth, employability, and enjoyment at work. They enjoy meeting new people, solving problems, facilitating teamwork, and sharing information. Unlike the helper, who sees the client as dependent, the self-developer sees help-seekers as equals, or potential equals, customers with a purpose toward which the self-developer can contribute.

Although self-developers are more interested in people than are experts, this interest is more gamelike and detached than that of the caring helpers. Self-developers want to read people and understand what makes them tick, because those activities are interesting and useful for problem solving or making a sale. They don't feel responsible for dependent people. They want people to treat others as independent adults, as they would like to be treated themselves. Self-developers define service in terms of productive relationships that involve:

1. Facilitating a team, so that each member contributes knowledge to arrive at good, consensual decisions.

2. Providing information, so that people can achieve their goals and make more informed choices.

3. Offering advice, or constructive criticism, so that people can do a better job.

4. Educating and teaching others so that they can provide for themselves.

5. Participating with others to understand and solve problems, or to try new approaches.

A 28-year-old management consultant from a large accounting firm says, "We do a lot of consulting on information systems. I help people say what they need, trace information flow, and so on." She goes into firms where she must gain trust and develop solutions with her clients. She likes her current assignment because she is "picking up a good technical background, which I figure has good resale value." By this she means she is helping the customer succeed and, at the same time, enhancing her own employability.

Self-developers turn work into a challenge, an opportunity for learning and, sometimes, a game. An IRS agent, age 46, says, "I try to look at the taxpayer as a whole person, to find out why they have a problem, and what to do to correct it.... I find the people fascinating, how they react to you. They don't like us all the time. Some shade the truth; some hide it. Some give you nothing. We're sizing each other up. It's a game of wits." Here she shows the self-developer's interest in understanding what makes people tick as she engages in a game of wits.

An AT&T middle manager, age 28, says, "I like the interface with people. I need to deal with programmers, headquarters, technical people, making sure the machines work. I like finding ways to get around hard-nosed people. I like dealing with people, solving problems, research." Again, the self-developer sees people as a challenge and work as a game with the goal of satisfying or besting others.

A Communications Workers of America (CWA) union steward, age 30, says, "A steward should be a problem solver, not a grievance filer. You try to find the fastest, quickest method to meet the employee's goals.... I make it easy for people to be open." Unlike the defender, the self-developer-helper defines the union role as facilitation, rather than defense against injustice.

A 38-year-old entrepreneur develops data systems for business and government. He hires people who want self-developing work and asks them to design their jobs. "I ask them what kind of service they would like to provide, and although I can't promise we will move into that business immediately, we always succeed within a year or so." Does he like to help people? He answers, "Helping is too personal. It is more development for our mutual interest."

In each of these cases, the service relationship adds value for everyone involved. This is achieved by understanding people and their needs and by facilitating ways of satisfying these needs.

Rewards From Work

The rewards that most motivate self-developers are those that further their goals, as well as satisfy their needs for independence and a good life. Self-developers believe in value for value and they are not afraid to negotiate. Although they are less interested than experts in recognition and medals from authority, they expect their fair share. A partner in a large Washington D.C., law firm, an institutional helper in his late 50s, contrasts the new-generation lawyers with his colleagues of 30 years before, "Then the senior partners made even more proportionately than we do now. But we never thought of complaining. We were disgustingly grateful when they gave us a bonus of $1,500. The self-developers demand a fairer distribution. But even more, they want to participate in the process of dividing up the profits. They want to know the criteria, and have no wish to please the old men."

Self-developers are disappointed by jobs where money is the only reward. In that case, as one telephone company clerk, age 30, says, "I feel I'm prostituting myself really, doing the routine. It's dull. I'd like more technical thinking, decision-making work. Now my work is repetitious and doesn't require any brains."

Those who feel most rewarded have jobs that allow the development and exercise of their skills and abilities. A 35-year-old lawyer considers his job "a lab of self-study and self-improvement." He admits, "I need friction. How can I work on how I relate to people if I don't work with people?"

Self-developers are rewarded by a sense of responsibility, creativity, and stimulation. They like to use all of themselves. A 32-year-old supervisor of sales at AT&T says, "What I like about my work is that I have complete responsibility for my own actions. I can develop something out of my own belief, implement it, see if it works." A 29-year-old financial systems consultant from a large accounting firm echoes this sense of individual responsibility, "What I like is that you get to be very independent. You have to pull your weight, and people you are working for have to delegate to you. You have a lot of demands put on you, often of a conflicting nature, so there is a high stress level. It's very stimulating."

Conversely, the self-developers are also rewarded by the sense of being needed, of having a unique, necessary, meaningful role. A 29-year-old auditor for an accounting firm says, "I've got to know that what I'm doing is meaningful. It's extremely important. The job you do has to be special, special to you."

A 31-year-old Library of Congress manager who provides information to senators and congressmembers says, "A psychic reward is that you see words you wrote written into laws, reports, used in speeches. I have a role but no real power, but the role is enjoyable. I do feel I'm giving the great leaders of the country their good ideas." Thus, for self-developers, stimulating and meaningful responsibilities and relationships are, in themselves, rewarding.

When The Workplace Is Frustrating

If stuck in dead-end or dissatisfying jobs, self-developers look for better work and, meanwhile, find new ways to express themselves inside or outside the company. They switch jobs more easily than other types. Sometimes they stay in the job only to finance their real vocations as struggling entrepreneurs, jazz musicians, artists, and artisans.

A telephone company clerk who has given up on her job is sharpening her writing skills at a local community college. Her goal is to write and be able to support herself from her writing. Another example of a frustrated self-developer is a woman of 40 who works as a statistical assistant to two economists in a federal agency. At age 29 she was extremely motivated to learn on the job. She says:

I went to work as a clerk so we could afford a house. At that point I didn't have any goals beyond earning money to buy a home. But as time passed I thought I could sharpen my skills. I asked my supervisors if I could take some courses. I took one in statistics and one in keypunch. The problem was not being able to use what I'd learned and rise up. It was a dead-end job. It wasn't my major interest, but it could have been. Since it was a job I was already in, I could have developed it, but when I saw this wasn't possible, I said, "What else can I do to develop myself?" So I switched from business to writing and drama. Maybe there's a chance to develop there. I went to school part time and got my degree. Now I'm involved with a group of graduates who are trying to start a production group. I acted in a play to raise money for the department. This position as a statistical assistant is at a dead end. Just knowing that I have something else that could materialize at any time gives me hope. The economists I work for come by now and then to check the numbers. I don't even know what they plan to do with my work. If I knew why, I would feel more a part of it. I've asked, but my question wasn't answered.

She keeps the job for the benefits in unemployment insurance, health insurance, and pension. She does the minimum in the office and takes night courses at a university where she writes plays, helps produce them, and acts. She identifies herself with the new generation:

My creative juices are always going, trying to fantasize how that can be put on paper. I'm observant of people, and describe them in my mind. I'm anxious to get to know them. I believe in opening up America to our young and letting the sky be the limit. My favorite people are the young ones. They are so candid, frank, and genuine. Older people get fixed in a mold. Younger people today are more flexible, and I love it.

In contrast to this woman whose creativity finds expression outside the office, a telephone company manager has been surprised to find his workplace so interesting. On the side, he owns his own jewelry business; he designs the pieces and cuts the stones. He also plays the jazz saxophone and has toured the country with a jazz group. Two years ago, he joined the company, he thought for a year, to make some money and get the medical benefits, but the job has become interesting. "I never did quit," he says. "I like the security; you don't have that with music." He enjoyed the excitement of "tracking down a problem on new computer systems, then deciding how to solve the problem." He also liked supervising five people and wanted to move into higher management. But a year ago, he was again thinking of quitting. There was "too much bureaucracy."

A Balanced Life

More than other types, self-developers say that work shouldn't be the most important thing in life. The ones with families want to keep a balance between work and home. They want "to be happy, both professionally and personally." Men don't want work to separate them from family; women don't want family to undermine career possibilities. A highly competent and motivated executive, age 38, says, "I work 50 hours a week. I come in early and go home late, but I leave it at the office. I am not going to push my little son off my lap because he is messing up papers from work." This executive has been competent enough and determined enough to maintain his values and his executive role. But he will never be CEO. That role demands being on call evenings and weekends.

For self-developers, both family and work require attention. So does physical well-being. Good diet and frequent exercise are essential to maintain the competitive work pace. They also help one to feel good. Sometimes self-developers skip lunch to work out or run. A 29-year-old manager says, "We watch the things we eat. We run. If you're a workaholic, after a while you're not really productive. You may work 75 hours, but how much work are you really getting done in 75 hours?" This depends on the individual and the job. For global managers at the top of large companies, 75 hours may be too much but 40 is too little. The optimum is more like 60.

At lower levels, self-developers can maintain the work-family balance. A technician, age 28, says, "I'm family-oriented. If the phone rang and my wife said I was needed at home, I'd go. Even if my supervisor said I shouldn't. I can always get another job, but I only have one family."

A 33-year-old manager at the U. S. Commerce Department says, "My overall philosophy is: Work comes second to family. Keep the harmony going at home, take care of those needs. Sometimes work does take precedence, but overall, the family gets the primary attention."

This manager turned down a promotion that meant traveling, which would interfere with family life:

> I don't really want the money. I'd rather have less pressure so I can live a long and full life than have a lot of pressures and live five more years and die with that.... I know I'm not at my maximum pressure level. When I get to my maximum pressure level, I don't want to go over that regardless of the money. A job that would demand travel 80 percent of the time would not have fit into my situation.... My outside life and inside life with my job are both important to me, and too much travel would mess up my outside life with my family.

An IRS agent, age 27, expecting her first child, says:

> I take the attitude that I can only do what can be done in eight hours. Right now I'm caught between being a wife and being a career person. Now I'm expecting my first child. I want to be so organized that I can achieve a balance between the things I want to do. I'm still very young. Some concentrate on their career and then later their family, but I wanted to taste a little of it all. It's harder to adjust to being a wife and mother,

but I have the determination to know that I won't give up on wanting to be a career person. It wouldn't have worked as well, I think, if I'd been a wife first.

A computer technician, age 30, sums up the new generation's concern, "At one time, I was concerned with my work being good, and then it was. And then I was concerned with my personal life, and then I got that in shape. The problem now is getting the two coordinated."

This coordination is not an easy task for self-developers seeking success in the competitive workplace. Many find that their resolve to achieve balance cannot withstand their drive to succeed. Or if they maintain balance, it is at the expense of moving to the top.

Character Formation

If we consider the traditional family of the bureaucratic-industrial age as one in which the father is the sole wage earner and the children grow up in one place, then self-developers come from nontraditional backgrounds. But these nontraditional families are becoming the norm of the '90s. We analyzed 45 interviews of self-developers. What this group shares is a background of continual change, mobility, and a lack of clear norms other than the value of continually learning to adapt to new conditions. Over half the self-developers came from dual-career families, another 20 percent from families broken up by death or divorce; only 30 percent came from families where the father was the sole breadwinner. This was the situation in the mid-'80s. Today, we would find even fewer self-developers from traditional families. In some of the self-developer families, mothers had semi-careers as volunteers. In others, the father's work was all-consuming, or kept him traveling constantly, so that the children didn't see much of him. About one-quarter of the mothers had high-level jobs as managers or entrepreneurs. The others were teachers, nurses, and secretaries in large corporations. These percentages are different from those of the expert, who was raised in a family with a sole male wage-earner. They are closer to the average for American society of the '80s, rather than the '50s or '60s, when these self-developers were children. The sense of balance of mother-father authority and lack of paternal dominance free the child from strong bonds of dependency and even facilitate peer relationships. Frequent parental disappearance may also cause self-protective detachment.

Unlike experts, self-developers do not need to please the father and copy his model of success. They do not have the expert's transferential relationship to bosses as father figures. On the contrary, some self-developers criticize fathers as too driven by work. Although they lack a clear model of authority for themselves, they have grown up in families where authorities negotiate decisions and share authority. This kind of activity becomes natural for them.

The self-developer does not have the maternal orientation of the helper, and does not want to create a family at work. Self-developers value friendly, helpful relationships, but they are uneasy with intimacy; it makes them feel trapped. They like the interaction of the team that plays together but splits at the end of the working day. Thus, the self-developers have been less overtly programmed for traditional work and family during childhood than the experts, helpers, or defenders. They see themselves as needing to create their own style of work and authority, which combines traditional male and female values. This means husband and wife both work, cook, clean the house, and care for the children. Rejecting both the paternal and maternal emotional attitudes of protective authority and unconditional care, what is emphasized by this group is equality of rights and responsibilities, as well as tolerance.

Role Models

Self-developers tend to admire people who have helped them along the way or who are models for their own development. These people are seen more as colleagues than as parental figures. In fact, self-developers are uneasy about admiring anyone, and some feel this detracts from self-esteem and a sense of equality. They are often critical of the people they admire. An example of admiring a mentor comes from a computer programmer in his late 20s who says, "One of my high school teachers had a great influence in my career, how it was started. He used to say, 'Set your goal and don't let anything turn you away.' He was more a buddy with adult wisdom than a teacher."

An example of an admired helper is also a model for a probation officer in her 30s who comments, "I admire my therapist, because she is 65 years old and continues to grow as a person. And she's helped me a lot." Here we see the self-developer using the therapist as a model and appreciating the help she purchases. Or self-developers may admire someone who is a model for them in the workplace. An AT&T salesman in his early 30s explains, "I admire Bill, my boss. He operates like I would like to. The way he handles people. He's able to communicate with people well enough so that he doesn't offend them when he says, 'No way.'"

Some self-developers admire people who have changed careers, or taken nontraditional paths toward independence. One mentions Albert Schweitzer, who had a career before age 30 as a successful musician, then went to medical school and theological seminary, eventually earning a total of four doctorates. But self-developers, more than any other types, can be critical of the people they admire. A 33-year-old manager of research admires Marie Curie, Eleanor Roosevelt, and Albert Einstein, but her admiration for the latter two is qualified:

> Eleanor Roosevelt...she was more problematic. A woman who achieved great things. Had broad interests. But she was not universally loved. Her personal life wasn't what I'd like my personal life to be...she didn't have a happy marriage. I value that a great deal. Einstein was a difficult person to live with. He didn't devote too much attention to his personal relationships.

For self-developers like this manager, achievement at work is not enough. Self-developers evaluate people as whole persons. Self-developers want to learn from but not copy models. Their ideal is to be "themselves," and to learn effective practice from good models but also know what to avoid from bad models.

The Self-Developer's Ideal Boss

It follows that self-developers want managers who help them learn and grow. However, because they expect less from bosses than do experts, helpers, and defenders, self-developers can be more objective, more understanding of their bosses' strengths, limitations, and constraints. They are clear about what they want from management: freedom to express their views, respect as adults, authority to make decisions, open information, participation in decisions, a clear contract as to expectations, competent leadership, support and coaching so that they can develop their potential. But they recognize that it is difficult for any manager to fully meet their expectations.

The telephone clerk says, "I want to be treated like an adult, make my own decisions whether right or wrong, because that's the only way I can learn." The computer technician comments, "I like supervisors who will work with you in a give-and-take relationship. As grown-up human beings we learn how to get along." An air traffic controller, age 27, says, "Managers must become more sensitive; some have not accustomed themselves to dealing with new employees who are forcing them to grow. Being more sensitive produces more. There is a need to instill confidence. Many managers are old Marine types; they don't want a bilateral relationship."

What he and others want is sensitivity to the individual's sense of dignity and more responsiveness to their need for information. Self-developers describe a good manager as a value-added resource when needed, a facilitator of teamwork, and a developer of people. They don't need managers to do for them what they can do for themselves. And they resent experts who act superior to them.

The 28-year-old AT&T manager was pleased with his boss in the mid-1980s. He said, "I'm given flexibility to change my job the way I want. I'm mechanizing the whole thing, with advanced office systems. It's a credit to my boss and district manager. They tell me, 'Here's the ball of wax, go for it.' I mold my job; I make major changes."

Self-developers appreciate real leadership. Like experts, they are contemptuous of laissez-faire management. Where they differ is in their emphasis on sharing information and its meaning, and facilitating teamwork. In contrast, the expert wants autonomy. The young manager at the Commerce Department complains, "I'd like a few more deadlines, even if they're arbitrary, just to keep me chugging along. My boss is too laissez-faire. I work better under pressure, as do many. We could benefit from regular meetings to keep us informed of all the issues before us and what needs to be pushed along."

Self-developers also complain about management that does not develop employees but leaves them in dead-end jobs without opportunities to advance and learn. A 27-year-old secretary at the Department of Agriculture says, "I wanted to be given an opportunity to see what my limitations are. If I do a good job, then I should be given added responsibilities, but that doesn't happen here."

A telecommunications manager, age 29, comments on management's performance in his firm:

> Management isn't developing people here. There's a lot of potential. If they were, maybe there would be more turnover, but people would also have incentive. Now, there's an overabundance of management. We lost a lot and it was a good thing. How many more are here that we don't need? At least 25 percent.

Since that time, many more have left his company. Indeed, the demands of self-developers in the '80s have become the common wisdom of business in the '90s. Sometimes new-generation self-developers learn to manage their bureaucratic-expert bosses. I was invited to speak to managers at a large company by a 30-old self-developer who was near the bottom of the management hierarchy. I asked how he was able to organize the meeting of top managers and invite me. He said, "I know what makes my boss run. I let him know how he will gain from my project. He's the kind of guy, if you wind him up and point him in the right direction, he goes straight ahead." Here the self-developer uses psychological knowledge to get things done.

While self-developers criticize bureaucratic management roles, they do not necessarily blame the individual manager. Rather, they are more likely to blame the system and see many management jobs as poorly designed or unnecessary because they involve paperwork or monitoring people who can manage themselves.

An IRS agent, age 37, says, "I'd like to see management as a facilitator, in a helping role to the revenue officer. Managers are given so much garbage to do; it directs them in the opposite way. When they're doing those reports, they can't manage the employees." Self-developers want managers who "have frequent meetings," are "always available for consultations," "work with you in a give-and-take relationship," and provide constructive criticism and coaching. They want managers who tell it like it is. They not only want information, but also want to know what it means. They want to understand. Self-developers want feedback from managers, co-workers, therapists (6 out of 45 mention seeking psychotherapy or psychologically-oriented workshops as a means to self-development). But they prefer to be measured by the market, because it is real and protects them from subjective evaluations by superiors who make them feel small. They are also disgusted by bureaucratic makework and meaningless measurements.

A high-level Washington bureaucrat, age 45, who worked in the Reagan White House, said:

> I once headed a federal internal consulting agency, which provided services to agencies on a reimbursable basis. This was lots of fun, a fascinating period really. Very entrepreneurial; feedback was from the outside. The goodies were to get contracts, and we did $600,000 on the books for that year, 1980. A very rewarding way to work, at least for me individually. The idea of the challenge, of having an outside opinion, getting outside appraisal. If we weren't attractive to an agency, we got no business. I like that; it just turns me on. I liked also that the only obstacles to doing a good job were those I put forward myself, such as not knowing how to do it. I like the enterprising feeling.

Self-developers rarely find this kind of work in government or in large businesses. That is one reason they are drawn to professions, and to starting their own businesses. They would really like to avoid having a boss, but even as independent business people, they look for good consultants and coaches.

Work Relationships

Although ambivalent about bosses, egalitarian self-developers enjoy the give and take of teamwork. They grew up learning the importance of cooperative peer relationships, and they recognize that without cooperation, technoservice becomes ineffective. For example, the research service manager at the Library of Congress says, "I need the cooperation of a lot of people, a lot of inputs on time. You need their help and ideas. I get help from other divisions a lot. When we have interdivisional projects, people really can say no; mostly they cooperate. If they say no, we end up with egg on our face, with a lesser-quality report." For this manager, cooperation is satisfying not because it feels good, but because it is essential for effectiveness.

The IRS agent also testifies to the value of interdependence. He says:

> You can't know all the aspects of tax law. If we didn't help each other we wouldn't be able to do it. And it involves interpretation, so we compare notes, how to research something, how to get something out of the computer. There are a lot of gray areas and you need help researching the manual. People have complex problems and you can't get it all in class. I've gotten a lot of help; I wouldn't have gotten as far as I have without people showing me that there is an easier way to do things.

A public health doctor, age 40, emphasizes the value of teamwork. He says, "I'm very strong on the team concept. I've learned as much about public health from the public health nurse and public health social worker as from any doctor. I really believe in teamwork. And I don't necessarily believe the doctor's always in charge of the team."

But teamwork requires trust based on respect and competence. According to the government auditor:

> What we do is an opinion based on what we dig up. I can bounce things off them if I have respect for the other person. If I don't like you or trust you, I can't

bounce anything off. It makes all the difference in the world. You need to work with people whom you're comfortable with. And who are comfortable with you. Respect is important. If you can't really like somebody, you can still respect them and work with them, and you can learn from them.

Another way of describing the meaning of teamwork for self-developers is that they value work relations that facilitate doing business effectively. They do not like work relationships that they consider heavy with emotion or sticky with sentiment. They want relationships to be freer and less attached than those of the familial helpers, more equal and less threatening to self-esteem than those of the hierarchical experts, more independent and less concerned with power than those of the suspicious defenders, and more down-to-earth and matter-of-fact than those of the ideological innovators who try to maintain continual excitement.

An AT&T systems analyst, age 30, says, "I think it's unhealthy sometimes to socialize with people you work with. It causes conflicts at work." An ACTION manager, age 35, says, "I'm a very private person. There's a difference between working with people and really being their friend. When I leave work, I like to get out of work. I try to leave it when I leave the building." She adds, "I think people need to be *friendly*, but you don't have to be friends, close friends, to work together." Put all this together and you have a type of person who fits in well with the requirements of technoservice: teamwork and partnerships with the customers and suppliers. They develop quick relationships, but are equally able to quickly drop those that do not work for them.

Self-Developers As Managers

Because of these qualities, as managers, self-developers like the role of facilitator. They are interested in other people's views and ideas. They are egalitarian, as one new-generation manager says, "I think of people working under me as working with me. I try to set the example." By avoiding the parental role, they diffuse transferential emotions, which make the subordinates of parental figures feel like children. But self-developers also frustrate the experts and helpers who want a caring leader.

Self-developers often mention fun as a valued ingredient of work. Like the gamesmen, they use humor as a managerial tool when they feel it necessary to lighten up the atmosphere. The 28-year-old AT&T manager says, "I'm people-oriented. I like to joke around a lot. I approach things seriously, work hard, but also have the sense when things get tight, let's joke around." Self-developers not only want to relieve tension, but also create in the workplace a playful spirit that supports intense competitive work.

Self-developer managers involve their subordinates in organizational goals and let them shape their own roles. Since the managers' need for information is so great, they are sensitive to this need in others. All this is not necessarily altruistic. Self-developers believe they create organizational power by providing opportunity, by using more human potential. For example, a TV executive, age 30, a former high-school teacher, describes how she manages:

> I like to give people responsibility. From teaching I've learned you have to structure for success, give steps for results. Then you must follow up. I'm motivated internally. I won't say I can do something unless I can do it perfectly. Most people say yes, even when they don't know how. There is a need to evaluate ongoing activity, to give feedback. People must feel they are important. But I like people who like to work and take pride in their work. Who don't need to be told 15 times a month they are terrific. You can't go overboard so they think they're wonderful and don't need to grow.

What all self-developer-managers do believe is that to succeed, they must create a motivated team. For them, being a team player does not mean group thinking. It means playing a special role on a team where each player has a say in how to implement strategy. For example, the service manager for a computer company says:

I'm moving from a management to a leadership role. Leadership requires greater delegation and accountability to others — being willing to compromise, greater sensitivity to support staff; but the best way to get the staff to do the policy is to get their participation. The best productivity comes if we have initial agreement on the way to do business. The challenge is to get the staff to buy into a policy, or figuring out how to improve the quality of life of the people in the office as well as improving the effectiveness of the work we do. I had been questioning the management of power, but, in fact, the more you share, the more you gain.

In the course of my experiences as a consultant, I have seen self-developers achieve teamwork through participation, when the experts have failed to do so. An example comes from the MITRE corporation, which does systems engineering for a number of government organizations including the armed forces. One division works with the air traffic control system. Jack Fearnsides who heads this division read the first edition of *Why Work?* and in 1989 called to say that it helped him understand resistances to transforming the air traffic control system. He invited me to work with his organization, which has since then made use of social character theory to increase mutual understanding and teamwork. Most of MITRE's technical managers have been experts. However, one of Fearnsides' younger managers, Margaret Jenney, a self-developer in her 30s, proved able to facilitate different experts in the air traffic control system to listen to each other for the first time and begin to engage their customers, the airlines, in a project to improve the system.

Self-developers like Jenney are comfortable with the technoservice mode of production: flattened team-based organizations, networking, and cooperation. In the late '80s, self-developers in law offices and even in government were talking like this professional:

I'd like to do away with all secretaries. During one of the spells when we didn't have a typist, I started doing my own stuff on a word processor. It eliminates a lot of paper drafts and I could see my ideas taking shape on the screen and in my head at the same time. If you put control of correspondence in the hands of policy makers, you have a different organizational structure. Then do you just drop out the lower half of the organization?

This explanation reflects the beginning of the downsizing and re-engineering that has become common practice in today's workplace. The self-developers were there even before consultants promoted this way of working. Even before Al Gore started to reinvent government, the self-developers were showing the way. Here a 32-year-old manager of volunteer programs for ACTION describes his management style. He is exceptional in that he combines the self-developer's objectivity, respect, and playfulness with the helper's caring and idealism. He says:

I have a really great staff. They need little supervision. What I like most is getting people to work together to get the task done, to set priorities and procedures. I like being a manager. My philosophy is getting people to work together as a team, to get them participating, and letting them do it, rather than dictating it. When there is a problem or a task, I present it to them, and a lot them figure out how to do it. We usually do this as a group, and I try to include the clerks.

He offers some specific examples:

Openness and honesty in the office are very impor-tant. They inspire people to do their jobs. A manager must trust employees to get the job done. Otherwise he tries to do it himself, and therefore he's not managing or he's a dictator. I share just about every-thing with my staff. First, I have a weekly circulating file where I circulate almost everything that comes in, but not everything, because I throw some stuff out. Second, we have a meeting about once a week. People know also that they can ask to have a meeting if they want. Then, and this is one of the advantages of being in a big, open room, I can make announcements immediately. If I have just talked to someone on the phone and heard some news, I just immediately tell my team. I prefer to tell them before they hear something by rumor. But I don't tell them about personal individual cases. They try to get me to, but I don't.

The main quality I look for in an employee is a person who will fit into our office. This means someone who is loose and relaxed, a person who is willing to do all the functions, including answering the phones. Someone who is not hung up on "That's not my job." Someone who is not hierarchical or status-oriented. I look for idealism, the desire to be of service....I'm going to continue hiring the kinds of people who have a background in volunteerism, but not those who are just here for a job. I want people with a basic liking and trust of people, an ability to create that atmosphere of trust and respect in the way they do business or in their lifestyle, and the ability to get people to work together.

He goes on to explain:

Evaluations I handle by having a one-to-one discussion with employees about any problems they may have, and I try to do that at least once every six months. But if something is changing either from outside or in the internal process, I might have sessions with them more often. And they can also talk to me at any time, and sometimes do. I usually have one of these one-to-one sessions in a private office, or we go for a cup of coffee, and it can last from five minutes to one or two hours, depending on the individual. I try to develop a mutual exchange of feedback, how they're doing and how I'm doing. Are there any personal problems? It's pretty open.

In the past, when I have had individual sessions with employees, I asked them, "What do you want beyond your job?" And if they said they wanted to become a manager, and some of them do, I've made sure to appoint them acting manager when I wasn't here, so they could get experience. I've tried to get them some visibility with others and to discuss their interests in the informal network. I've also tried to get them to take some courses when there was money. Actually, two people from this office have become placement managers and two have become area managers.

This government manager learned management not from books and courses but from experience and from applying his own set of values. He remembers:

I learned to be a manager from my other jobs. My first job as supervisor was awkward because I was managing friends and peers. Then when they left and we got new people, I managed mainly as a technician, saying, "I have done this work before and so I know it and I can help you learn it." I try to give public credit for work. If someone has come up with an idea and I write it up, I say, "Harriet had this idea."

While many self-developers believe in providing an open team atmosphere and opportunity, they are less likely than this manager to take a paternal-like coaching role. They are not comfortable with getting too personal. They don't have the expert's need for father-son/daughter mentoring. On the other hand, they lack the expert's need to know more than subordinates. They expect and want to learn from subordinates, clients, and customers. They succeed best when, like this manager, they institute good practice: frequent evaluations, team meetings, and training in group process and problem solving. We shall return to this point in Chapter 10.

I would like to add here that I find self-developers making their presence felt in all parts of the world. In Beijing, in 1993, I interviewed a 28-year-old sales engineer and asked his view of a good manager. The answer of this self-developer was, "Someone like my basketball coach at the university. He knows each person's strengths and puts them in the right role. He gives feedback on your performance. He is a good strategist and can adapt strategy to whatever team we play."

In *The Leader*, I described the ideal leader for the new generation as a developer of organizations, products and services, and people. Since 1981, when that book was written, I have found no reason to discard that ideal. I have seen, however, that managers approach their version of an ideal leader differently, according to their dominant character style. Those most likely to reach the ideal combine values of innovator, expert, helper, defender, and self-developer. Those least likely are the ones dominated by a single orientation.

Weaknesses of Self-Developers

Although self-developers are the type most adapted to the new workplace, both as employees and managers, many of them also have weaknesses. These are, as with the other types, the reverse of their strengths. Flexibility can mean lack of commitment. Easy relationships can imply emotional shallowness. The concern for employability can cause the self-developer to become a self-marketing personality, trying to make him or herself into a package that sells at the expense of personal integrity.

The weaknesses of self-developers, like their strengths, are rooted in their childhood adaptation to insecurity and continual change. More than any other type, they describe their strengths as intellectual, rather than moral or emotional. They sometimes rely on intellectual flexibility too much. Typically, they describe themselves in terms like: "I am considered intelligent," or "I am open and eager to learn." Indeed, they have learned to be quick studies, fast learners, flexible team players. But compared to traditional types, self-developers' speed can make them superficial and shallow. They tend to overestimate their strengths and underestimate the importance of judgment, experience, caring, extensive and in-depth knowledge, as well as commitment to and defense of values.

Some feel they have unlimited possibilities and are consequently unrealistic about what they can achieve and how much work such achievement demands. Starting in the '70s, the critics of the new generation focused on its pathology: narcissism, lack of loyalty and commitment.[1] In the '90s, I still hear these complaints from expert-executives. Indeed, these are the criticisms of Bill Clinton, a self-developer who has brought personal development coaches into meetings of his top aides and has consulted with Stephen Covey and other self-development coaches.

The critics of self-development have a point. Without a purpose beyond the self, without a larger meaning, self-development becomes an unfocused search for self-realization. For some, compulsive self-development seems an anxious drive for elusive self-esteem. For example, one 35-year-old IRS agent expresses the compulsive quality of self-development:

> Self-development is very important to me. It means reaching a point in your life where your self-esteem is at a level that's admirable. That you feel good about yourself. That you owe it to yourself to go on and make progress. If you stopped self-development, you'd be vegetating, you wouldn't be living. You owe it to yourself.

A lawyer, age 35, describes the underlying anxiety of a self-developer in search of his center, "My only goal is that I become everything I have the potential to become. My big anxiety is that I could be missing out in developing a potential in me." This man's father died when he was

---

[1]The most dramatic was Christopher Lasch, who, in *The Culture of Narcissism* (New York: W. W. Norton, 1979), excoriated the new social character from the point of view of a moralistic expert.

six. He had to take on a mature role in the family before he was ready and without a paternal model. He became extremely self-critical and self-demanding. "As a lawyer, a logician, I'm brilliant," he says. "I'm very critical of myself first, then others. Mine is a critical approach rather than accepting. I always think, here's what's wrong rather than what's right." He seeks self-acceptance through psychotherapy and feels he has begun to understand himself better. "My character is unfolding. The more secure I get, the more solid I become, the less critical." He is finding a self that he can develop.

Some self-developers seek meaning in compulsive unfocused activities, "forcing myself not to stand still, be dependent or stagnate." For example, a financial consultant, age 36, divorced, with an MBA, is running away from boredom and meaninglessness into a frenetic life of achievement and uncoordinated "learning experiences." She describes the self-developer's inability to commit herself to projects:

> I'm what you call achievement-oriented. It drives me crazy not to get things done. An industrial psychologist told me I'd be happier if I just failed at something. I guess I'm afraid of failure....I guess I'm too other-directed, I should have a life plan. I never figured out where I want to be....You can't plan in a vacuum. I'm just a normal healthy girl. I'm fairly intelligent. Have an active mind. I'm continually frustrated because I don't have enough time to do what I want to do. I try to balance things, you have to in this business; if you don't, it becomes dull.

What is self-development to her? She answers:

> Forcing yourself not to stay still. To learn and do new things. Anything, I guess. Like if I go through with my resolution of today, it would be to get a copy of the *Iliad* and read it, or my resolution in Hawaii was to learn wind surfing. I assume I'm more interested in self-development than the average person. I watch maybe two hours of TV a week. You have to not allow

yourself to vegetate. Particularly if you have a challenging job. Life is too short. I love to cook gourmet meals. It depends on how you define self-development. It's more important to keep moving and growing, learning more. It makes you more interesting and your life is more interesting.

I don't have a great plan. This year I've been reading a lot of technical computer journals. I started taking aerobic dancing. I should stop smoking. What does my poor body think, when I go from aerobic dancing to smoking? Going to Hawaii was self-development. Going to a new place and exploring.

I still don't know what I want to do when I grow up. Part of me would like to have my own business, but I don't know what that business would be. I'd like to learn more about data processing. It never hurts to develop expertise at anything. And it's our most salable product and it enhances my career path, if you want to call it that, if there is a career path.

I regret not reading more than I do. At the end of my day, I'm too mentally tired. I do well analytically and it's intellectual, but I'm not so good at creating something. It's the difference between playing scales and writing a symphony like Beethoven. I've always shied away from abstract thought. Work does get you to think about things like "Why is this important?" I'm afraid of getting mentally lazy.

I believe she is afraid to face her sense of meaninglessness. As a compulsive performer and experience seeker, she avoids listening to herself, to her deeper needs for intimacy and commitment. Her response to people is shallow. Her interests are diffuse and confused. Without commitment to meaningful projects, her energies are wasted in a search for information and experiences that seems more self-indulgent than developmental.

Some of these compulsive self-developers seem like neglected, hyperactive children. A 28-year-old accountant says, "I can't stand to wait, to hold on a phone, stand in a line, or wait for a check in a restaurant. I'm just hyper. I always like to be doing something. In the first grade, the teacher wanted to put glue on my seat. There's been no change."

Self-developers seek help, sometimes in psychotherapy, to find their centers. A 24-year-old account executive appreciates her husband because he helps her to be "more accepting, easy-going, patient, and to just enjoy life." Otherwise, she can't stay still. She enjoyed painting, but gave it up because "it keeps you by yourself in a room," not out making contacts, building her network in case she needed it.

Even though some of the most successful self-developers have disciplined themselves and gained a sense of independence, they still remain detached and lonely. The following is the story of a highly successful woman, a self-developer, age 38, in 1987 when she was vice-president of a data services company in Chicago. Her parents were both business people in a small city; both believed in education. In college in 1968, she became involved in the antiwar movement and joined protests. As the New Left sputtered to a halt, she and her husband began a series of successful businesses, starting with restoring inner city houses and reselling them for big profits. She remained liberal in terms of foreign policy and antinuclear politics, but economically she moved toward the neoliberal view that government must be concerned with creating wealth, not just distributing it. Many of her friends became extreme Republican libertarians. All of them shared a critique of bureaucracy and big government.

As their business grew, her husband wanted her to stay at home and raise their child. She felt he neither understood nor appreciated her, so she took their daughter and left him, went back to school, got an MBA, then joined a large company for the experience. Today, her second husband runs their five jointly-owned businesses, including a trailer park, a car wash, and a beauty salon, while she operates at the top of a major corporation. I watched her in action for three days. In her activities, she gets to the point, demands concrete examples, is flexible and open. But she seems all intellect. There is little human resonance. She does not get emotionally involved with people at work.

I asked her what self-development meant to her. "I call it 'working on myself,'" she answered. "It includes education. I'm taking philosophy courses. It includes health, running. It includes team experiences, like Outward Bound, where you get feedback on your interaction with people."

"Don't subordinates find you tough?," I asked her. "Yes, they say they are sometimes frightened of me. They don't know where I am coming from." Her boss, a 64-year-old paternal expert, felt she was too driven. Is there any meaning for her beyond constant self-development? She values the creation of wealth. She enjoys the excitement of the game, and the support of the team. She has money enough so that she feels she can turn down a job without fear. Beyond self, she supports improved education and health care. But something is missing, a sense of caring. One feels she could leave everything, her husband as well as her job, and start a new adventure without missing a beat. She does not seem happy. Is there a happy person who does not care about people? I have not met one.

Some self-developers seem to be struggling for deeper spiritual meaning, to transcend the self, to reach the state of mystical, pure being. A member of the Reagan White House staff, who came from a broken home said, "Some of the more difficult parts of myself are that I'm a person who has a tendency to be self-centered and who probably has a fragile sense of self-esteem. I can be compulsive and a perfectionist."

She declared, "St. Francis is a model for me. He talks about 'self-dying'; it's the burden, it's the dealing with the 'me,' this thing which I carry around this 'self' and 'I.'" She goes on to explain, "I seek this because my very happiest moments are when I have forgotten myself. His prayer is very beautiful; he asks the power to understand, rather than being understood, 'for it is in self-forgetting that we become true persons...and become alive in dying of self.'"

Another self-developer also compared his quests for spiritual, physical, and mental development with that of St. Francis, whom he admires "because he had a controlled mind and purifying thought." But neither of these self-developers practiced St. Francis' style of life or discipline of the heart. They leave out love, serving God by giving even when it is not a good deal for them. They are too isolated in their own struggle for self-esteem to care deeply about other people.

Commitment and intimacy are problems for self-developers. Of the people we interviewed in the mid-'80s who saw themselves as self-developers, a high percentage (25 percent) have been divorced and fewer than half were in their first marriage (48 percent); 22 percent were single; 2 percent were widowed. This breakdown compares to only 6 percent ever divorced in the *Gamesman* sample of high-tech managers surveyed in elite companies in the '70s. It compares with 16 percent divorced for experts, and 9 percent for helpers who were also interviewed in the mid-'80s. Given that self-developers were on the average younger than the other types, the differences may be even greater in the '90s, as more self-developer marriages break up.

Self-developers describe their marriages in terms of doing things together, traveling, sailing, going out to dinner, taking courses. Few speak of trust, caring, or deepening knowledge of each other. Some, as we have mentioned, do look for a parental kind of support in spouses. This is the kind of unconditional love they yearned for in childhood.

Based on self-developers' backgrounds and my clinical experience with the new generation, I can speculate about the cause of this problem. Some self-developers as children lacked consistent, caring parental experiences. Insecure about their own worth, they doubt others can really care for them. Needs for love and acceptance are suppressed, hidden by the compulsive quest to prove their worth. Intimacy is threatening, not only because one may be rejected, but also because one may be too needy, dependent, and trapped. One rejects and represses needs that make one feel vulnerable and weak.

Describing the breakup of his first marriage, a 40-year-old manager says, "I could not say no to anything. That sort of thing destroyed my first marriage. When you can demonstrate real feeling and not worry about the other person skipping out on you, the relationship grows."

A lawyer describes his anxiety-reducing mechanisms for avoiding intimacy, "I withdraw. I get into a neutral experience — movies, hanging around with safe people, drinking too much."

Traditional types lecture the new generation about their lack of altruism. However many self-developers are not insensitive to social problems, but they are suspicious of solutions that increase bureaucracy and offer help that keeps people dependent. Many self-developers are idealistic and struggle with consumerism and materialism. They want their work to help make the world a better place. But rejecting traditional paternal and maternal roles, faced with the freedom to choose, they have not found an inspiring model of maturity.

A self-developer manager in his mid-30s says, "The main thing wrong with our society is that the nuclear family and extended family have disappeared and we haven't developed a new contract or learned how to behave. Our values were a by-product of the extended family. We have to learn to help other people and to get help from other people in new ways."

Since 1970, I have been a volunteer and board member of an orphanage, Our Little Brothers and Sisters (*Nuestros Pequeños Hermanos*) founded by Father William Wasson, an American priest in 1955 in Mexico. There are now branches in Haiti, Honduras, and Nicaragua. I have interviewed or examined questionnaire responses from a few hundred young people from the U.S.A., Germany, Holland, Switzerland, and Ireland, who volunteer to help with the children. Increasingly, these volunteers are self-developers from dual-wage-earner families, who combine the desire to help with that of self-development. The following are the statements from self-developers in 1995. Here is a 22-year-old whose father is a lawyer and mother a teacher. She writes: "I am interested in spending some time in a Latin American country doing something productive besides traveling, and ideally, I would like to teach or to work in some form with children." Another 21-year-old whose father is a manager and mother a teacher describes her eagerness "to participate in a supportive, caring environment where the education and personal development of children constitute the primary foci." She also wants "to meet novel challenges outside of my routine daily existence in the States and to learn the way of a new culture and community." Another whose father is a psychologist and mother a manager writes, "My primary goal at this point in my life is to stretch beyond my own limits, not only so that I may grow personally, but also so that I can reach out into other people's lives and make a difference in them." She and other idealistic self-developers combine the wish to help develop the children and make a difference with the drive to develop themselves and enjoy the experience.

There is evidence that families producing self-developers will be the norm, at least in the families of professionals and managers. In 1992, I participated in an interview study carried out by SIFO, a Swedish research and consulting company, of families with incomes over $75,000 a year in the U.S.A., France, Sweden, and Germany. We found the nontraditional family with divorced parents to be considered normal, and that work-family roles shared by men and women were becoming the norm, except in Germany where the patriarchal ideal remained. However, in all the countries, an emphasis on education and self-development was characteristic of the most successful families.

The challenge for self-developers is commitment, but, whether at work or in relationships, this commitment will not result from moralistic pressure, a sense of loyalty, or a desire to please the boss, but by free choice based on reciprocal self-interest. Self-developers will commit themselves to meaningful projects rather than to institutions, which they distrust. Their commitment is not just to material goals, but to emotional and intellectual development as well. To commit themselves, they require at work unambiguous contracts that describe mutual expectations in terms of both rights and responsibilities. The rules of the game must be made clear to them. Beyond this, self-developers need knowledge of what is required to gain their goal of wholeness and happiness. They must be willing to invest in their emotional as well as intellectual development. This knowledge starts with a better understanding of what self-development actually implies, an exploration which will begin in the next chapter.

CHAPTER 8

SELF-DEVELOPMENT

The quality of intrinsic motivation depends on how people develop their needs. Productive motivation, to understand and create, results not only from formative experiences, but also from individual decisions that develop competence, good relationships, and meaning.

The productive motivation of the self-developers — learning, teamwork, solving problems — fits the technoservice workplace. The self-developers' values of independence, networking, and maintaining employability are adapted to the new economy. Given global competition and changing technology, neither companies nor people can predict the future or guarantee employment. To maintain employment security, experts and helpers must follow the lead of self-developers. They must continually sharpen their skills and prepare themselves for continual change.

In the late 1980s, a clerk, age 28, defined self-development as "taking responsibility to train yourself." He said, "For six months I was getting frustrated. These guys aren't developing me like they told me they would. Then I thought, `Hey, I've got to do it myself,' so I went to my supervisor and asked, `What courses should I take? How should I change?' It's up to you to do it." As a part of its Workplace of the Future process, bargained in 1992, AT&T and its unions, the Communication Workers of America (CWA) and International Brotherhood of Electrical Workers (IBEW) have agreed to provide employees with opportunities for career planning, but people must take advantage of these offers.

Self-developers will not move ahead by modeling themselves on experts who made it in the past, who were taught to define development in terms of success in passing exams, being promoted, achieving status, or pleasing the boss, with the goal of job security at a company. Indeed, some of the most gifted of the new generation avoid large companies and look for opportunities in professions or small, entrepreneurial ventures. As one executive, age 37, who left a large company for a smaller one, states, "To succeed in a large organization, you've got to put on a mask and tuck part of your true self away. I'm not willing to do that."[1]

Furthermore, many self-developers aspire to more than economic success. They want to balance work with other values, to be successful parents and to enjoy a stimulating life, full of interesting experiences. The dual-career family increases this sense of freedom. Dual-career partners resist sacrificing the other's career for their own promotion, believing that each has equally legitimate demands. Of course, their double income allows them to take more risks at work.

However, many members of the new generation know more clearly what they do not want at work than what they do want. They dislike having power over people, but rightly fear powerlessness and stagnation. They believe that power corrupts, but are also learning that powerlessness perverts. It causes anger, regressive narcissistic self-protectiveness, and inflexibility. It results in the addictive needs described in Chapter 2. This is more obvious in the violence of unemployed black teenagers from city ghettos, less obvious in the passivity and helplessness of the middle class, made powerless by their own inability to take advantage of their affluence.

We shall see in the next chapter that to achieve success, companies need to empower employees. But the purpose of self-development is, in a major sense, one of self-empowerment. Indeed, development can be defined as *increasing people's power to shape their needs and to satisfy them.*

---

[1]"Kissing Off Corporate America," *Fortune*, February 20, 1995, pp 44-52. The article cites a survey that "just 1% of 1,000 adult respondents said they would freely choose to be corporate managers. Careers that carry a high degree of independence, such as medicine and law, were far more popular."

Wholeness And Power

Just as the innovator creates strategies for organizational development, so can people create strategies for their own self-development. Individuals must begin by asking, "What are my goals?" They should ask this question not just in terms of career goals, but also in regard to the development of one's needs and the ability to satisfy them. Many young people tend to view their lives in terms of vague and sketchy plans, not serious strategies. Just as a corporate strategist describes an end state and the steps that must be taken to reach it, so individuals need to ask themselves, "What is my vision of self-development? And what precisely must I do to achieve it?"

Some members of the new generation speak of a new aesthetic, moral, and religious ideal: wholeness. The traditional experts tend to scoff at this as new-age psychobabble. Indeed, for most people, it is easier to define the feeling of the absence of wholeness in their inner lives, rather than the presence of its positive development. Wholeness, which comes from the old English *hal* (as in *hale*), is the root of health. It is the opposite of feeling like a partial person in a narrow work role. It includes integrity, which has to do with being faithful to one's commitments. But it is more than this. It is the expression of creative potential at work, or in other words, feeling motivated because one's work is meaningful. Employees who feel they are stagnating, not developing themselves, do not feel whole. Furthermore, people do not feel whole if they let their bodies disintegrate due to poor diet and lack of exercise. People do not feel whole if they passively accept the disintegration of mind and body, if they give in and do not fight for themselves when they are treated disrespectfully. Nor do people feel whole if they are unwilling to reach out to others and do not develop their ability to love. Wholeness means making one's values clear, taking responsibility for one's needs, and practicing the discipline needed to satisfy them.

I believe the new generation's aspirations can be summarized as a striving for power to master self, understand, create, love; power to gain respect from others, to establish satisfying relationships and maintain a sense of dignity and integrity, while making enough money to enjoy the good things in life. This kind of power is not the same as power over people. Where the new generation seems to me most confused is in understanding how to gain this kind of power at work and in intimate relationships.

Five Conditions for Human Development

What is known about the conditions necessary for developing one's needs, one's productive motivation? Values expressed at work are formed in the family and in school. As I said in Chapter 2, I have come to believe that we can view human development in terms of the eight value drives that all human beings share. From Stone Age tribes to 20th century civilizations, these drives — survival, relatedness, pleasure, information, mastery, play, dignity, and meaning — have been shaped by culture into needs. What are the conditions that lead people to channel these drives for their personal development and not their destruction, to realize their brightest potential, to achieve a sense of wholeness and potency instead of internal conflict, stagnation, perversion, and addiction? What are the conditions that transform drives into developmental instead of addictive needs? What leads people to make good developmental choices in life?

In every society, five conditions must be met for human development. The conditions are:

care vs. neglect

freedom from and to vs. oppression and scarcity

discipline vs. indulgence

balance vs. excessiveness

commitment vs. diffusion

Family, school, and work organizations either succeed or fail in satisfying the first two conditions. Individual understanding, knowledge, and responsible choice determine how the last two conditions are resolved. The third condition is a combination of individual and social institutions. Remember, the opposite of each condition causes perversion, which is defined as channeling the drives into addictive needs that weaken us rather than into the developmental needs that strengthen us.

The first two conditions, care and freedom, are created in a positive family environment, and re-created in good schools and places of work. The third condition, discipline, is strongly influenced by family, school, and workplace, but also by individual understanding, knowledge, and choice. The final two conditions, balance and commitment, are largely determined by informed choice, especially in a free and open society like ours.

Care

The first condition for development is care. To gain a sense of trust, infants must have a secure, nurturing adult who helps them express themselves and satisfy their needs.[2] Infants cannot survive, gain pleasure, affection, and a sense of security all by themselves. The caring parent helps them master their bodies and contain strong feelings. Satisfying this first condition is one requirement for positive expression of drives. Without this experience of being able to count on help, a child is damaged in the ability to trust and create relationships essential for development. For adults who have lacked this experience, psychotherapists try to provide in a healing encounter a basis for building caring, trusting relationships.

Neglect, especially in the first year of life, causes drives to turn back on the self. Frustration when no one responds causes rage. Social drives can be perverted into narcissistic needs. Narcissists are typically hypochondriacs whose attention focuses on their bodies rather than on the world of other people. When I use the term neglect, I do not mean just giving infants too little food, shelter, and playthings. Neglect is much more a psychological problem of absent child care. Rene A. Spitz,

---

[2]Erik H. Erikson, in *Childhood and Society* (New York: W. W. Norton and Co. Inc., 1963) has described the stages of development from a psychoanalytic standpoint. The above explanation builds on his work, that of Anna Freud in *Normality and Pathology in Childhood: Assessment of Development* (New York: International Universities Press, 1965), and that of Jean Piaget (see Chapter 2).

a psychiatrist, studied abandoned children and found that even when well fed, institutionalized infants who were not hugged and talked to became autistic and uninterested in the world, aimlessly playing with their own feces. Because these infants were preoccupied with their own bodies, their drives become increasingly directed toward themselves, not the world. In contrast, babies in a nearby hospital, with less food but more cuddling were healthier, both physically and emotionally.[3]

Less severe emotional neglect of children by inadequate, infantile parents or uncaring guardians can produce a semischizoid character, seemingly devoid of feeling, because the needs for relatedness are frustrated and repressed. That is why some seemingly cool and detached new-generation people are shocked by the intensity of their needs and dependency once they move close to another person. For such people, intimacy is understandably frightening, and they feel safer maintaining minimal contact.

The importance of care in childhood makes it imperative to provide good day care for the young children of parents who work. People who have received good care as children respond positively to caring teachers, managers, co-workers. There is a feeling of reciprocity, of wanting to respond to care with care. (One personal note: Some conservatives argue that society would be better off if mothers stayed home to care for their children. My own mother ran a business before marrying and staying home to care for her children. She was frustrated and miserable at home. Everyone would have been happier if she had continued to work.)

Neglect in the workplace, an uncaring management, provokes egotistical strategies of self-interest. In such environments, employees feel unprotected ("If they don't care, why should I?"), as did a director of nursing who described the lack of caring about nurses on the part of doctors and administrators, "People do not feel good about each other....There is a feeling of stagnation....The nurses have not kept up

---

[3]Rene A. Spitz, *The First Year of Life* (New York: International Universities Press, 1965), pp. 227-281.

with advances and changes in the way nursing is delivered. Some of these areas are technical, some are management....There is a feeling of worthlessness, individually and collectively. Powerlessness."

Freedom

The second condition for development is freedom. At about the age of two in our culture, the issue of freedom arises in a child's struggles with parents. The child must master bowels and limbs to avoid shame, gain social approval, and maintain a sense of dignity. Notice how two-year-olds express dignity and a growing wish for independence through negativism. They demand to choose the clothes they wear, the stories they hear. They enjoy saying no, to the despair of uncomprehending parents. By five or six, if not before, the child must learn to leave home for the day, act with initiative toward strangers, and begin to master the symbols necessary for knowledge — reading, writing, and arithmetic. The parents or teachers help motivate a child toward mastery by setting goals that are challenging but attainable. Goals that are too low bore children; goals that are too high discourage them.

To gain a sense of initiative and develop a need for achievement, the child must be free of overcontrol and be free to experiment through play. The children who become most cooperative are those who feel secure enough to criticize authority, but also protected enough to leave an oppressive peer group. Adult approaches to work reveal the importance of these early experiences and resulting attitudes. The future expert is too impressed by adult authority, while the future helper may withdraw from the contest into protective relationships.

Neglect and oppression can deform and distort character and self-perception. British psychoanalysts W. R. D. Fairburn and Harry Guntrip describe cases of parents whose oppressive behavior causes a splitting of the child's self.[4] What results in the child is an inauthentic conforming self that hides feelings of humiliation and anger. My clinical experience supports these observations. Rather than blame parents,

---

[4]For example, see Harry Guntrip, *Schizoid Phenomena: Object Relations and the Self* (New York: International Universities Press, 1969); W.R.D. Fairburn, *An Object Relations Theory of the Personality* (New York: Basic Books, 1952).

patients who have been neglected and oppressed will blame their condition on their own "bad" drives, accepting the parents' view that they had impossible, selfish demands. Otherwise, the rage they feel against their oppressors threatens to break the fragile ties that bind them to their parents. This syndrome has become generally accepted as common by therapists in the '90s.[5]

Oppression takes forms of domination, control, and seduction. Historically, whole groups or classes have been oppressed as slaves or exploited workers, children of bondage brought up to submit, to repress their need for dignity. Submission is not the perversion; submission may be necessary for survival. The perversion of dignity is servility and sadomasochism. Erich Fromm's analysis of sadomasochism describes this perversion in the authoritarian character who compensates for submission and humiliation by identifying with a powerful and punishing organization or leader in order to maintain a sense of dignity.[6] The masochistic child may later gain mastery, a sense of relatedness, and pseudodignity through sadism, expressing power over those who are weaker.

The destructive effects of oppressive control extend to the workplace. For example, oppression in the workplace can cause angry sabotage or discourteous treatment of customers by those unable to quit their jobs. It can also bring out the sadomasochistic tendencies in bureaucrats. Studies of government workers show that some sadomasochists rise in the civil service because they flatter insecure, inexperienced political appointees and promise to get results by "kicking ass."[7] What they get from employees is either servility or sullen compliance, putting on a mask and doing the minimum.

---

[5]For example, the influences of J. Weiss, H. Sampson, and The Mount Zion Psychotherapy Group, *The Psychoanalytic Process: Theory, Clinical Observations and Empirical Research* (New York: The Guilford Press, 1986).

[6]Erich Fromm, *Escape from Freedom* (New York: Rinehart, 1941).

[7]See Michael Maccoby, *The Leader*, (New York: Simon and Schuster, 1981), Chapter 8; as well as Douglas LaBier, *Modern Madness: The Emotional Fallout of Success* (Reading, Mass.: Addison-Wesley, 1986).

Members of the new generation will not tolerate such oppressive management. To avoid being oppressed or stuck with a bad boss, they seek independence and opportunity at work. To maintain independence in the unstable organizations of today, they must maintain marketable skills, but also the willingness to quit their jobs if these jobs become oppressive. The dual-career family helps to fan the spirit of independence by increasing the opportunity and freedom to try new ventures.

Discipline

The third condition for productive development is discipline. To develop a sense of power as potency, children must learn to manage themselves and master various disciplines. In common language, we use the term *discipline* in two ways. One meaning refers to punishment. Either an oppressive authority demands unquestioning obedience, or a benevolent authority sets limits, thus expressing indignation toward bad behavior that transgresses the rights of others. Parents who understand the feelings of children, and especially their need for dignity, find that the child responds more positively to reasonable discipline, and learns early to understand the difference between just and unjust punishment. This is especially the case if the parent explains that he or she understands the child's feelings.

The second meaning of *discipline* refers to the training or development of individual skills. The disciplines required in the new workplace include more than those that are intellectual, physical, or artistic. The term *discipline* also includes the trained power to resist the seductiveness of a consumer society, to concentrate despite distractions, to listen carefully, and to discriminate among claims, propaganda, and sales pitches. Discipline for freedom requires critical thinking, and discipline for success requires self-restraint and good habits that keep the mind sharp and the body in shape for long hours and frequent travel.

The opposite of discipline, indulgence, can cause perversion. This I have observed most dramatically in patients who were brought up without sufficient discipline in very rich families. Easy satisfaction by servants feeds limitless, addictive needs; mastery becomes too easy.

Without discipline, people fear tests of competence and avoid them, thus causing a vicious circle of avoidance and failure to develop competence. The drive for effortless pleasure comes to dominate their existence, weakening their will and causing self-contempt. Indulgence is not limited to the very rich, and, of course, some rich people (like John D. Rockefeller and Joseph Kennedy) create a disciplined family culture with strong values of public service. There are different causes of indulgence. Neglectful parents may indulge children to compensate for their own sense of a deprived childhood, mistakenly believing this indulgence will make the child happy. Liberal parents may indulge because of a vague Rousseauean belief that the "natural needs" of the child should be met and that whatever the child wants is "natural." Busy parents may indulge to salve their consciences for not giving more real attention, not aware that they are depriving their children of the discipline essential for freedom.

Parents may also indulge children to try to keep them dependent and close, a form of oppression and seduction. Parents can pervert the child's drive for mastery by manipulating with extravagant praise and attention, inflating self-esteem, and making greater performance demands that tighten the bonds of dependency. Positive reinforcement has its value, but it may feed an addictive need. To get a quick fix of adulation, children are driven to achieve not for themselves, but for the parent. The child has been robbed of an authentic sense of dignity, which has been replaced by a grandiose self-image. This false sense weakens intrinsic motivation at work.

Balance

The fourth condition for productive motivation is balance between work and love, mastery and play, mind and body, head and heart. When a single value directs the personality, one drive then dominates at the expense of the whole person, and the individual loses the capacity for growth. Other drives do not disappear, but are repressed or undeveloped. Experts intent on mastery lose the ability to play, innovate, and create. Gamesmen obsessed with winning lose the capacity for human understanding, caring, and loyalty. They may be daring but lack courage: the knowledge of the heart, the quality that is essential to a sense of integrity.

A strength of Swedish culture is the concept of *lagom,* which means balance, not too much or too little, but just right. The concept comes from the Viking practice of passing a horn full of beer around the campfire. Everyone was supposed to take a swallow but there should be enough left for the last person. Swedish parents teach children that putting too much on their plate is not *lagom.* This balance is an underpinning to a sense of fairness that strengthens Swedish organizations in terms of wage differentials and working conditions.

We shall see in Chapters 9 and 10 that balance of values is also a key to a motivating organization and leadership.

Commitment

The fifth condition for development is commitment. Many self-developers struggle against the limits that commitment implies. Both the search for and the escape from commitment dominate the discussions of self-developers about work, family, and relationships. "How much of myself am I willing to commit?" is a popular question for the new generation. Of course, our potentialities are greater than we can realize in a lifetime. We must focus our energies, commit ourselves to some projects and people, and not to others. When these commitments engage our intrinsic motivation, they allow for satisfying self-expression, stimulate development, and create meaning rather than a sense of diffusion, superficiality, and meaninglessness.

Of course, self-developers fear commitments that are entrapping, freezing development in oppressive relationships or rigid ideologies. But they sometimes guard their flexibility at the cost of superficiality and diffusion of energy. The most productive self-developers struggle against self-indulgence through exercise and diet. They seek balance in mind and body, work and family. They are used to negotiations and trade-offs and, when necessary, cutting their losses. They are less clear about the discipline of the heart, the courage to fully experience oneself and others, and to act on the basis of felt conviction. Many lack the sense of hope generated by commitment to projects that improve life, that develop not only the self, but also the larger world. Their skepticism about government and organizations in general turns them inward to self and family life.[8]

Toward Balance and Commitment

The new generation supports the transformation in the workplace that furthers development. While skittish about intimacy, they want people in the workplace to treat each other with respect. They resent overcontrol and refuse to submit when respect is lacking; rather, they may fake compliance, do the minimum, and start looking for better opportunities. Where they seem most in need of guidance is in understanding the developmental issues of discipline, balance, and commitment.

Poor adult choices cannot all be blamed on childhood. Self-development is less a matter of satisfying needs than forming good ones. Young people with many opportunities make bad choices. They may avoid the hard work and self-restraint necessary for mastery and achievement. They may pursue pleasure at the expense of mastery and dignity. Alternatively, they may become addicted to one-dimensional mastery at the expense of relationships. They may invest all their energies in success at any cost.

Self-development today calls for an inner dialogue based on strategic questions about one's life: "How can I balance my drive for success with a commitment to satisfying human relationships? How can I gain a sense of security and at the same time experience a sense of creativity at work?" To answer questions such as these, one needs to become aware of one's real values and understand the conditions — care, freedom,

---

[8]As Robert D. Putnam writes, this trend threatens the underpinnings of democracy in America, which has been based, to a large degree, on many formal and informal associations. "Bowling Alone: America's Declining Social Capital", *Journal of Democracy*. v 6 n 1, Jan. 1995, p. 65.

discipline, balance, and commitment — that reinforce developmental needs. Then it is essential that one acts to create the conditions for personal growth through supportive relationships and wise choices.

To summarize, development requires taking responsibility to create the conditions that shape developmental needs and strengthen one's ability to satisfy them. The following are suggestions for guidelines.

1. Caring relationships establish a sense of emotional security. Relationships based on shared meanings and mutual respect are the basis of the trust that is essential to building good developmental friendship. In such relationships, caring and empathy are balanced by support for each other's positive values and developmental needs, and intolerance of each other's addictive needs. One's closest relationships should be evaluated in these terms.

2. To maintain a sense of freedom, people must develop their marketable skills. In avoiding addictive dependency, they must guard against the illusion that they can do it all by themselves. A certain amount of dependency can be developmental if one is helped by trustworthy people who share values and goals. However, only with a sense of independence can one challenge the corporate experts and join with others in transforming the workplace.

3. Self-discipline is never-ending. Self-control requires self-understanding. To frustrate addictive needs, one must recognize them and admit they rob one of potency. To reinforce developmental needs, one must commit oneself to challenging goals and push oneself to practice good habits. Without intellectual and artistic discipline, self-expression remains primitive and unsatisfying. Few of us are blessed with great talent,

but we can all practice those disciplines that enhance self-expression throughout life. Once a technique has been mastered, we can express ourselves spontaneously. Mastering academic technique in their youth, painters, like Turner and Monet, and composers, like Scarlatti and Verdi, expressed themselves in old age with an exciting sense of freedom. Those of us who are less gifted can still gain satisfaction in disciplining intellectual, musical, and artistic talents, writing, learning to speak in front of others, even cooking and gardening. This discipline strengthens us not only at work, but in all of life.

4. We can all reflect on the balance in our lives by charting our values. Which of our "needs" and values are developmental and which addictive? To become whole, hale, healthy, potent, and powerful, in the sense of consciousness, capacity, and energy, we must frustrate the addictive needs, reach for higher values. Do not forget fun. If there is none in work and love, a person is in the wrong place, with the wrong people. But fun itself, linked with playful experiment and dialogue, is developmental. Those who want to become leaders might benefit from comparing themselves with the leadership styles described in Chapter 10 and asking these questions: What are my strengths? How can I build on them? How can I compensate for my weaknesses by working with others who have the strengths I lack?

5. Energy is generated when we engage our intrinsic motivation. It is spent and drained when there is conflict, unresponsiveness, deadness at work. Some of the most effective leaders in business and government today are the entrepreneurs who followed their own interests rather than someone else's prescription of what would

lead to success. As one successful professional phrased it, "My goal in life is to do work that I enjoy and to get someone to pay for it."

Development requires commitment to meaningful projects that engage intrinsic motivation, develop one's skills, and involve coming together with people with common principles. It is unwise to invest all one's hope in promotion; no one can predict the future of any company. Rather, one can envision the competencies one wants to acquire and develop them, envision the life one wants to lead and plan to create it. We should all ask ourselves what kind of environment, community, society we want to live in. How will it be created? If we don't participate in building the future for ourselves and our children, who will? Through our work, we are forming ourselves. By our work, we are creating the world.

Once we understand these challenges, we gain a sense of meaning at work, and we are forced to take greater responsibility for ourselves. In a sense, each of our lives is a project. Either it may just happen, and be over before we know it, or we can plan to make it meaningful and adventurous. This challenge requires not only living well and developing skills when one is young, but also continuing mature development by accepting responsibility, authority, power to influence others, even power over others. The new generation rejects the older models of authority, but has not yet found one that is meaningful for itself. In fact it cannot do so without a willingness to defend the values of freedom and dignity, which are essential to self-development. Nor can it gain authority in the minds of others without commitment to projects and people. To become leaders in the information age, self-developers must also become educators and developers of others. The workplace provides opportunities for this kind of leadership.

The Technoservice Organization and Self-Development

The technoservice organization needs people who can continually learn and adapt to changing conditions. Management should welcome those who want to be whole persons, as opposed to narrow experts. Chapter 9 proposes tools for satisfying developmental needs which, at the same time, motivate people to help the company succeed. Development requires a corporate culture that balances care, freedom, discipline, and mutual commitment to meaningful projects and continuous improvement. No company or government agency will ever fully succeed in achieving this ideal, but there are some, which come much closer than the average organization to a point where the meaning of work includes self-development and creating useful services. There is a growing understanding that these are the workplaces that are most effective in motivating the new generation.[9]

---

[9]As of 1995, corporate executives are aware of this fact intellectually, but not ready to act according to what they say they believe. According to a survey of 300 executives from large to medium-sized companies conducted by Towers Perrin Co., a New York-based management consulting firm, 98 percent of these executives agreed that improving employee performance would significantly improve their companies' productivity. In addition, 73% claimed employees were their companies' most important investment. But when these same executives were asked to rank their business priorities, investing in people ranked fifth on a six-item list. The top three priorities listed by executives were customer satisfaction, financial performance, and product and service quality. See *The Washington Post*, Business Section, February 5, 1995. See also *The New York Times*, Business Section, February 19, 1995.

CHAPTER 9
THE MOTIVATING ORGANIZATION

In the motivating organization, people are engaged by their responsibilities, by the challenges that are part of their jobs. They feel supported by their relationships, and satisfied by their rewards. Furthermore, they understand organization goals and find them meaningful, worth achieving. In such a situation, the organization connects with both intrinsic and extrinsic motivation. It engages the whole person at work.

The managers who lead the organization should be evaluated by how well they create and lead a motivating organization. Indeed, the term manager comes from the Italian *maneggiare* (from Latin *manus*, hand), to handle, to wield, to touch, to manage, to deal with, to break in horses, to handle horses — to train and direct animal forces. For human beings, these forces combine mind with body, head with gut and heart. Directing human motivation requires understanding values and needs and creating opportunities to express, satisfy, and develop them. This approach is as true for managing ourselves as it is for leading others.

Companies hire people who have shown that they can work hard and well. These people come to work with strong intrinsic motivations. The task of management is to understand these motivations, develop rather than frustrate them, and direct them to work that needs to be done. Although radical individualists may consider this approach to be manipulation, most employees welcome leadership that provides them the opportunity to exercise their skills, develop their competencies so that they can get better jobs, and play on a winning team.

People at work want bosses to use power, but they want it used productively, to create power for them also. Leaders who claim they have no power or do not want it are not seen as becomingly modest; they are considered weak leaders who should be replaced by those who do have power. However, people at work eventually resent a leader who manipulates, motivating by seduction, false promises, and unreal visions of opportunity. Chapter 10 describes leadership style for the new workplace. This present chapter discusses the organizational practices that motivate, the conceptual tools that leaders can employ. These are: *responsibilities, relationships, rewards,* and *reasons* — the four Rs.

The Four Rs

The Motivating Organization graphic summarizes the relationship between the four Rs and the eight value drives. Responsibilities typically engage values and needs having to do with mastery and survival (developing competence that guarantees employability), information (learning), and play (opportunities to innovate). Rewards typically satisfy needs for survival (pay and benefits) and dignity (recognition). Relationships not only satisfy the need for communication and coaching, but also may involve information (learning), survival (sense of support from others) and pleasure (celebration of success, the give-and-take group process). Good relationships create the trust essential for teamwork. And reasons refer to needs for information (goals, results, feedback on performance) and the meaning of the work one does.

Let us consider each of the Rs.

Responsibilities

Responsibilities is the ambiguous term that describes both tasks and challenges on the one hand, and authority or turf on the other. Managers sometimes define responsibility in terms of control. "I am responsible for this organization" means, "I am in charge here." "This is your responsibility" means, "These are your tasks," and sometimes, "This is your turf." But responsibility has another meaning, the ability to respond. In this sense, we speak of accepting responsibility to meet a challenge, solve a problem, or serve a customer.

The Motivating Organization

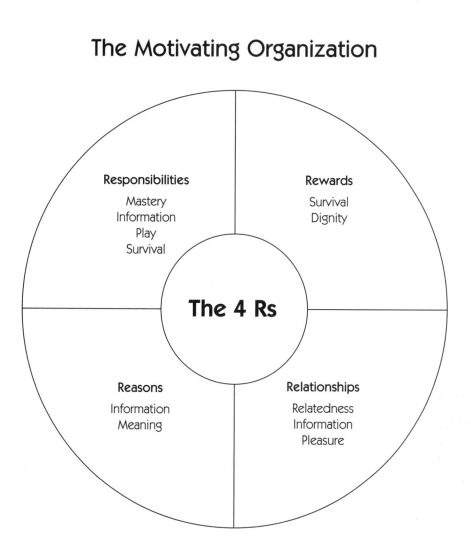

People are motivated by opportunities to express themselves through work. This fact implies that responsibilities should engage the intrinsic needs for mastery and information, in terms of learning and developing competence. Needs for play should be engaged by opportunities for innovation. And the need for dignity should be met by opportunities to participate in decisions at work. Responsibilities should be neither beyond competence nor beneath it. Without competence, people are unable to respond adequately, and responsibility becomes a burden, not a motivator. The need for mastery is frustrated by tasks beyond one's capabilities. Without competence, people do not willingly accept accountability for their performance. A beginning medical student does not want responsibility for a surgical operation. Conversely, despite all the ideology about everyone's sharing work roles, the highly qualified pilots at the now-defunct People Express did not want the responsibilities of baggage handling. To motivate productively, a manager must match person with job, facilitate learning, and define the rules of the game to encourage taking responsibility to satisfy customers, avoid costly accidents, and present ideas for continuous improvement. If small errors are punished, people will avoid responsibility; if errors are not understood, people will not learn. A motivating match between people and tasks is more likely to occur if people participate in designing their jobs.

Most people are motivated by opportunities to develop their competencies through experience and education. To continue motivating a person whose competence has increased, managers need to see that the individual's responsibilities are expanded. In the traditional workplace of the industrial bureaucracy, this is done by promotion to a higher level with "responsibility" for and authority over more people. In the traditional workplace, experts carry out this responsibility by narrowing the responsibilities of those beneath them, frustrating subordinates. The paradox of industrial bureaucracies is that to motivate the careerist through promotion, subordinates must become demotivated through loss of responsibility. For example, managers are typically given the job of checking on the quality of front-line employees who are, in fact, capable of checking their own work.

In the new workplace of information-age service, motivation does not require promotion up the hierarchy. Responsibilities can be expanded, for example, to deal with more customers, teach other employees, and solve problems that bureaucracies usually hand over to specialized experts. For example, a front-line bank employee can determine whether a customer meets credit requirements and decide whether or not to loan money, within limits. In this type of workplace, there is less need for management, since individuals and teams learn to manage themselves, and share most management functions, such as planning and quality control. This arrangement may be frustrating for the expert, who measures success by promotion and status, but not necessarily a problem for self-developers, more interested in learning from new experiences and expanding their options for employment by gaining new skills.

In the technoservice workplace, front-line employees need to have the tools, knowledge, and support to satisfy customers. They must be enabled and motivated to use their judgment and to care about satisfying the customer. This is the meaning of *empowerment*, a term that is often used but seldom defined. The dictionary defines empowerment as giving someone authority, both *authorizing* and *enabling* them to act. But this definition leaves out motivation. Formal authority alone does not guarantee that someone will accept responsibility. For empowerment to be meaningful, employees not only require the competence to recognize problems, the tools that enable, and the authority to take action; they also must be willing to act and accept responsibility for the result. Empowerment requires both motivating employees to accept responsibilities and instilling freedom from the fear of exercising them.

Unless employees are empowered, they will remain frozen in hierarchical roles. Unless front-line technicians are empowered, there are likely to be more accidents like that at the Three Mile Island nuclear power plant where an employee close to the problem lacked the authority to close a valve. He had to ask for approval before he could act. Nor were the technicians at an AT&T switching center in Manhattan empowered to prevent a power failure in September, 1991, an event which brought down communication in the air traffic control system.

Empowerment has to do not only with front-line employees, but middle- and upper-level managers as well. When I was teaching a series of day-long seminars in leadership to senior executives at one of the largest American companies, I asked members of the executive committee what it was they most wanted the seminars to achieve. "Get them to stop delegating upward," said one executive vice-president. He complained that most of these highly paid divisional and department managers lacked courage. He described how as a plant manager he had risked his career by refusing to manufacture a product he considered unsound. His own boss had declined to support him and made him argue his case with the CEO. Putting his career on the line, he persuaded the chairman that his decision was in the best interests of the company. He said, "Most of these officers would just delegate upward and accept the boss' decision. That's why our company is in trouble today."

Of course, the opposite of willingness to take responsibility is fear of making a mistake and risking bad personal consequences. When I next met a group of senior executives at this company, I presented them with a scale of fear — responsibility and asked them to indicate by a show of hands where they would put the company's management overall.

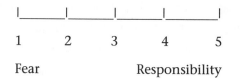

The median was two. I have repeated this test with managers at that company and at a number of others. The results are the same. Incidentally, when I ask where they should be on the scale, most managers say 4, not 5. They are uneasy about completely fearless people who might be loose cannons on the corporate deck. Whether or not they are right about this, closing the gap between 2 and 4 requires either an increase in courage by individuals or of support by their managers so they do not need to feel afraid.

To better understand the conditions that support empowerment, Berth Jönsson of SIFO, a Swedish survey and consulting company, and I proposed two dimensions. One has to do with the employees' formal responsibilities and the other with their willingness to accept responsibility. We hypothesized that both these conditions must be met to ensure that employees are in fact empowered. We constructed questions to probe these dimensions, and tried them out at a multinational company with business units in both the U.S.A. and Sweden.

One set of questions asked employees about their responsibilities, whether or not they had the authority and training to reject products not up to standard and fix quality problems. Were they expected to use their judgment to satisfy customers? Did they understand business goals? The second set, questions on willingness to accept responsibility, asked whether they were afraid to take action to solve problems. If they did act, would they be supported? Were they afraid to say what they think? Could they criticize bad decisions? Or, fearful of making the wrong decision, did they delegate upward?

Answers to the two sets of questions were made into scales that define the two dimensions. One dimension has to do with formal responsibilities, including training to fill a responsible role. The other dimension has to do with the relationships with managers who are either supportive and drive out fear or instead increase the employees' fear of taking responsibility, because they would be punished for making mistakes.

The Empowerment Matrix on the next page describes four types of organization based on correlating the two dimensions with each other, making a matrix with four quadrants. In the upper right quadrant is the *empowered* organization. People have the training and authority and take responsibility to satisfy internal and external customers, recognize quality problems, analyze their causes, and solve them.

In the lower right quadrant is the bureaucratic organization. Although people have authority, they protect themselves, stick to the rules, and when in doubt delegate upward. It is like the government agency in which I once worked as a consultant. For two weeks, no one changed a light bulb. When I asked someone why he did not do it, he said, "It's not my job."

In the lower left quadrant is the *compliant* organization. People lack authority, and they are not expected to take initiatives. They follow orders, generally doing a simple, repetitive job. At the extreme this is the traditional assembly line of Henry Ford and of Charlie Chaplin's *Modern Times* where people were expected to act like parts of a machine.

In the upper left quadrant is the *anarchic* organization. People are not afraid to take responsibility, but they lack the training and guidelines to do so effectively. They are emboldened to take initiatives that are not aligned with company goals. I have observed companies where

Empowerment Matrix

Organizations can be placed within a matrix based on both responsibilities and relationships.

Responsibilities
Are Broad
And Enabled

Relationships Drive Out Fear
(Taking the Initiative Is Supported)

Empowered

People have the business understanding, competence, and support to satisfy internal and external customers. They take responsibility to analyze causes of quality problems and solve them.

Bureaucratic

People have authority, but they do not accept responsibility. They protect themselves, stick to the rules, and when in doubt delegate upward.

Relationships Cause Fear
(Mistakes Are Punished)

Anarchic

People are not afraid to take responsibility, but they lack the training and guidelines to do so effectively.

Compliant

People are not expected to accept responsibility. They follow orders and when in doubt, delegate upward.

Responsibilities
Are Narrowly
Formatted

managers have become intoxicated with the vision of everyone's becoming an entrepreneur, but have failed to communicate goals. Roles are unclear. What happens is that people take initiatives and make deals, which cause problems for others, and suffering for the company. An example is an R&D organization, where entrepreneurial engineers devoted their energies to developing technology without first connecting it to the world of business. The fault was not in the entrepreneurial inventors, but in the laissez-faire management, which failed to define their goals and responsibilities.

When Jönsson and I recently applied our empowerment survey to a number of business units in the U.S.A. and Sweden, measures of empowerment were correlated with those of profitability. Those business units where employees scored in the empowered quadrant made money. Those that fell in the bureaucratic, compliant, and chaotic boxes showed zero or negative results. Undoubtedly those managers who were able to create a culture of empowerment also did other things well to produce good results. However, we should not underestimate the ability of a motivated and empowered workforce to implement corporate strategy by continuous improvement of quality and productivity. Such progress does require attention to both responsibilities and relationships.

Relationships

People are motivated by relationships with bosses, peers, subordinates, customers, and suppliers. We have noted that supportive relationships drive out fear. The trust essential for teamwork in the new workplace also depends on a sense of security and respect for individual dignity. In the past, employment security was a key element in building trust. Today, no company can guarantee employment. Instead, employees need to take responsibility for their own futures, but they also need opportunities to upgrade their skills and knowledge. Trust is also developed by clearing away nonfunctional status differences and symbols of authority that wound the sense of dignity and divide people. Managers also build trust by listening to criticisms nondefensively and responding to ideas for improvement.

While everyone is motivated by relationships that provide support and drive out fear from the workplace, different types of people vary in terms of the relationships that motivate them most intensely. Experts develop attachments to father-figure bosses whom they try desperately to please. Brief expressions of approval and disapproval have a powerful motivating impact on experts, because the father figure's judgment is so important to them.

But paternal approval is not a satisfying relationship for self-developers, who are more motivated by encounters with customers and colleagues where they have a chance to increase understanding and knowledge. Helpers are motivated by a feeling of family, solidarity, and mutual support that seems mushy to the self-developers. Innovators are motivated by an excited team. However, all types are motivated by relationships marked by respect for individual dignity, recognition of good work, and opportunities to learn and participate. In Sweden, where government benefits used to assure workers they would not lose money by being absent from work, the corporate doctors at Volvo found that when they felt needed and their views were solicited, workers came to the factory or office even with mild symptoms of illness. Workers who lack this kind of relationship stay at home with mild symptoms.

Rewards

Rewards are extrinsic motivators, but as we note with bonuses, their power depends on individual values. Different types of people view rewards differently. Consciously, experts want rewards to represent the fair market value of their performance and prove their achievement. Unconsciously, they experience rewards as parental approval and a bonus cements transferential loyalty to the boss. However, if an expert considers that a "sibling's" higher reward is unfair, the result can be disgruntlement. For this reason, some companies, like IBM, would keep salaries and bonuses secret and forbid employees to compare them.

Helpers, however, feel that material rewards contaminate good relationships and should be the same for all, or based on seniority. Union leaders who are helper-defenders distrust reward systems that allow managers to play favorites. They believe reward systems should be developed with the participation of all employees involved. Helper-teachers resent merit pay schemes. They believe that no administrator can measure the value of help, and that differential pay undermines solidarity. And the innovator-gamesmen treat their rewards as the score, and money as a liquid resource to be used, like any other resource, to create wealth and independence. Self-developers see money as part of the total reward package they would like to negotiate, individually. They weigh money against other rewards: opportunity to develop skills, time off, health care, child care, exercise facilities, and a friendly atmosphere. These self-developers want clear commitments from management concerning responsibilities, relationships, and rewards. They want explicit performance and profitability goals, and they want to know how they will be rewarded as individuals and team members.

Money is not the only, or necessarily the most effective, reward for motivating employees. (For instance, the State Department finds that the Germans they hire at the U.S. Embassy in Bonn sometimes prefer a higher-sounding title to a job with more money.) Experts will extend themselves to win plaques, professional validation to frame and put on their walls. Helpers will work long hours, weekends, and holidays for signs of love and appreciation. Once self-developers earn what they consider essential, some of them may be motivated by the promise of gaining more free time.

I first became aware of the motivations of self-developers in the early '80s. I was visiting a factory in Southern California where managers asked apathetic young workers what it would take to make them really productive. These workers felt they had interesting craft jobs and fairly good relationships with each other and with management, but they were not motivated to work harder to make more money. One of them said, "If you are serious, what I want is a chance to enjoy life more, with more time off." The others agreed. "We have seen our fathers old and tired at 50 because they worked too hard, and did not learn how to have fun. Don't expect us to wear ourselves out. If you want us to really work, give us at least three months a year unpaid leave, so we can live another life in the woods or on the beach. We might build a house or sharpen our surfing skills. Just guarantee our jobs will be available when we return." I sat in on the meeting of company management when this idea was proposed and rejected by grim-faced experts for the reason that "it would be treating workers like school kids getting a three-month vacation and it would undermine discipline."

Although there are differences in which rewards are most motivating for each type, there are common principles that should be considered in designing rewards for the new workplace. Rewards should reinforce the behavior that is needed by the organization, and employees should feel that they share in the company's success. This approach implies rewards based on profitability, but for these to be credible, employees must understand the business and the direct relationship between their work and profitability. Rewards such as team bonuses should reinforce cooperation.

To look at the other side of the rewards issue, does punishment or the fear of punishment motivate? The answer depends on both the degree of punishment and the type of person. If punishments for failure are too severe, people will play it safe, and the result will be a bureaucratic or compliant rather than an empowered workforce. But even less severe punishment may backfire. Some people, particularly expert types who are motivated by rewards, are disturbed by punishments. They feel they have done their best and should not be punished for failure. Others, particularly gamesmen, are motivated by risks and perform better if failure means punishment. The adrenaline fear seems to energize them like it does for professional football quarterbacks who turn the fear into super-alertness.[1] Gamesmen do well when a large part of their compensation depends on the score. But this is not true of the other types.

When AT&T introduced pay based on sales performance to employees who had before been paid on a fixed salary, there were two results.

---

[1] I have been interested in different reactions to reward systems for over 40 years. In an experiment I did as a college student on using information to solve problems, I found that anxious people did better when rewarded for success but not punished for failure. However, less anxious people (like gamesmen) did better when the stakes were higher—when they were punished for failure and rewarded for success (M. Maccoby, "The Pay-Off Matrix in Concept Attainment," unpublished honors thesis, Harvard University, 1954).

Many employees were motivated to sell more, and they earned more money. But some employees who felt pressured by the pay scheme left the company. This reaction showed that a reward system may be used not only to motivate, but as a way of selecting gamesmen and self-developers for sales roles, as contrasted to choosing more traditional types.

To summarize, although there are differences among types, the following three principles are essential for motivating everyone at work:

1. Rewards should be meaningful. People should feel they have been compensated, recognized, and appreciated for a real contribution. They should understand the relationship between their performance and the reward they receive.

2. Rewards should be considered fair by everyone in the organization. This means that differences in pay should be considered equitable. One person's gain should not wound another's sense of dignity. As leadership asks for higher levels of motivation, employees will become more sensitive to salary differentials. In American companies, CEOs make 40 or 50 times as much as a skilled employee, compared with a ratio of from 5:1 to 10:1 in Japan or Sweden. That huge difference undermines the motivation of employees who are asked to perform as though they were owners of the company. Corporate leaders tend to compare their compensation with each other, but not with that of the company's front-line employees.

3. Rewards should reinforce the behavior that produces value added for customers, employees, and owners. If managers want to reward individual achievement, they must describe the criteria so that the whole team understands what behavior is expected. Ideally, the team will participate in defining the criteria so that everyone considers the process to be fair. People should not be punished for failing when they take the kind of

risks that are necessary for success. They should only be punished for unethical behavior. The well-known global engineering company, ABB (Asea Brown Boveri) has the right approach to this. According to ABB's corporate policy, it is best to make a right decision at the right time. Next best is the wrong decision at the right time, which is quickly corrected. The worst action is to do nothing.

Reasons

Reasons play a significant role in motivation. We are motivated to do what we believe is worth doing, and that includes what is important for the organization's success. Managers have to communicate the reasons why they set goals and develop strategies. Many people at work do not know about competitive realities; if they know their jobs are at stake, that company survival depends on good service, quality production, or lower cost, they become motivated to achieve these goals. People also want to play on a winning team and to be known as winners. Information about what competitors are doing can persuade people that they must cut costs to compete. People like to know how they are doing against the competition.

By explaining reasons for decisions and actions, leaders can manage meaning. One task of managers, then, is to provide reasons that are meaningful to each type in terms of their values. Experts find meaning in the search for excellence in products and processes; they are motivated by management that supports this goal. For helpers, it is the chance to make a real difference in the lives of those they serve. For innovators, it is adventure, challenge, and the chance for glory by doing something to change the world. Self-developers, more than the other types, are motivated by knowing the reasons why things are done, and thereby seeing possibilities for personal growth and improved practices.

A group of software programmers, self-developers, left a computer company. They were not dissatisfied with their pay and benefits. But they were not informed about the reasons why they were doing their jobs, how their work fit into the business. In contrast, AT&T's Workplace

The Value Creating Circle

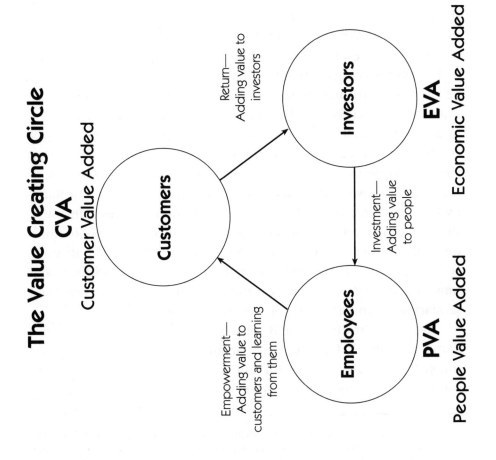

CVA
Customer Value Added

Return—
Adding value to
investors

Customers

Investors

Investment—
Adding value
to people

Empowerment—
Adding value to
customers and learning
from them

Employees

EVA
Economic Value Added

PVA
People Value Added

of the Future, initiated in 1992 with the cooperation of the Communications Workers of America (CWA) and the International Brotherhood of Electrical Workers (IBEW), provides education for all employees, not only about business strategy, but also about how the company measures success in terms of satisfying AT&T's three main stakeholders: customers, owners, and employees.[2]

The Value Creating Circle graphic describes the process that benefits the three stakeholders. It works as follows. Customers pay for those products and services that add value for them. This produces profit that is used to provide a satisfactory return to investors; it also pays salaries, and allows the company to invest in developing the competence of the people who must provide the products and services to customers. To evaluate its executives and determine their bonuses, AT&T uses the measures they call CVA, EVA, and PVA. The first measure, CVA, or "customer value added," is based on surveys of customer satisfaction with quality, service, price and other factors customers consider essential in deciding whether or not to buy from AT&T. The second measure, EVA or "economic value added," tracks return on investment. Investors should receive a return that is competitive with competing opportunities to invest their money. AT&T's third measure, PVA or "people value added," estimates both employee empowerment, the competence and support necessary to achieve CVA, and motivation, the engagement and satisfaction essential to energize the organization.

The Value Creating Circle is consistent with the findings of John P. Kotter and James L. Heskett of the Harvard Business School. Their study shows that the most successful corporate cultures practice values to balance the interests of customers, employees, and investors.[3]

---

[2]An example of empowerment is the billing inquiry group at AT&T's Corporate Information Technology Services center in Orlando, Florida, where a Workplace of the Future team, re-engineered responsibilities, thereby benefiting customers and the bottom line. A number of jobs were no longer needed. However, the team found new jobs for practically all those who were displaced. They reduced the workforce from 128 to 70 people. With 30% fewer people, they improved productivity 40%, customer satisfaction 38%, and associate satisfaction 75%. Of the 30 surplus people, they were unable to find jobs for only two.

[3]John P. Kotter and James L. Heskett, *Corporate Culture and Performance* (New York: The Free Press, 1992).

The 4 Rs and Dominant Values

	EXPERT	HELPER	DEFENDER	INNOVATOR	SELF-DEVELOPER
Responsibilities	Autonomy and challenge	Opportunity to help	Righting wrongs	Opportunity to innovate	Learning experiences
Rewards	Awards	Appreciation	Increased power	Glory	Competence and Independence
Relationships	Like-minded experts	Caring people	Loyal people	Supporting team	Networks
Reasons	Excellence	Improving people's lives	Justice	Changing the world	Self-development

There is also a fourth stakeholder of companies and that is the community in which people work. The well-being of the community should be important to companies, but it usually only becomes so when government and interest groups (e.g. environmental protection) make it so through law and pressure. Otherwise, most people will first try to maximize their personal and organizational gain, even if this means moving work out of the community or damaging the environment.

The 4Rs and Dominant Values

To summarize, in the motivating organization leaders use the 4Rs to produce empowered, enabled, and engaged people who are motivated to make the organization succeed. For each type, there are differences in what most motivates as The 4Rs and Dominant Values graphic shows. For experts, what most motivates is autonomy and challenge, the promise of awards and recognition for excellence, and the chance to work with like-minded experts, preferably the best in the world. Helpers are motivated most by opportunities to help, appreciation for work that improves people's lives, and the chance to associate with caring people. What most motivates defenders are challenges to right wrongs, and being able to work together with loyal people who share a common view of justice. The reward for defenders is increased power to achieve their goals. For innovators what most motivates are challenges and opportunities to find new ways of doing things, to change the world, sometimes alone, sometimes with a supporting team and as a result, gain glory. And for self-developers the opportunity to learn and grow is what most motivates, combined with the chance to extend networks and in the process increase one's competence and independence.

For the motivating organization to function, motivating leaders are required. In the next chapter, we put together what we have learned so far and consider different leadership styles. In this final chapter, we address the question: what are the leadership values and practices essential for motivating the new workforce?

CHAPTER 10
MOTIVATING LEADERSHIP

Leaders are needed to transform the industrial bureaucracies, to create and continually improve motivating organizations for the age of technoservice. How can we best describe the kinds of leaders who are needed? According to the dictionary, a leader is someone who leads, directs, or commands. But there are many different ways to lead, and how well people are motivated to follow an organizational leader depends in large part on the fit between the motivation of the leader and the motivation of the led.

In every culture, the ideal leader is one who is motivated to achieve the common good. However, the attributes of the ideal leader are different in different cultures and historical eras. In the Confucian cultures of Taiwan, Singapore, Korea, and to some extent, Japan,[1] the ideal leader appears to be a benevolent father figure. People in those cultures want to follow such a leader, even if he is demanding and even depostic. As long as followers are convinced that the leader is acting for the good of the organization-family, these people will follow a benevolent despot, like Lee Kuan Yew who is credited with building Singapore into a prosperous city-state. In contrast, the ideal Swedish leader is first among

---

[1]Japan, of course, is a complex culture, and there are different models of leadership there. Compare, for example, Toyota and Honda. Toyota is like a feudal empire, which grew up in semirural Ngoya. When a worker joins the company, he is brought by his parents and formally handed over to Toyota management, which acts *in locus parenti*. At all levels, leaders are expected to be teachers, which fits the Confucian ideal. Honda in contrast, draws employees to its Tokyo plant from a city culture that is more egalitarian. The ideal is heterarchy in which leadership functions are shared and shift to the person who has the relevant knowledge.

equals, an admired expert who builds consensus through participation. In Germany, the ideal corporate leader is the master craftsman who expects subordinates to provide fact-based views on issues. He then analyzes this feedback and arrives at a decision, which must be obeyed quickly and efficiently. In each culture, people want to follow a leader who exemplifies the best in the social character, while still working for the common good. Such a leader will give people a feeling of hope and a sense of meaning. Although he may have to govern with a firm hand, particularly in a time of change, it will be with the consent and approval of the governed.

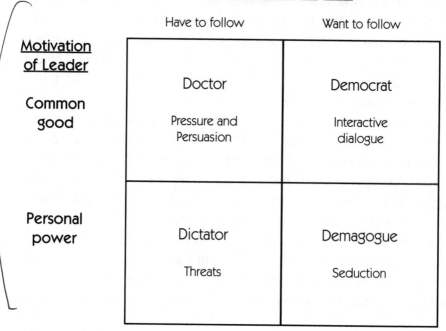

Leader Relationship to Led
Motivation of Led

	Have to follow	Want to follow
Motivation of Leader **Common good**	Doctor Pressure and Persuasion	Democrat Interactive dialogue
Personal power	Dictator Threats	Demagogue Seduction

Relationships of Leaders to the Led

What about the U.S.? In this country, people are ambivalent about leaders. We know we need them, but we are quick to criticize them. At heart, most Americans want to be their own boss, and we rightly fear becoming overly dependent on strong leaders. However, the possible relationships between leader and led in America can be described in terms of the Leader Relationship to Led graphic. One dimension on this chart is the motivation of the leader, which is either the common good or personal power. The other dimension is the motivation of the led, either having or wanting to follow the leader. The ideal leader is the democrat in the upper right quadrant whom all the stakeholders of a company — employees, customers, and owners — would elect if they had the opportunity to vote.

In the upper left quadrant is the leader motivated to change the organization for the common good, one who faces employees who are threatened by change. Such a leader becomes like a doctor who tells overweight patients with cardiac problems that they must either change their eating habits or die. The doctor uses a combination of pressure and persuasion to change the patient's behavior. In an organization, although the followers are not happy about it, they may be forced to accept the "doctor"-leader's logic that if they do not change, the company will not succeed. In the lower right section of the chart is the demagogue or "Pied Piper" who seduces people to follow by false promises. People believe these leaders are motivated for the common good, but in the end, like Napoleon or Hitler, such leaders demonstrate that their true motivation is personal power at any cost to their followers. In the lower left quadrant is the dictator, whose motives for personal power are evident to the led, who follow only because of threats; they are afraid of what will happen to them if they do not follow.

Why do Americans want to follow a leader? In my book, *The Leader*, I describe ideal American leaders as having promoted and defended the most productive values of the age. People wanted to follow leaders like John Winthrop, George Washington, and Abraham Lincoln because they affirmed values that made the followers feel more valuable, that gave meaning to their lives and work. These values defined the work ethic of the era. In Colonial Massachusetts, this was the Calvinistic Puritan ethic of hardworking service to God, which Benjamin Franklin then secularized into the craft ethic. In the late 19th century, the stories of Horatio Alger described an entrepreneurial ethic of business success that

Lincoln had earlier articulated. In the early 20th century, the career ethic expressed by corporate leaders, like Alfred Sloan of General Motors, promised that hard work would be rewarded by promotion up the corporate ladder. At the end of the 20th century, the self-development ethic promises that continual learning and self-renewal will result in employability and personal growth.

In companies today, people want to follow a leader who appeals to the work ethic of our time. They look to leaders who offer the realistic hope of personal success and at the same time, stimulate motivation for the common good, including the motivation to understand and satisfy customer needs and create an organization that contributes something useful to society.

How democratic can a corporate leader be? This depends on our definition of democracy and the type of company involved. In a small partnership or cooperative, it is natural for the owner-workers to make decisions based on voting or consensus. To some degree, small, self-managed teams in large companies can do this within guidelines set by corporate leadership. However, their decisions can be overruled by management. In large companies, democratic practice is limited not only by questions of ownership, but also because everyone does not have the information and knowledge to participate in all decisions. Even in the most democratic of worker-owned companies, the Mondragon cooperative in northern Spain where all employees are owners, democracy is constrained by the understanding that experts are required for marketing and investment decisions.

There is a much-debated view that the ideal for a corporation is direct democracy, meaning open debate and voting on major decisions. I believe that even if a corporation adopts some democratic practices, there are limits set by size, knowledge, and ownership that may give authority to one person, a small group, or many shareholders. Even though the workers were to own a company and have the power to replace the leader, they must invest that leader with the power to make some decisions unilaterally. There are times when corporate executives must move quickly, like a ship's captain, to avoid a collision. There are times when negotiations should remain secret to avoid publicity that might unravel a deal. The leader has to be empowered to act for the benefit of all the stakeholders — owners, employees, and customers.

Democracy should be seen as a means toward an end or mixture of ends, rather than an end in itself. As James Madison argued in Federalist Paper No. 10, democratic decisions by majority vote tend to strengthen larger interest groups, sometimes at the expense of minorities. The vision of the founding fathers of the United States was a government that protected individual liberty without damaging the common good. To this end they devised a republican government of checks and balances. While some parts of this government were elected by direct democracy (that did not include women and slaves), other parts, including U.S. Senators, were appointed. Over the last two centuries, the U.S.A. has expanded democratic practice, but interest groups sometimes wield disproportionate power.

A corporation, of course, is not a country. It is more like a subculture that seeks to attract some of the most gifted, motivated, and highly trained members of the society and organize them to create wealth. To do this, it must respect the values these people bring with them. It must also compensate for skills that are not developed so strongly outside a corporation, particularly skills of communication: writing and reading, speaking and listening, dialogue and problem solving. The large corporation has become the leading institution in modern society for defining the skills and values that families and schools should teach the young.[2]

However, the aim of the corporation is not to guarantee individual liberty to pursue happiness, but to satisfy customers in such a way that their purchases generate a competitive return on investment compared to alternative uses of capital, while operating within the boundaries of law and national custom. We join a corporation because we see it to be in our interest.

The corporation in turn needs people who implement its strategy. It demands more discipline than does the general society, more precision,

---

[2]See Michael Maccoby, "The Corporation as a Part-Culture," in *Anthropological Perspectives on Organizational Culture*, Tomoko Hamada and Willis E. Sibley, eds. (Lanham, Maryland: University Press of America, 1994).

and a greater concern for excellence. It demands that highly ambitious individuals temper their drives and work together for common goals. It requires that employees who might be happier doing something else see their own futures as involved in the company's success. It needs to transform intrinsic motivation into motivation for corporate success.

The corporate vision must satisfy all stakeholders and be meaningful to employees if they are to be optimally motivated. In the past, it might have been enough to feel part of a powerful army, to identify with the elite, to feel protected, well-rewarded, and highly regarded. Doubtless, this is still a part of corporate appeal. People want to belong to a winning team. However, the most independent and creative of the new generation do not find these meanings to be sufficient. In increasing numbers, the young seek to develop themselves at work intellectually and emotionally, but they do not want the workplace to dominate their lives. Their aspirations fit the needs of companies for innovative projects and profit centers, provided that leaders can inspire them.

A motivating leader for organizations will use the four Rs — responsibilities, relationships, rewards, and reasons — (see Chapter 9) sometimes as a doctor and ideally as a democrat who designs an ideal future for the organization and engages interactively in a dialogue with an organization concerning how to interpret and implement it.[3]

The Workplace of the Future, which has used this approach, has been part of a major transformation in leadership style at AT&T. Driven by the competitive marketplace, the company has recognized that motivating the workforce requires participation and empowerment and that the unions can make a difference in creating communication and trust with the more than 100,000 employees they represent. Although only the union leaders are subject to removal by vote, the goal of the managers is also to lead with the consent of the governed. In those parts of the company where the most progress has been made, this has been the case.

---

[3]See Russell Ackoff, *The Democratic Organization* (New York: Oxford Press, 1994) for a description of interactive planning.

Leadership Style

The old leadership style at AT&T was quite different. Before the breakup of the Bell System in 1984, a group of AT&T executives invited me to help them change their management style. These executives agreed that the style that had propelled them to the top when AT&T was a regulated monopoly would not succeed in the new competitive telecommunications market. Like most managers during the period when American industry dominated world markets, these executives had learned to be administrators of industrial bureaucracies. They administered a system of anonymous authority based on rules. They did not have to do much leading. They had reached the top because their superiors had felt comfortable with them and trusted their judgment. They had maintained a good track record, and had avoided mistakes. They knew how to look like leaders, and represent the company in the community. They spoke in terms of "we" rather than "I." They exuded an aura of optimism, confidence, and toughness. At best, they were coordinators of experts, fair scorers, responsible gatekeepers, judicious arbitrators, intrepid fire fighters, and conservative policy makers, advocates of high standards of conduct, and protectors of the public interest. At worst, they were monitors and martinets, jungle fighters who jealously guarded their turf; or alternatively, loose, laissez-faire figureheads. They all saw that the future of deregulation and global competition would require from them a new approach to management, new attitudes and skills. In the competitive world, they believed they would have to be entrepreneurs, enterprisers who led a change process.

Using the questionnaire as reproduced in Appendix D of this book, Bob Gaynor, then vice-president for human resources, and I interviewed 60 top executives of AT&T, vice-presidents and above, about their leadership practices. I found that while many of the executives were administrators, with the values of experts and institutional helpers, a few were entrepreneurs, and they were the ones who proved able to survive in the competitive world. (Of the 60 we interviewed, only 5 are still at AT&T.) Subsequently, I have used these questions in the other companies where I have been a consultant to senior management. This questionnaire is meant to stimulate managers to reflect on their style and its effectiveness. In categorizing differences in style, I started out with the dichotomy suggested by the AT&T executives: administrator versus entrepreneur; with their help I expanded and refined the dichotomy to include four types of entrepreneurs, expressing different value orientations. They are: expert, protector (helper-defender), facilitator (self-developer), and innovator.

Although each type has strengths and weaknesses, the best entrepreneurial leaders at the companies I work with today combine and balance styles. The managers most easily stereotyped are the ones who are least effective, for reasons we will see. The ideal leader in the U.S.A., Canada, Western Europe, and Scandinavia should combine the best elements of each style. The extreme exemplars of one style almost invariably express the negative as well as the positive traits.

Four Entrepreneurial Types

Here is a description of the four entrepreneurial types.

Expert-entrepreneurs are decisive, competitive risk takers who invest in products and services based on market research and sometimes on their own hunches. They want in-depth knowledge so they can extrapolate what has worked in one market and enhance it for another. Then they can establish managerial processes they feel they control. They are fervent salespeople who take pride in performing at meetings. They value their skill at negotiating deals and are no-nonsense cost-slashers. They pick good people, usually experts just like themselves, set demanding goals, and try to delegate. But it is hard for them to keep their noses out of everything. Sometimes they are hip-shooters, overvaluing their knowledge as they make too-quick decisions. Expert-entrepreneurs tend to be poor at listening, unless they are sucking up information for their own purposes, and then they listen selectively to confirm their theories. They are impatient and overly controlling and are unaware of how they bruise dignity and turn people off, especially those who do not relate to them paternally or share their values.

Typically, expert-entrepreneurs who start their own businesses get into trouble when their companies start to grow and require significant delegation. They second-guess subordinates, and cause a sense of insecurity in the company. Some of the best people leave. The Apple Computer board had to replace Steve Jobs, the co-founder of the company, who was this kind of entrepreneur and could not delegate decision making. (Jobs has since founded a new computer company called NeXT.)

Protector-entrepreneurs believe they will gain organizational strength not only by sharing power but by creating it. They do not merely delegate. Protectors encourage people to expand their functions. They share information freely and explain its meaning, thus creating a common understanding of goals. They care about their people, and coach and protect those subordinates who share their values. People are motivated not only by responsibilities and opportunities, but by their trust in the leader.

One such top executive defines his managerial philosophy:

> Most people will not give their best because they feel you don't care. We need to send a message that we do care. Most work relationships are like cool business transactions at best. Usually there is not even much trust. I motivate and encourage by creating big jobs with clear role definitions, and then by getting out of the way. But I am there when I am needed. I see myself as a coach, counselor, and barrier remover so that my people can do their best.

The weaknesses of protectors include softness and loose management. People tend to become too dependent on them. Protectors become overprotective and lose their objectivity about subordinates because they want them to do well. They avoid facing necessary conflict within the team and fail to maintain discipline because they want to be loved by everyone. However, to defend their own people, they may cause conflict with other parts of the organization.

Facilitator-entrepreneurs avoid these weaknesses. They work for consensus on strategy and action, but they are not coaches or protectors. They like to solve problems with subordinates, and are skillful in making sure that everyone contributes knowledge and experience. More than other types, they are egalitarian. They listen. Used to seeing things from different points of view, they work easily and effectively with different types of people. At best, they are good organizers. Their weakness as leaders lies in a tendency to believe that consensus guarantees good decisions and that harmony is always better than conflict, which is not always the case. While they are more objective about people than are the protectors, facilitators remain more emotionally distant from subordinates. While they are tolerant of value differences and like to try new approaches, they do not take responsibility for coaching those subordinates who cannot take advantage of the opportunities they offer. In contrast to the entrepreneurial expert or protector, they are uncomfortable in a parental-type role. Goal-oriented, they measure success in profitability, not esteem or applause, but in so doing, they deprive people of reassurance and inspiration.

Innovator-entrepreneurs such as Lemasters, Nagel, and Carlzon (discussed in Chapter 3) offer strategic visions that integrate customer service and participation. They have an intuitive sense of workable wholes, and they take risks to prove their theories. They energize the organization with their enthusiasm. As their vision creates hope, they may become charismatic leaders; as people respond with trust and put their hopes in the leader, this response injects the leader with a sense of certainty and spontaneity; the leader's glow of ease and self-confidence then further strengthen people's trust, and correspondingly, the leader's charisma.

The weaknesses of innovator-entrepreneurs are the other side of their strengths: utopianism, seductive promises, intolerance of other visions and value orientations. They need help in team building and maintaining trust. Real participation, however, can bring them down to earth and improve their visions.

Each entrepreneurial type must beware of its own characteristic tendencies to sabotage good intentions in moments of stress. Experts become autocratic and unsympathetic to the weaknesses of others. When things go wrong, they grab back authority. They make decisions too quickly and pay for them later, because subordinates do not buy in and decisions are not implemented. Protectors exhibit the opposite failing: taking too long to gain everyone's buy-in, procrastinating until it is too late to solve problems, rationalizing their unwillingness to make tough decisions that will hurt some people. Facilitators work well with project and marketing teams, but lack the inspirational leadership that pulls an organization together. In a crisis, they appear uncommitted and uncertain, and may settle for a superficial consensus. The weakness of innovators is falling in love with their creations, becoming true believers in their visions, and losing their experimental playfulness and flexibility. Instead of engaging people in rethinking the strategy and perhaps compromising with approaches that are less pure and more pragmatic, like Don Burr of People Express, they exhort and preach the true faith as the plane crashes.

Matrix of Management Styles

With the help of the AT&T executives, I constructed the Management Style Matrix as shown on the next page. I asked the executives to first circle the behaviors that most characterized them. These could be in any of the lists of entrepreneurial types or under the heading "administrator." Then I asked them to circle the behaviors they would like to develop. I have used this matrix in other companies to begin a strategic dialogue with managers about how to change themselves and their organization. I invite the reader to do the same.

Many of the executives I've interviewed see themselves as experts, but they believe business goals require them to become better team builders and innovators. Most experts can imagine themselves learning the skills of the facilitators, but less so the behavior of the protectors, perhaps because they fear they will be too soft if they start caring about people. One expert said, "To do my job (that involved closing factories and laying off hundreds of people), I have had to cauterize my heart."

On the basis of observing organizational leaders in the U.S.A. and Europe, I find that the extremes of each type cause problems and ultimately impede the change process. I would like to emphasize that the best organizational leaders combine the positive values of expert, protector, facilitator, and innovator. And they work at self-development.

Management Style Matrix Graphic

Positive Traits

	Administrator		Entrepreneur	
EXPERT-PROTECTOR	EXPERT	PROTECTOR	FACILITATOR	INNOVATOR
COORDINATOR	PROBLEM SOLVER	COACH	ORCHESTRATES CONSENSUS	VISIONARY
SCOREKEEPER	DEAL MAKER	LOYAL, CREATES LOYALTY	OPEN—LEARNS FROM CO-WORKERS AND CUSTOMERS	ENTHUSIASTIC
MENTOR	DEMANDS EXCELLENCE	REMOVES ROADBLOCKS	EGALITARIAN	INSPIRING

Negative Traits

	Administrator		Entrepreneur	
	EXPERT	PROTECTOR	FACILITATOR	INNOVATOR
AUTOCRATIC	HIP-SHOOTER	AVOIDS CONFLICT WITHIN TEAM	DIFFUSE	UTOPIAN
TURF DEFENDER	KNOW-IT-ALL	WE vs. THEY MENTALITY	SUPERFICIAL	MANIPULATIVE
LAISSEZ-FAIRE FIGUREHEAD	MICROMANAGER	SOFT ON LOYAL SUBORDINATES	UNCOMMITTED	GRANDIOSE

At AT&T Business Communication Services today, I find top executives place a high priority on becoming better leaders. They recognize that while they must be innovators, they must also remain humble enough to keep learning about new technology in order to create new offerings that will add value for customers. These leaders recognize they must develop good relationships and learn from each other. They must be interactive. They must balance their expert eagerness to know the answer with the patience and skill to facilitate team problem solving. But they also recognize they must learn to be persuasive. When others hesitate to accept conclusions they are convinced are correct, they cannot gain results by command. They must explain the logic of their strategy.

There are different reasons that motivate these leaders. Some enjoy the game itself, the excitement of the play. But some inspire others because they communicate their belief that they are creating a better society through the business enterprise, "using the organization to contribute to the betterment of customers, employers, and the larger society." This same viewpoint characterizes the best leaders at other companies I have been working with: ABB, the global engineering company, Swedbank, the largest bank in Scandinavia, the MITRE Corporation of high-tech system engineers, and Cultor, the food, sweetener, and animal nutrition company headquartered in Helsinki, Finland.

Becoming a Leader for Information-Age Companies

The great danger for executives of large companies, especially for experts, is that as they move in a Wall Street world driven by numbers, they become alienated from the productive values essential to corporate success. The only stakeholders that influence them are not even real owners, but dealers in shares. Isolated from the front-line employees who must make any strategy work, they wrongly assume people can be motivated by extrinsic rewards and inspiring speeches about being #1.

Entrepreneurial leadership can be messy and uncomfortable. While elation and satisfaction are the rewards of success, there are also times of weary self-doubt. From the outside, the top managers of international companies seem confident and unassailable. From the inside, the best feel insecure. They recognize that their companies have no inherent right to exist. They have seen powerful companies like IBM and GM stumble when they became complacent and arrogant. Often, corporate leaders must push themselves to the limits of competence and physical endurance. When leaders have to become pushy doctors to mobilize human energy that has been frustrated by outmoded bureaucracies, inevitably they will also provoke resistance in those experts and helpers who were comfortable doing things in the traditional way. They must be prepared to hear criticism and, at times, angry, bitter feelings from those who have been losers because of change. There is always the danger that leaders will protect themselves from anger and hostility by retreating behind omniscient, narcissistic self-images that cloud perception. The developmental need for achievement and knowledge can become perverted into the defensive addiction for applause and reassurance that further alienates the leader from the employees.

It is cleaner and more comfortable to be an expert-administrator in a stable world than an entrepreneurial leader thrust into the hurly-burly of continual change. It is safer to be an uncommitted self-developer than to invest oneself in risky projects and the education of others. Can the experts change? Will the self-developers commit themselves to a larger project? Only if they are convinced that change and commitment are necessary. This conviction is growing as managers realize that to compete in the global market, to satisfy demanding customers, they must motivate the organization. They need to be understanding and responsive both to people on the front lines and to their managerial colleagues. Motivating an organization in the age of information requires managers who are continually learning, not only about customers, competitors, technology, and the global business environment, but also about the people at work who yearn for leaders whom they want to follow.

Values and the New Workplace

To answer the question, Why Work?, we have explored intrinsic motivation, the values that drive human behavior and how these connect with the new workplace. In a time of transition from the bureaucratic-industrial to the technoservice mode of production, both people and organizations struggle to adapt. Even the most advanced technology created by brilliant engineering innovators will be of little use if the workforce is not motivated to use it. We have seen that the self-developers are more in tune with the new workplace than are the experts and helpers, but the latter offer values of excellence and care that remain essential for quality work and good leadership. Although different people bring different intrinsic motives to work, all want to express themselves and satisfy a combination of needs for survival, mastery, dignity, sociability, pleasure, understanding, caring for others, and creativity. All want their needs for fair pay and good working conditions satisfied. But they will be motivated only if organizations empower them to carry out their responsibilities, and if leaders present them with visions and goals that make their work meaningful and give them hope for a positive future. In the final analysis, most people need to work, not only for material rewards, but because they want to exercise their abilities and feel valuable to themselves and to others. A major challenge of our time is to create meaningful work for all those who want it.

APPENDIX A

ON METHODOLOGY

The first edition of this book began with research to study social character and leadership in the new service workplace. My earlier books studied managers in high-tech industries, workers and managers in manufacturing and government, and peasant farmers in Mexico.[1] The approach taken in all of these books combined the study of human development with the factors that improve effectiveness at work. I have sought knowledge that can be used to improve work relationships in terms of two different criteria: economic/technical and social/human. The first pair concerns the forces that make companies competitive so that they can create wealth and provide employment. It has to do with managing resources more productively and satisfying customers and clients. The second has to do with the conditions that improve working life: what stimulates the fullest development of human skills and character, and what strengthens democratic values in the surrounding society.

There is, of course, a serious question about the degree to which these two criteria are mutually compatible, or conversely, the degree to which trade-offs must be made between them. My purpose for undertaking these projects in the workplace is to further both economic and human goals. The research I conducted for this second edition is one segment of these projects.

Why Work? uses three methodologies—surveys, interviews, and participant study. Chapters 3 through 7 are based in large part on a survey on those values that motivate people at work. Over 3,000 employees from 1981 to 1986 at 8 companies and more than 10 federal, state, county, and municipal agencies answered this survey. These employee samples were not random, but were composed of volunteers who took the survey with the understanding that they

---

[1]See my previous books, *Social Character in a Mexican Village*, with Erich Fromm (Englewood Cliffs, N.J.: Prentice Hall, 1970); *The Gamesman* (New York: Simon & Schuster, 1976); and *The Leader* (New York: Simon & Schuster, 1981).

would receive the group results. In the companies and in three of the agencies, I discussed the findings in the context of motivation and resistance to organizational change. In the other agencies there was no such discussion, either because the leadership that had sponsored the survey changed, or there was insufficient interest among the group and the findings were never reported back.

The questions used in the survey were based on an analysis of more than 100 interviews on the topics of what satisfies and dissatisfies people at work, how they want to be managed, how they relate to customers, clients, and co-workers, and about their family background and goals at work. These interviews were administered by myself (thirty interviews) and the research associates I have trained to study social character, who were members of the Seminar on Social Character of the Project on Technology, Work, and Character, which from 1970-1990 was affiliated with the Kennedy School of Government at Harvard University. The interviews were given during the period from 1977 to 1982 at AT&T, an insurance company, three federal agencies, and a county health agency. The interviews were analyzed in meetings of the Social Character Seminar. On the basis of these discussions, I formulated the survey questionnaire, which is reproduced in Chapter 1.

We were invited by the Merit Protection Board of the U.S. Civil Service to administer the survey to seven different samples representing all levels of the federal bureaucracy. After each testing, people who answered the questions discussed the survey's validity. For example, they considered whether the choices did, in fact, reflect their values. I then fine-tuned the wording of the questions until everyone felt comfortable with the questions before I gave the questionnaire to business groups and federal agencies.

The *reliability* of the survey was established by retesting a sample 12 months later. Agreement was found in 62 percent of first choices; in 96 percent of the cases, either the first or second choice remained the same. Reliability was also checked with seven different samples of managers from AT&T, and no significant differences were found in the response pattern among the samples. Indeed, we have found that the pattern of responses is always similar for companies in the same line of business, and that differences can be explained by the values that are selected for and reinforced by organizations (see Appendix C).

To further test the *validity* of the questionnaire, those interested in a confidential follow-up were invited to write in their names and telephone numbers on a second page, attached to the questionnaire. Fifty-two percent responded. This percentage was higher for managers (66 percent), who wanted feedback that might improve their effectiveness, and lower for clerical workers (31 percent), who might have been either wary that their answers would be traced and used against them, or merely less hopeful that the interview would be useful to them. A sample of 130 from government and business, representing each self-selected value type, was interviewed by my research associates. They were asked questions about their family background, attitudes toward work, supervision, service, and self-development. Members of the Social Character Seminar and I found that in almost all cases, our view of the person from the interview fit his or her view of self in terms of dominant values. Parts of these interviews and others used to explore management style are quoted verbatim in the chapters in this book on character types, with minor editing to make them grammatical and reduce repetition.

We also made use of a managerial style interview that began in 1979, when I worked with a group of U.S. State Department diplomats led by Harry G. Barnes, Jr., then director-general of the Foreign Service, to define good leadership for the State Department by studying its existing leaders. The group agreed that the fact of reaching top positions did not guarantee that a person was a good leader. He or she might merely be a clever climber. Together with the group, I designed a series of interview questions to be used in the study. The questions explored the diplomats' strategic goals, their styles of communication and decision making, their motivating values, and their work histories. The group then set out to identify good leaders within the department. First they described personal experiences with good managers. Then they formulated general criteria for good leaders, including skills such as communication, negotiation, waging interbureaucratic power struggles, and knowledge of the political and economic subject matter of foreign policy. They also included character traits such as perseverance, a drive to achieve, fair-mindedness, objectivity, a sense of humor (the emotional equivalent of a sense of reality), high tolerance for frustration, optimism, enthusiasm, the willingness to listen to different viewpoints, capacity for growth, and high energy. This list led to nominating 15 good leaders who were interviewed and compared to a control group of 12 people in similar positions. The research team then analyzed the results and arrived at the conclusion that good leadership depended on values as much as competency, or to put it another way, competency combines skill and values.

During 1983-1985, I used a version of the State Department managerial interview questionnaire in Sweden to interview 28 national leaders, including 8 chief executives of large companies, 6 political leaders, 7 heads of national unions, and 7 general directors of national government agencies. This was part of a study that the Swedish Council on Management and Worklife Issues asked me to help design to determine the kind of leadership Sweden needs for the future. The results of that study have been published in Swedish.[2]

During 1985-86, Robert H. Gaynor, then vice-president of personnel for AT&T Communications, and I used a customized version of the managerial questionnaire to engage sixty AT&T executives in 3-hour interviews where they explored their approach to management and their own careers. This AT&T questionnaire is reproduced in Appendix D. Altogether, I have interviewed over 100 business executives and 30 government leaders with a version of this questionnaire.

The interviews with Russ Nagel of Westinghouse Furniture Systems used in Chapter 3 resulted from his invitation to me to go to Grand Rapids to study his innovative leadership.

In four of the businesses and three of the government agencies, where I have given surveys and interviews, I had been invited as a consultant to help improve management and the quality of working life. As a result I was able to carry my research beyond the survey and interview, and place it in the context of attempts to change organizations.

As a consultant to AT&T, I learned about the leadership of Larry Lemasters, described in Chapter 3. In 1981, Lemasters asked me to help him begin the process of transforming AT&T's Stock & Bond Division, which eventually became American Transtech.

In my role as a consultant, I have tried to maintain my objectivity as a researcher. This goal is helped by making my values clear from the outset and by engaging those I work with in the study process. I categorize consultants into three varieties: off-the-shelf, interactive, and participative. Although at different times consultants can be all three kinds, usually they specialize in one of these approaches. Off-the-shelf consultants have a product or service to sell, such as total quality management, re-engineering, zero-based budgeting, a training package, or a workshop on motivation. Interactive consultants are called in to help solve a problem. Typically, successful interactive consultants work with worried leaders and help them calm their anxiety with new

---

2 Anders Edström, Michael Maccoby, Jan Erik Rendahl, and Lennart Strömberg, *Ledare för Sverige* (Lund: Liber, 1985). The interview with Jan Carlzon of SAS in Chapter 3 was part of that study. Some of the material in that book was published in Michael Maccoby (ed.), *Sweden at the Edge* (Philadelphia: University of Pennsylvania Press, 1991).

processes and techniques. They study the problem, interview a number of managers, and craft solutions that appeal to the values of managers. (Examples of solutions they employ include reorganization, decentralization, turning cost centers into profit centers, and changing the incentive pay system.)

Participative consultants join project teams, bringing not a product but the skills and knowledge needed to address the problem. They do not just provide reassuring solutions, but rather become part of the team, adding a missing competency to the group. In the process they teach their skills to people in the organization. As a participative consultant, I have worked with managers and union leaders to develop greater employee participation. I have applied the methods of psychoanalysis and anthropology, by exploring the conscious motives and unconscious values that determine approaches to work and social relationships, and by attempting to help leaders understand the interrelationship of psychological, social, economic, and technological factors in creating successful organizations.

In my previous books, I have used the Rorschach test to explore cognitive style and unconscious themes. Despite the Rorschach's value, I decided not to use findings from the test in this book because I wanted a methodology that can be understood by readers who do not have the specialized training needed to interpret the Rorschach for themselves.

In 1980, I became the sole joint consultant to the Bell System and the Communications Workers of America (CWA) in their attempt to improve the quality of working life by giving employees greater freedom and involving them in management decisions. Since 1984, I have continued as consultant both to AT&T and CWA and have been the principal consultant to the Workplace of the Future. (See Appendix E for the contract language.)

Businesses where employees were studied for the first edition of this book include AT&T, U.S. West, a large accounting firm, an innovative insurance company, a TV broadcasting company, a large supermarket chain, the information services division of a large oil company, and a company producing high-tech services. The government agencies include the Internal Revenue Service, the Commerce Department, ACTION (Peace Corps, VISTA, Older Americans Volunteer Programs), the Federal Aviation Administration, National Aeronautics and Space Administration, the Departments of State, Agriculture, Justice, and Defense, the Federal Trade Commission, the Library of Congress, a statewide health department, two hospitals, a county health department, a city tax office, a social-work office in California, and a municipal library. Besides these, I surveyed high school teachers and seniors, and drew on interviews conducted by research associates and students of social character with police officers in two metropolitan departments, entrepreneurs in the United States and Sweden, employees of SAS (Scandinavian Airlines), and middle managers in Japanese banks and trading companies.

For the second edition, I have made use of interviews at AT&T, ABB (Asea Brown Boveri) (including over 200 managers in 20 countries), Swedbank, Ford, Cultor, MITRE, and Battelle.

In summary, I have studied people in organizations that have hired me to help them become more effective, and I have administered surveys in those companies and government agencies where I have been invited to speak about the issues described in this book.

From surveys, interviews, and consulting I have found that work has different meanings for people and that they are most strongly motivated when the demands made on them fit their values. To learn what motivates people at work, I find I must study both the individual and the organization, and especially the role of leadership. Correspondingly, if people are to develop themselves at work and realize their potential for leadership, I believe they must understand themselves and others in relationship to a changing workplace. I have written this book to contribute to this understanding.

APPENDIX B

A NOTE ON VALUE DRIVES

There is no ideal word to use when talking about the forces that move us. We cannot see them or directly measure them. We experience them. If *need* is a misleading term, because it implies the lack of something, so is *instinct*, which is too biological. The inner forces that drive us are both inborn and shaped by culture. They are weak instincts. We might call them desires or passions, but these terms are too hot, too suggestive of sex or irrational drives. To speak of a passion for mastery or for play suggests abnormal compulsiveness, although some managers like to talk about a passion for quality or excellence. The term *want* is an alternative, but it is commonly used to indicate conscious acceptance of one's impulses, when, in fact, once irrational strivings become conscious, they are often rejected as dangerous, inappropriate, or inconvenient. We might just call the forces that move us values. By itself, however, the term *value* does not suggest emotional strivings or intense appetites, even though these express values. Deep values, or emotionally driven values, would be more precise. The concept of *value drives* seems to be useful, because it combines the commonly used term *drives*, suggesting force and energy that can be either conscious ("I am driving toward the goal") or unconscious ("I feel driven to repeat these patterns of relationships"), with *value*, a word used in ordinary language to indicate what is important to us, what determines our priorities. We commonly speak of motivated people as "driven," as people with "drive," and this always implies that they have aims and values.

In the nineteenth century, William James postulated the existence of human instincts and described them as inborn reflexes or impulses that become drives through early learning. He described social drives as rooted in man's instincts to imitate and to love, but he also described how other "instincts" like anger, acquisitiveness, and fear can conflict with sociability, thereby forcing us to make choices. There were problems in James's approach, particularly in distinguishing instinctual from learned behavior. Unlike the fully patterned instinctual behavior of insects, fish, birds, and reptiles, and even of some mammals, human instinctual reflexes, in large part, become shaped by learning, and are eventually largely controlled by the neocortex, the upper part of the brain where thinking takes place.

Freud used the concept of drives (in German, *trieb*) to describe the dynamic, intense nature of behavior, the expression of passionate impulses in symptoms and dreams. His concept of drive as directed psychic energy connects seemingly unconnected strivings and usefully explains development and perversion, intensity of feeling, and emotional attitude. The problem with Freud's theory of drives is that he makes them too biological and reduces them too much, finally subsuming them under two forces, Eros (love) and destructiveness.

Of course, drives are rooted in biology, but the mechanisms are more complex than Freud was able to show, particularly since dynamic human strivings combine the lower and higher brain, the hypothalamus and limbic system, the seat of emotions, and the neocortex. Although we can infer the connection between the thinking and emotional parts of the human nervous system, no one has traced precisely how the emotions, reflexes, and purposeful activities of infants become human drives. From a biological point of view, we can observe the following: although each of us is born with different constitutional levels of energy, i.e., different intensities of dynamic tendencies, intensity also varies with age; all value drives are affected by cycles of ebb and flow, excitation and satiation. The intensity of value drives also depends on exciting stimuli, such as sexual arousal. Threats to life trigger flight or fight with strong infusions of adrenaline or noradrenaline; good-tasting food excites appetite.

As we mature, intensity varies not only because of the aging process, which erodes drive, but according to whether we strengthen or weaken drives through good or bad habits, skills and competencies, activating or addictive needs, and a good or bad fit with other people and the environment. Work and intimate relationships are especially important in developing our value drives. Indeed, Freud was said to have defined mental health as satisfaction in love and work. Value drives when expressed productively are strengthened. Those individuals invested in dissatisfying activities or relationships deplete energy, causing, as it were, emotional bankruptcy. Value drives that are continually frustrated and suppressed, because of either the environment or conflicting drives, may eventually weaken, although they may maintain their force through perversion.

Parsimony is a criterion for designing a usable theory, because the human brain cannot easily remember more than seven or eight categories. I have grouped the value drives into eight categories: *survival, relatedness, pleasure, information, mastery, play, dignity,* and *meaning.* I made separate categories only when it was necessary to maintain a causal distinction, keeping in mind the typal analysis rule that each concept in a category should be more like each other than like one in any of the other categories. The end result is still arguable. I debated the idea of considering self-expression or individuation as a separate value drive. After all, babies show a dynamic tendency to express themselves through speech, singing, making marks. With discipline this activity develops into speaking, art, writing. However, including self-expression not only adds a category, but it separates this concept from mastery and play, when the expression of these value drives is, in fact, self-expression.

The value drive to reproduce the species has been left out of this group of eight. This drive affects motivation to work in complex ways, depending on cultural factors. Men have traditionally been driven to provide for their children, while having and caring for children have been women's work. In every society, as women gain independence and enter the workforce, they limit their childbearing. There are two reasons for this, egotistical and altruistic. Children tie them down, and by having fewer children, they can provide each child with better opportunities.

How the value drives are grouped is open for discussion. There is no scientifically precise way. Indeed, this grouping is as much poetry as it is science. I have grouped value drives according to concepts that can be experienced and understood by people in every culture. In discussing this grouping, I have tried to avoid technical language where possible, and yet include the best evidence from psychology and anthropology.

A recent *Journal of Social Issues* focuses on "Human Values and Social Issues" (Volume 50, Number 4, Winter 1994). It includes a discussion of the theories of the social psychologist Milton Rokeach who defined values as enduring prescriptive or proscriptive beliefs that a specific mode of conduct (instrumental value) or end state of existence (terminal value) is preferred to another mode of conduct or end state (p. 3). This translates into beliefs that in some sense drive or push us to think or behave in determined ways. Values direct our decisions. Shalom H. Schwartz a social psychologist at the Hebrew University of Jerusalem defines values in terms of guiding principles (p. 21). Schwartz proposes ten types of motivational values: Power, achievement, hedonism, stimulation, self-direction, universalism, benevolence, tradition, conformity, and security. There is considerable overlap between this list and the eight value drives. Power and Achievement are both contained in *Mastery*. Hedonism is included in *Pleasure*. Stimulation is included in *Information*. Benevolence and Conformity are included in *Relatedness*. Security is mentioned in both our lists. Universalism, by which Schwartz means "understanding, appreciation, tolerance, and protection of all people and for nature," combines *Dignity* and *Meaning*.

Self-direction meaning "Independent thought and action-choosing, creating, exploring" combines *Play* and *Mastery*.

Tradition defined as "Respect, commitment, and acceptance of the customs and ideas that traditional culture or religion provide" has to do with *Meaning* (p. 22).

What are the differences between the concept of motivational values presented in this book and those of Schwartz? To some degree, the two approaches are different ways of cutting the same cake. Besides differences of emphasis, *Why Work?* considers each of the values in terms of positive (developmental) and negative (addictive) expressions. It also describes how these values are developed into social character types, and how they influence motivation at work.

APPENDIX C

RESULTS FROM THE VALUES AT WORK QUESTIONNAIRE

The Values at Work questionnaire has been administered to over 3,000 people. The results from 9 interesting samples are given in this section. The first sample combines 650 employees from 10 different service sector businesses and government agencies (Service-Sector sample). The second describes about 300 middle and upper managers from a telecommunications and information service company (Telecommunications sample). The third includes 180 middle and upper managers in a high-tech service company that designs information systems (High-Tech sample). The fourth is a sample of 135 agents and managers of the Internal Revenue Service (Government sample); the fifth includes about 700 managers from the National Aeronautics and Space Administration (NASA sample). The sixth presents 46 leaders (80% under age 40) brought together for a seminar by a major foundation (Young Leaders sample), and the seventh consists of 106 college students who were summer interns at a major technology company (College Interns sample). Besides these, the survey has been given to other groups from business, government agencies, and schools. Since the publication of the first edition of this book, my colleagues and I have used the survey to help management groups understand themselves. As examples, the eighth sample includes 64 technical managers from a national laboratory in 1993 and the ninth sample includes 65 sales and marketing managers from a global engineering company; this group was surveyed in 1995.

The distribution of character types varies among samples because organizations can be considered as *psychostructures*. That is to say, types are selected and select themselves to fit the styles required by a role that serves a particular organization's goals. For example, a higher percentage of teachers (75%) than IRS agents (51%) say that the phrase, "I want to help people" describes them very well. On the other hand, a much higher percentage of the IRS agents (44%) than teachers (8%) check "defender" as describing them very well. This is not surprising. People go into teaching because they want to help people learn. IRS agents are more likely to be motivated by the desire to uphold the law. In my experience, the percentage of innovators is higher in business than in government. Indeed, most of the innovators I have met in government eventually left for business.

Different types approach the same job differently. Revenue agents or government auditors who are defenders are more aggressive in attacking suspected criminals than are the experts. Teachers who are helpers show more interest in slow students than do experts, who respond most to achievers like themselves.

Almost everyone surveyed identifies to some degree with each of these values, because all are important for organizational effectiveness. However, the most important values to most people in both business and government are, first, those of the expert (about 50%), and then the self-developer (20%).[1] These two types express the individualistic values of traditional and new-generation Americans. Helping (15%) or helping leaders (7%), innovating (8%), and defending organizations (1%) are less frequently chosen as most important. The Service-Sector and High-Tech samples are even more expert-oriented, with 92 percent of the NASA managers indicating that the expert description fits them very well, and 72 percent listing it as most important. The Young Leaders and College Interns samples identify most with the self-developers. (Over 90% of the young leaders and 93% of the interns say this statement describes them very well.)

Most employees of all types, especially those at higher levels, feel they can express their preferred orientation at work. Three-fourths of all the samples believe their job allows them to take their favored approach very much or some-what. What dissatisfied about 60 percent (very much or somewhat) is weak leadership, lack of communication with and too little participation in management.

This finding means that although most American employees feel they can be experts or self-developers at work, the majority of workers also believes that the system and its leaders keep them from working as productively as they can. This seeming contradiction can be easily explained. Most Americans have a basically positive attitude toward work. In companies and government bureaucracies, there is room for expertise and self-development. But people feel that red

---

[1]Checking an approach as "most important" is considered to indicate the primary way people see themselves.

tape and over-controlling management limit them. Although there has been a movement to increase participation over the past five years, employees are still dissatisfied with organization and authority, although the meaning of this dissatisfaction is different for the different types.[2] Studies at AT&T in 1994 showed that those employees who were able to participate through the Workplace of the Future joint union-management program were 10-15 percent more satisfied with work and management than those who did not participate.

During the past 10 years, the percentage of people who see themselves as innovators has grown in response to pressures for change in both business and government. In the 1980s, 10 percent of the top managers saw themselves as innovators, versus 6 percent of middle managers, 2 percent of skilled workers, and 0 percent of clerical workers. In the Telecommunications sample, 17 percent of upper management saw themselves as innovators, versus 6 percent of lower management. In the '90s the percentage of managers who see themselves mainly as innovators has doubled. However, as we discussed in Chapter 3, not all who see themselves as innovators really innovate.

Most of the types are distributed fairly evenly among the age groups—with two noticeable exceptions. There are fewer female helpers among the younger generation than the old. That is to be expected now that women are gaining options beyond the traditional helping roles.[3]

The major difference between younger and older employees has been seen in the self-developers. They comprise a higher percentage of the under-40 employees (25%) than of the over-40 group (14%). At age 30, it is 30 percent. This difference between younger and older employees held for all samples, and among the young leaders, there was an overwhelming emphasis on self-development. We also found an even higher percentage of self-developers among the sample of college interns (40%) and high school seniors (35%). In 1990, I surveyed 70 youth leaders from the U.S.A. and Western Europe and found 50

---

[2] The Worker Representation and Participation Survey directed by Richard Freeman and Joel Rogers and conducted by Princeton Survey Research Associates in the fall of 1994 is reported in the Report of the Dunlop Commission on the Future of Worker-Management Relations, 1995, U.S. Department of Labor.

[3] However, in the IRS sample, more women (17%) than men (4%) see themselves primarily as helpers, and this difference is reinforced by second choices (women, 40%; men, 22%). The difference is explained by the fact that women have traditionally been selected for helping roles in the IRS, such as service specialists who give information to taxpayers. More of the men were in revenue agent and criminal investigator roles that called for defenders.

percent identified themselves as self-developers, and these were more likely to be the offspring of dual wage earning families. This age pattern fits my thesis in *The Leader* (1981), which states that values among new-generation careerists would become more oriented to self-development than to merely moving up the hierarchy.[4] Of course, the pattern might indicate that older people have become less interested in self-development, and there is evidence that some self-developers became innovators, but the first explanation is supported by the correlation of self-developer with the two-wage-earner family, which has become the norm. This explanation is also underscored by the interview findings reported in this book; these results demonstrate how these values were formed in childhood as people adapted to different family constellations and social mores.

STATISTICAL RESULTS FROM
THE VALUES AT WORK QUESTIONNAIRE

Overall Results

Most Important Approach to Work (1983-1987)

	Service Sector	Tele-com.	High-tech.	Gov't.	NASA	Young Leaders	College Interns
Expert	47%	48%	59%	64%	70%	20%	43%
Helper	15	13	10	9	4	24	3
Defender	1	2	1	6	1	0	1
Institutional Helper	7	7	4	2	6	4	7
Innovator	5	8	12	0	4	17	5
Self-Developer	20	20	12	19	12	35	41
No Choice	5	2	2	0	3	0	0
	100%	100%	100%	100%	100%	100%	100%

---

[4]This thesis was also presented by Daniel Yankelovich on the basis of his surveys in *New Rules* (New York: Random House, 1981).

Telecommunications Sample *N=295
(This describes me) (1985)

	Very Well	Some-what	A little	Not at all	Total
Expert	76%	22%	2%	0%	100%
Helper	55	38	7	0	100
Defender	25	31	32	12	100
Institutional					
Helper	44	40	14	2	100
Innovator	30	41	22	7	100
Self-Developer	51	35	12	2	100

*N is the sample size, the number of people who answered the questionnaire.

High-Tech Sample *N=180
(This describes me) (1985)

	Very Well	Some-what	A little	Not at all	Total
Expert	75%	23%	2%	0%	100%
Helper	36	49	15	0	100
Defender	7	19	35	39	100
Institutional					
Helper	23	48	26	3	100
Innovator	26	46	20	8	100
Self-Developer	36	46	16	2	100

*N is the sample size, the number of people who answered the questionnaire.

Government Sample   *N=135
(This describes me) (1985)

	Very Well	Some-what	A little	Not at all	Total
Expert	88%	12%	0%	0%	100%
Helper	51	36	10	3	100
Defender	44	31	14	11	100
Institutional Helper	30	35	25	10	100
Innovator	10	31	26	33	100
Self-Developer	48	38	10	4	100

*N is the sample size, the number of people who answered the questionnaire.

NASA Sample   *N=706
(This describes me) (1986)

	Very Well	Some-what	A little	Not at all	Missing†	Total
Expert	92%	6%	1%	1%	0%	100%
Helper	51	34	9	3	3	100
Defender	28	22	23	22	5	100
Institutional Helper	61	28	6	2	3	100
Innovator	31	35	19	11	4	100
Self-Developer	58	26	10	3	3	100

†For the other tables, missing questionnaires were taken out in calculating percentages. This table was prepared by a taskforce sponsored by the Academy of Public Administration. "Equal Opportunity and Management Practices in NASA Headquarters" (Washington, D.C.: National Academy of Public Administration Report, January 1987).

*N is the sample size, the number of people who answered the questionnaire.

Young Leaders Sample *N=46
(This describes me) (1987)

	Very Well	Some-what	A little	Not at all	Total
Expert	85%	11%	4%	0%	100%
Helper	60	29	11	0	100
Defender	9	29	27	35	100
Institutional Helper	36	34	23	7	100
Innovator	35	30	30	5	100
Self-Developer	91	6	3	0	100

*N is the sample size, the number of people who answered the questionnaire.

College Interns Sample *N=106
(This describes me) (1987)

	Very Well	Some-what	A little	Not at all	Total
Expert	84%	14%	2%	0%	100%
Helper	40	42	18	0	100
Defender	10	37	34	19	100
Institutional Helper	34	52	12	2	100
Innovator	40	42	15	3	100
Self-Developer	73	21	5	1	100

*N is the sample size, the number of people who answered the questionnaire.

Service Sector Sample   *N=658
(Business and Government)
(This describes me) (1983-1987)

	Very Well	Some- what	A little	Not at all	Total
Expert	82%	16%	1%	0%	100%
Helper	65	29	6	0	100
Defender	26	34	25	15	100
Institutional Helper	46	38	12	4	100
Innovator	25	40	21	14	100
Self-Developer	57	31	9	3	100

*N is the sample size, the number of people who answered the questionnaire.

Engineering Management Sample   *N=108
(This describes me) (1995)

	Very Well	Some- what	A little	Not at all	Total
Expert	74%	22%	4%	0%	100%
Helper	63	30	7	0	100
Defender	19	30	35	16	100
Innovator	67	31	2	0	100
Self-Developer	44	45	10	1	100

*N is the sample size, the number of people who answered the questionnaire.

National Laboratory Managers *N=64
(This describes me) (1993)

	Very Well	Some- what	A little	Not at all	Total
Expert	78%	17%	5%	0%	100%
Helper	45	36	19	0	100
Defender	8	20	52	20	100
Innovator	69	25	6	0	100
Self-Developer	36	48	13	3	100

*N is the sample size, the number of people who answered the questionnaire.

Approaches to Work †
Significant intercorrelation of approaches to work
at 1% level of significance
Telecommunications sample: * N = 295

	Expert	Helper	Institu- tional helper	Defender	Innovator	Self- Developer
Expert	—	X	X	.16	.18	.24
Helper	X	—	.34	.28	X	15
Institutional Helper	X	.34	—	.34	.29	X
Defender	.16	.28	.34	—	.37	.17
Innovator	.18	X	.29	.37	—	.24
Self-Developer	.24	.15	X	.17	.24	—

†This table reports product moment correlations based on a scale of identification with each type ranging from very well (4) to not at all (1). I report those correlations that are significant at the one percent level (meaning that there is less than one chance in a hundred that they are caused by chance). The significant correlations indicate which combinations of types people tend to choose. They show that many people identify with more than one type. They also describe patterns of choice that are explained in this book. For example, all types except helpers tend to identify with innovators. Institutional helpers tend to identify with helpers on the one hand and with defenders and innovators (leaders) on the other. Self-developers identify most with innovators and experts, very little with helpers, and not at all with institutional helpers.

*N is the sample size, the number of people who answered the questionnaire.

A full explanation of the product-moment correlation can be found in any standard textbook on statistics. However, a general understanding of its meaning will be useful for the reader. For example, the correlation between innovator and self-developer is .24. A possible numerical product-moment correlation can range from -1.0 to +1.0. If checking innovator always implied that the individual also checked self-developer, the correlation between the two variables would approach +1.0. In contrast, if checking innovators always implied not checking self-developer, and checking self-developer always implied not checking innovator, the correlation between the two variables would move toward -1.0. If there were no systematic relationship between checking innovator and self-developer, the correlation would be 0.0, meaning in effect that some innovators checked self-developer and some did not, and there was no way of predicting whether an innovator was likely to be a self-developer.

In practice, correlations between character types seldom approach the certainty of 1.0 or -1.0. Generally, the investigator looks for correlations large enough to be considered "significant," meaning that the value of the product-moment r cannot be attributed to a chance relationship. The significance level is found by a formula that takes into account the size of the correlation and the number of cases on which it is based. The formula is used to arrive at the probability that the correlation could be attributed to a chance relation, rather than to a systematic relation between the variables, given the assumption that there is only a chance relationship between the variables. This assumption is called the Null Hypothesis, and traditionally in statistics it is rejected when the significance level is less than 5 chances in 100. Thus, a significant product-moment r (correlation) is large enough so that if there were really no systematic relationship between the variables, a correlation made from a random sampling from the same population with the same number of cases would produce an r that large or larger less than 5 percent of the time.

Besides looking at the significance of a correlation, we should also take account of the fact that it provides a way of determining the percentage of variance in one variable that can be accounted for by the other variable, or, in other words, the percentage of variability that they hold in common. This percentage is found by squaring. Thus if the correlation between innovator and self-developer types were .24, it could be stated that innovator accounts for 6 percent of the variance of self-developer or vice versa. It is important to keep in mind that a correlation may be significant but low. With 295 cases, a significant product-moment correlation can be as low as .15 meaning that, although only 1 percent of the variance between the variables has been taken into account, it is still true that a significant relationship exists between the variables. A significant but low correlation might indicate that the measures used to gather data were not fine enough to discover what is in reality a higher correlation. Or it might indicate that in reality the two variables account for a small but significant mutual variance that would remain the same no matter how fine the instruments used to measure the variables. It is important to stress the fact that even significant correlations must be understood in the light of both theory and the assessment of the instruments used.

APPENDIX D

THE AT&T MANAGERIAL INTERVIEW QUESTIONNAIRE

I. INTRODUCTION

Describe your current job.

II. MANAGERIAL APPROACH

1. What are the main goals of your organization? Do you think your subordinates see the goals as you do? How do you communicate them?

2. How do you give feedback and evaluation to your subordinates, and how do you get it from your own boss?

3. How do people in your organization give you feedback?

4. Describe your activities as a manager — what do you actually do?

5. How are decisions made in your organization? Do you have any process for involving others in the decisions you make? (Give examples.) What decisions have you delegated?

6. What are your views about sharing sensitive information with those who work for you?

7. To what extent are lower-level people involved in the work usually allotted to senior individuals?

8. What is it that is challenging in the work in your organization for employees? Is it different for different types or groups of people? What do you do about it?

9. How do you apportion new work that arises that doesn't fit the existing structure?

10. How do you conceive of your role regarding the morale of your organization?

11. How do you share credit? Give examples.

12. Do you have a managerial philosophy? What is it? How did you develop it? (Reading, etc.)

13. What is your definition of leadership? What words and/or behavior most inspire employees in AT&T?

14. Is it important, useful, or necessary in your leadership role to have symbols of authority, rank, and prestige?

15. What individuals have been the greatest influence on you and your managerial approach, either as role models or in what they have said to you or taught you?

16. What are the criteria you use to evaluate subordinate managers? Do you communicate these criteria? If so, how?

17. Do you talk about management with subordinates? (Give examples.)

18. What specifically are you doing to help the people who report to you to develop themselves?

19. What do you see as your role in regard to the development of those two levels down from you, and of others down to the lowest levels?

20. Assuming a responsibility on the part of supervisors, do you think that any other part(s) of the organization has a responsibility to help individuals develop their capabilities? What should be the nature of that help?

21. In your experience, are there some individuals whose management style makes them good leaders in one situation but poor leaders in a different situation? (Give examples.)

III. STRUCTURAL CONSTRAINTS

1. Are there things you believe you ought to be accomplishing in your position, things you feel you could do and that the organization needs to have done, that you are not doing? If so, what are these things, and why are you not doing them?

2. If you are accomplishing what you feel needs to be done, are you doing it with satisfaction, and as efficiently and effectively as you would like? Do you have a sense of accomplishment? If not, what are the reasons (institutional and personal)? What needs to be changed?

3. Do you have what you need in the way of authority to structure the work and organize people to accomplish the tasks at hand (e.g., determining the proper number of positions and the areas to which they are allocated)? If not, what would have to be changed for you to have what you need?

4. In general, when you think about the things you feel should be done, do you feel blocked by structural constraints? If so, what needs to be changed?

5. What are the strengths and values in AT&T that we need to protect, that should be preserved?

IV. BACKGROUND AND CAREER DEVELOPMENT

1. Describe your family background and work history.

2. What experiences or training would you like to have had to prepare you for what you are doing now? Is it possible for you to provide such experiences or training now for the people who work for you? (Give examples.)

3. What strategies have you employed in planning your own career?

V. What are your views of the goals of AT&T in the broadest sense? (Describe the company's strategy and your organization's role in achieving it.)

APPENDIX E

WORKPLACE OF THE FUTURE: 1992 CONTRACT LANGUAGE[1]

AT&T, CWA and IBEW recognize that AT&T's business of tomorrow will be characterized by intense global growth and competition. In order to meet this global challenge and to respond to the desire of the Unions for a meaningful voice in decisions that affect its members' jobs, AT&T, CWA, and IBEW agree to institute this innovative model, the WORKPLACE OF THE FUTURE, to facilitate greater participation by the Unions in human resource and business planning, benefit AT&T's market position and transform our traditional work systems to customer responsive work systems.

The parties share the goals of establishing a world class, high performance organization and protecting employment security through market success.

The parties agree to the following principles to ensure success of the WORKPLACE OF THE FUTURE:

a)   The Unions and management must mutually agree on roles and responsibilities, objectives and goals, how the relationship will be described and communicated, the substance and providers of training, and other key issues.

b)   The Unions shall select all Union representatives who participate in the various components outlined below.

---

1 Workplace of the Future was reaffirmed in the 1995 contract between AT&T, CWA and IBEW.

c) The Unions shall have access to information needed to participate in a meaningful way in the process as jointly defined by the Company and the Unions.

d) At each component level, the Company and the Unions may jointly agree to appoint special task forces to address specific issues and to make recommendations.

AT&T and the Unions agree to develop the four components listed below in order to implement the WORKPLACE OF THE FUTURE.

1. WORKPLACE MODELS will encourage Local Union officers and AT&T managers to identify and develop new approaches to managing change in the workplace. These cooperative efforts should be viewed and leveraged as models for transformation. The workplace models will be focused on quality, customer satisfaction, quality of work life and competitiveness in the marketplace, thereby protecting and enhancing employment opportunities within AT&T.

Workplace models will be jointly defined by the Company and the Unions and changes will not be implemented unless jointly agreed to by the parties.

This will require a radical transformation in the roles of managers, occupational employees and Union leaders to initiate, sanction and encourage new methods of working together to achieve customer success. The Company will provide training and opportunities to management to make this transition, as appropriate.

Workplace models would include, but not be limited to (1) employee participation initiatives, (2) self-managed/self-directed team environments, (3) continuous quality improvement efforts, (4) flexible, highly-skilled work environments, (5) information sharing, and (6) Union involvement in the development of new systems of work organization.

2. BUSINESS UNIT/DIVISION PLANNING COUNCILS will be formed by the Company and the Unions to:

- design "ideal futures" for specific marketplaces to achieve customer satisfaction, quality of work life, employee professionalism, and development of cooperative work styles,

- support pilots to assist employees in achieving customer satisfaction and marketplace success, improve quality of work life and expand employment opportunities,

- invest in employees through education, support and leadership styles,

- influence decisions that determine production technology, work organization, job content and employment.

This process will facilitate participation by the Unions in business decisions regarding the development and deployment of new technologies and work structures which will help achieve the goals of enhanced service quality and employee job satisfaction.

The Company recognizes that gaining employee involvement and commitment to the WORKPLACE OF THE FUTURE model, which targets customer satisfaction and market flexibility, requires the Company to be sensitive to employees' needs regarding employment security. This is an appropriate issue for Business Unit/Division Planning Councils to address in their assessment of business unit market conditions, planned technological changes, and future force management requirements. It is not the Company's intention for employees to be negatively impacted by workplace innovations resulting from employees' ideas.

This requires that management and the Unions be committed to a relationship where information is openly exchanged, problems are solved mutually and cooperatively, critical differences are accepted and accommodated, agreements are developed in good faith and commitments are honored.

Joint training, jointly designed, will be essential to develop common understandings, describe business strategies, and develop union expertise in new technology. The make-up of planning councils will be determined by management and the Unions. The Unions shall select the Union representatives. Union representatives shall participate on company paid time.

3. The CONSTRUCTIVE RELATIONSHIP COUNCILS (CRC), established in 1989 bargaining and consisting of four (4) members (two Company, two Union) from each of the national bargaining committees, will continue to function to facilitate the leveraging of Workplace Models and Business Unit/Division Planning Councils. Any question or issue which may arise in the Planning Councils may be brought to the CRC for resolution. The CRC may also initiate the formation of special task forces to address specific issues. Special task forces shall slice across all appropriate corporate entities to involve the most appropriate group of problem solvers as determined by the CRC.

The CRC will continue to meet periodically to review progress and, as appropriate, to approve specific cooperative ventures or trials.

4. A HUMAN RESOURCES BOARD will be formed to review key human resources issues worldwide and provide input to the Executive Committee of AT&T. Specifically, the Human Resources Board will:

- leverage the "best practices" that most effectively engage and develop people to uniquely position AT&T with its customers and be competitive in every dimension (e.g. leadership styles, education/training, employee involvement and communication, self-directed teams, reward and development processes),

- address the needs of employees and treat them as "whole persons", i.e., as members of families, communities, and Unions,

- address external systems that impact AT&T's ability to be competitive (e.g. education, health care, environment).

The Human Resources Board will be comprised of three (3) AT&T executives, one Union leader from the CWA, one Union leader from the IBEW, and two distinguished leaders in the field of human resources from outside the Company and the Unions. The Unions and AT&T shall agree on the choice of these distinguished leaders.

The Human Resources Board will address broad, strategic, global human resources and business issues within the context of the external environment over long range time frames. In contrast, the Workplace Models will deal primarily with customer, employee and technology issues in the workplace in short tactical time frames.

INDEX

Burlingame, Hal, 75
Burr, Donald, 104, 249
Burt, Dan, 162
Bush, George, 159n
Business Week, 130

care
  as a condition for human
    development, 208, 209-11
  helpers and, 135, 136
Carlzon, Jan, 74, 82-89, 101, 103,
  105, 106, 107, 248, 258n
Castle, The (Kafka), 113
Challenger disaster, 121
challenges, experts and, 113-15
Chaplin, Charlie, 57, 227
character formation
  of defenders, 158-63
  of experts, 112-13
  of helpers, 138-39
  of innovators, 100-4
  of self-developers, 183-84
chief executives (CEOs), 87, 88, 129,
  233
  at American Transtech, 82
  as economic men, 12-13
  at Scandinavian Airlines, 86
children
  dignity of, 55-56
  discipline and, 213
  independence and, 211
  meaning and, 60
  play of, 53, 101-3
  value drives and, 46, 51
Chrysler, 93
Churchill, Winston, 161
civil rights, 31, 157
Clinton, Bill, 30, 94, 95, 159n, 197
Cocke, John, 69, 72
Commerce Department, U.S., 157,
  163, 168, 182, 187
commitment
  self-developers and, 196,
    197, 198, 199, 202, 204

strategic self-development
  and, 208, 209, 215-19
communication, 51, 123
Communications Workers of
  America (CWA), xii, 48, 82, 169,
    177, 205, 236, 259
company men, 22
competition, 2, 93, 234
  in airline industry, 83
  dignity and, 57
  global, 205, 245, 252
  Lemasters' vision of, 81-82
computer-aided design (CAD)
  systems, 90
computer systems, 69, 77, 80, 103
Congress of Racial Equality, 146
consultants, categories of, 258-59
Continental Airlines, 104
cottage industry, electronic, 47-48
Covey, Stephen R., 127, 128, 197
craftsmen, 22, 24, 45, 240
creativity, 71, 127, 207
  innovators and, 66, 67
  play and, 53
  self-developers and, 179, 181
cuero quemado (burnt leather), 102
Cultor, xiii, 251, 260
culture
  dignity and, 57
  leadership models in, 239-40
  value drives and, 3-4, 20-21,
    39, 50, 60
Cummins Engine, 77
Curie, Marie, 185
customers
  focus on, 106, 109
  satisfaction of, 81, 83-84, 85,
    89, 93, 225, 236, 243, 252
  technoservice and, 74
customer-supplier relationship, 1
Dana Corporation, 77
Death of the Bell System, The (film),
  75

gamesmen and, 101
sadomasochism and, 212
wholeness and, 207-8
Presidents, as defenders, 159
Prince, The (Machiavelli), 14
problem solving, 77, 80, 176
productivity, 220n
profits/profitability, 229, 231, 232,
236, 244, 248
Carlzon and, 83-84
Lemasters and, 80, 81
Nagel and, 94
project teams, 76, 77, 80-81, 83
promotion, 113-14, 163, 224, 242
protector, innovation and, 73
protector-entrepreneurs, 247, 248-49
psychoanalysis, 40, 46, 198, 200
psychological man, 12, 15-19
punishment, 213, 232
Puritan Ethic, 49, 241
Putnam, Robert D., 216n

quality, 106, 229, 234
experts' drive for, 109-10
Nagel's views on, 89, 90, 91,
93, 94
Quality of Worklife projects, 143-44
Quality Program, 169
questionnaires
AT&T Managerial Interview,
275-77
Barometer, 91-95
Values at Work, 28-29,
265-74

Rabi, I.I., 72
Rabinow, Jacob, 69, 70, 72
Ransom, John Crowe, 162
re-engineering, 89, 193
Reagan, Ronald, 38, 93, 160
reasons, as motivating factor, 1, 223,
234, 237, 244
reduced-instruction-set computer
(RISC) technology, 69, 103

reinforcement, *see* rewards
relatedness, 41, 42, 43, 46-49, 61, 62,
208
defenders and, 154
experts and, 110
helpers and, 133, 134
innovators and, 66
relationships, 1, 9, 223, 229-30, 237,
244
of helpers, 139-41
religion, 59, 61, 130, 138
responsibilities, 1, 9, 30, 98, 124,
174, 179, 191, 222-29, 237, 244
rewards, 1, 15, 37, 126, 222, 223,
230-34, 244, 251
of defenders, 9, 237, 238
of experts, 8, 113-15, 230,
231, 232, 237
of helpers, 8, 142-44, 230,
231, 237
of innovators, 8, 66-67, 231,
237
of self-developers, 9, 178-79,
231, 237
Riesman, David, 40
risk taking, 175
Rockefeller, John D., 214
Rokeach, Milton, 263
role models
of defenders, 161-62
of self-developers, 184-85
Roosevelt, Franklin Delano, 38, 139,
159
Roosevelt, Eleanor, 139, 185
Rorschach test, 71, 259

sadomasochism, 212
Samhall, xiii
Scandinavian Airlines (SAS), 73, 74,
82-89
chief executives at, 86
customer satisfaction and,
83-84
philosophy of, 85